ENGLISH TEACHERS' ACCOUNTS

This book looks at the figure of the English teacher in Indian classrooms and examines the practice and relevance of English and India's colonial legacy, many decades after independence.

The book is an account of the varied experiences of teaching English in universities in different parts of the country. It highlights the changes in curriculum and teaching practices and how the discipline lent itself to a study of culture, historical contexts, the fashioning of identities or reform over the years. The volume presents the dramatic changes in the composition of the English classroom in terms of gender, class, caste and indigenous communities in recent decades, as well as the shifts in teaching strategies and curriculum which the new diversity necessitated. The essays in the collection examine the distinctiveness of English practice in India through classroom accounts, which explore themes like post-coloniality, feminism and human rights through the study of texts by Shakespeare, Beckett, Doris Lessing and poetry from the Northeast.

This book will be of interest to academics, researchers, students and practitioners of English Studies, education, colonial studies, cultural studies and South Asian studies, as well as those concerned with the history of higher education and the establishment of disciplines and institutions.

Nandana Dutta is Professor of English at the University of Gauhati, India. Her teaching and research interests are in American studies, gender, postcolonial theory and literature, travel writing and the discipline of English in India. Her publications include *Questions of Identity in Assam: Location, Migration, Hybridity* (2012), *American Literature* (in the 'Literary Contexts' series, 2016) and *Mothers, Daughters and Others: Representation of Women in the Folk Narratives of Assam* (edited with an Introduction, 2013).

ENGLISH TEACHERS' ACCOUNTS

Essays on the Teacher, the Text and the Indian Classroom

Edited by Nandana Dutta

Routledge
Taylor & Francis Group

LONDON AND NEW YORK

First published 2022
by Routledge
2 Park Square, Milton Park, Abingdon, Oxon OX14 4RN

and by Routledge
605 Third Avenue, New York, NY 10158

Routledge is an imprint of the Taylor & Francis Group, an informa business

British Library Cataloguing-in-Publication Data
A catalogue record for this book is available from the British Library

Library of Congress Cataloging-in-Publication Data
A catalog record has been requested for this book

ISBN: 978-0-367-61056-2 (hbk)
ISBN: 978-0-367-70419-3 (pbk)
ISBN: 978-1-003-14620-9 (ebk)

DOI: 10.4324/9781003146209

Typeset in Sabon
by SPi Technologies India Pvt Ltd (Straive)

To our students who tolerate and enrich us.

CONTENTS

CONTRIBUTORS

Jinan Ashraf is a doctoral candidate at the School of English, Dublin City University. Her doctoral dissertation explores key formal, thematic and postcolonial concerns in the modern novel.

Jeetumoni Basumatary teaches English at Cotton University, Guwahati. She has also taught at Ramjas College, University of Delhi. She has translated a collection of poetry and a novel from the Bodo language into English. She has written two plays in the Bodo language. She has also contributed a number of articles and chapters to various academic volumes. Her current research interest is in cultural nationalism and literature.

Sukalpa Bhattacharjee is Professor of English at North-Eastern Hill University, Shillong. Her publications include *Human Rights and Insurgency: The North-East India*, (2002), *Ethno-Narratives: Identity and Experience in NE-India* (2006), *Postcolonial Literature: Essays on Gender, Theory and Genres* (2004) and *Society, Representations and Textuality: The Critical Interface* (2013).

K. Narayana Chandran has been a teacher of English for 40-odd years. He has held teaching and mentoring positions in IIT-Bombay, St Berchmans' College, Kerala, and the erstwhile Central Institute of English & Foreign Languages, Hyderabad (now EFLU). He has been Professor of English in the School of Humanities at the University of Hyderabad for the last 34 years. He is currently the Institution of Eminence Chair in Literary and Cultural Theory, Department of English, University of Hyderabad. His published work includes critical studies of poets and poetry and the problems and prospects of teaching English at advanced levels in India.

Nandana Dutta is Professor of English at the University of Gauhati. Her teaching and research interests are in American Studies, Gender, Postcolonial Theory and Literature, Travel Writing and the discipline of English in India. Her publications include *Questions of Identity in Assam: Location, Migration, Hybridity* (2012), *American Literature* (Series: Literary Contexts, 2016), *Mothers, Daughters and Others: Representation of Women in the Folk Narratives of Assam* Edited with an Introduction (2013), *Communities of Women in Assam: Being, Doing and Thinking Together*, Edited and Introduced (2016) and essays in several national and international journals. She is currently working on a book on English Studies and a history of African American Literature for Indian students.

Lakhipriya Gogoi teaches in the Department of English, Dibrugarh University. She received her PhD degree from Gauhati University with a dissertation on "Self-Narration and Identity Formation: A Critical Study of Women's Autobiographical Writings in Assam". She has translated an Assamese novel *Seuji Patar Kahini* by Birinchi Kumar Barua into English as part of her M.Phil research and some of her translations are awaiting publication from Sahitya Akademi. Her other areas of interest include postcolonial literature, women's studies and writings from the Northeast of India.

Payal Jain teaches in the Department of English, Cotton University, Guwahati. Her areas of interest are gender studies, Indian English Fiction and Narrative Theory. Her doctoral thesis was on "The Paradox of 'Writing the Body': Reading Contemporary Indian English Women's Fiction". She has published several research papers and presented papers in national and international conferences on various aspects of women's narratives and everyday lived experiences.

Anna Kurian mainly teaches courses in canonical Anglo-American Literature in the Department of English at the University of Hyderabad. Her areas of interest include Children's and Young Adult Literature, Shakespeare Studies and Early Modern Drama, as also pedagogic issues related to English Studies in India. She has published in these areas in journals such as *ANQ, Radical Teacher, English Teaching: Practice and Critique*, etc.

Pramod K. Nayar teaches at the Dept. of English, University of Hyderabad, India. Among his recent books are *Human Rights and Literature: Writing Rights* (2016), *The Extreme in Contemporary Culture: States of Vulnerability* (2017), *Bhopal's Ecological Gothic: Disaster, Precarity and the Biopolitical Uncanny* (2017), *Brand Postcolonial: 'Third World' Texts and the Global* (2019), *Ecoprecarity* (2019), *Indian Travel Writing in the Age of Empire* (2020), *The Human Rights Graphic Novel* (2021), and *Essays in Celebrity Culture* (2021) besides essays on graphic novels, Human Rights and other subjects in *Orbis Litterarum, Narrative, Image & Text* and *Journal of Postcolonial Writing*.

Namrata Pathak teaches in the Department of English, North-Eastern Hill University, Tura Campus, Meghalaya. She has an MPhil and PhD from English and Foreign Languages University (formerly, CIEFL). Her research interests include Performance Studies and Indian Writing in English. Her essays have appeared in national and international journals and she has so far written four books. She is currently working on a book on theatre and an anthology of poems from Northeast India.

Binayak Roy teaches in the Department of English, University of North Bengal. His research interests include the Indian English Novel, Postcolonial Literature, Literary Theory and the Cinema of Satyajit Ray. He has done his PhD on the novels of Amitav Ghosh. His papers have been published in journals like *Postcolonial Text, South Asian Review, Asiatic, Nordic Journal of English Studies, ANQ: A Quarterly Journal of Short Articles, Notes and Reviews, Journal of Postcolonial Cultures and Societies, Asian Cinema Journal, Film International, Crossroads,* etc. His article "Exploring the Orient from within: Amitav Ghosh's River of Smoke" (*Postcolonial Text.* Vol 9, No. 1, 2014) was included in *The Years' Work of English Studies* published by Oxford University Press, 2016.

Dolikajyoti Sharma teaches English at the University of Gauhati. Her PhD work was on the problematic of female identity in the novels of D. H. Lawrence. Her research interests and publications are in the areas of women and literature, contemporary South Asian Literature, literature and the environment, and twentieth-century literature.

PREFACE AND
ACKNOWLEDGEMENTS

All of us who work as teachers of English probably cherish secret desires to draw all of the concerns together and write that nice and neat summary and overview of the field. We all have thoughts and opinions about what constitutes English in India and would like to test our views against those of others. We are a huge community united by our reading and interests and the English texts we teach. And yet doubts and questions and differences are as big and frightening as are the certainties and similarities.

The diversity of locations where we work, the influence of regional culture and politics on our disciplinary practices, the nature of the many classrooms we enter, the peers we work with and against have been important factors in the way we have positioned ourselves as teachers of English, and the exchanges I have had with the writers in this volume have convinced me that it is here in the small corner, in the specific site, in the particular classroom, that English literary culture in India is being transformed and remade.

Four of the essays are from Hyderabad University, one from North Bengal University, two from North-Eastern Hill University (NEHU), Shillong, and one each from Gauhati, Dibrugarh and Cotton Universities. The initial field was larger but these were the ones that finally got written. However, since I don't believe it is possible to have a representative selection anyway from a site as vast and varied as India, these are as good as any to provide a glimpse of what might be happening in the classroom.

I began thinking about this volume as a spin-off from a different book on English in India. It is a collaborative work, a conversation we began about how to frame the teaching experience. By then some of us had already published essays that sought to give a sense of this. K. Narayana Chandran has written often and with great eloquence on the teaching of English, almost singlehandedly giving shape to this new kind of critical essay on English in India, while Anna Kurian has written several essays on the teaching of Shakespeare in today's India. Pramod K. Nayar turned his hand to this form of writing with his usual ease and style. I am privileged to have their essays in this volume. My other contributors, who had not perhaps thought about writing of their classroom experiences, responded with enthusiasm to the challenge and put in what might actually be seen as 'reports from the field'. I thank them for being part of this conversation.

I would like to thank Shashank Sinha of Routledge, India, for being supportive of this project and always tolerant of my often unproductive intentions. Antara Raychaudhury, Anvitaa Bajaj and Shloka Chauhan handled the official processes of publication with patience and courtesy. Thank you girls.

INTRODUCTION
The teacher, the text and the Indian classroom

In 2008 when Rosinka Chaudhuri's edition of Derozio's works was published, it went largely unmarked outside a limited readership. But this event, if one may call it that, should be a critical point in the history of English in India. For too long we have been trying to make sense of the pan Indian scene and seminars and books on the field have been caught up in such exercises. There have been interesting reports from the ground and accounts by teachers of their many and varied experiences of teaching English in different parts of the country but the overall intention of such efforts has been to give a broad picture of all the things that are of relevance to the issue of English in India. The Derozio book is unique in focusing on the writings of an English teacher who played a crucial role in the gradual establishment of the discipline. And it suggests that this is one area we might well examine more closely to understand how English came to be taught and understood and what investments were made in it at different points in its journey. The lives and works of teachers of English, memoirs, essays, monographs and anthologies are sites that merit more attention than they have received. These would reveal the trajectory of the subject from the exclusively textual focus that was a convenient and practical teaching method in the early years of its life in college and University departments to the growing concern with historical and national issues that resulted in readings that were deeply embedded in the contexts of both the writer and the reader. The English teacher's perception of her role in response to these shifts might then be tracked in different cultural and linguistic regions. The figure of Derozio is exemplary in this situation, showing how an English teacher read the time in which he was teaching and interpreted his responsibility towards his students in relation to it.

Thomas Edwards in his biography of Derozio (1884) represents a crucial moment in the intellectual development of the time – Derozio's performance of his role as the English teacher who was also much more than that: someone who captured the imagination of his pupils and left a lasting impression on them. Many of the students who passed through Derozio's classroom did not even pursue English. They went on to become scientists and mathematicians but always remembered the influence of Derozio.

DOI: 10.4324/9781003146209-1

1

Edwards points to the breadth of learning that Derozio brought to his classes as well as his deep concern for his pupils with whom he interacted outside of college hours at the Academy he founded:

> The teaching of Derozio, the force of his individuality, his win-ning manner, his wide knowledge of books, his own youth, which placed him in close sympathy with his pupils, his open, generous, chivalrous nature, his humour and playfulness, his fearless love of truth, his hatred of all that was unmanly and mean, his ardent love of India, evidenced in his conversations and recorded in his lines, " My country! In thy day of glory past /A beauteous halo circled round thy brow," his social intercourse with his pupils, his unrestricted efforts for their growth in virtue, knowledge and manliness, produced an intellectual and moral revolution in Hindu society since unparalleled.
>
> (65)

In the qualities listed here are concerns not only with teaching literature – which was what he was expected to do in the job he held – but with deep nationalist feeling and desire for social transformation that involved helping students develop into exemplary human beings.

The 'short manuscript history' of Hindu College by Baboo Hurro Mohun Chatterji, which Edwards refers to as a source for much of Derozo's life and influence, records that students attended daily, a '"Conversazione estab-lished in the schools by Mr. Derozio where readings in poetry, literature, and moral philosophy were carried on. The meetings were held almost daily after or before school hours"'. The history refers to "'Derozio's disinterested zeal and devotion in bringing up the students in these subjects' and his 'love and philanthropy'". It credits him with having:

> fostered their taste in literature, taught the evil effects of idolatry and superstition; and so far formed their moral conceptions and feelings as to make them completely above the antiquated ideas and aspirations of the age. Such was the force of his instructions that the conduct of the students out of the college was most exemplary, and gained them the applause of the outside world, not only in a literary and scientific point of view, but what was of still greater importance, they were all considered men of 'truth'! Indeed, the 'College boy' was a synonym for truth, and it was a general belief and saying among our countrymen, which those that remember the time must acknowledge, that 'such a boy is incapable of falsehood because he is a College boy'.
>
> (in Edwards 1884: 66–68)

We see here the English teacher who perceived his role as one of inculcat-ing in students a spirit of disinterested enquiry on life and the world around them. The 'College boy' as being synonymous with truth is an impressive achievement for a 'mere' English teacher. But perhaps even more important in this account is the historical moment that demanded of the teacher like Derozio an effort towards social transformation.

The historical moment is indeed worth thinking about because the discipline as it has developed in different parts of the world has always been tied to a national cultural goal, to social developmental processes and to the fashioning of the citizen at a crucial point in a nation's history. If a colonial agenda was at work in "the beginnings of literary study in India" (Viswanathan 1989), colonising compulsions were behind the assertion of racial-civilisational superiority in the processes of the discipline's development in Britain, especially in its concern with "social and ethnographic issues" (Court 1992: 2), and in the concrete outcome of literary study in the making of the British imperialist. Alongside the energies of Empire were internal social imperatives represented in works like *The Social Mission of English Criticism* by Chris Baldick (1983), *English and Englishness* by Brian Doyle (1989) and Terry Eagleton's chapter on "The Rise of English Studies" in *Literary Theory: An Introduction* (1983).

A similar concern with the making of national consciousness is implicit in Jeffrey Sammons' claim about the source of American education in a German model whose goal is "the cultural formation of the self so that it might reach the fullness of its potentialities" (Sammons 14 cited in Fish 1989: 16). The compulsions behind the setting up of English Literature departments in universities in the United States, the individuals involved and the debates on how literature should be taught are recounted in Gerald Graff's *Professing Literature: An Institutional History* (1987/2008) while John Guillory looks at the socio-economic contexts of literary education in *Cultural Capital: The Problem of Literary Canon Formation* (1993).

In Australia, as Leigh Dale demonstrates in her historical account of the establishment of the discipline and the profession, "universities were focal points for cultivating and expressing ... race patriotism" (2012: 281) and the many decisions on individual texts and curricula, setting up of departments, and the rise of Australian Literature all finally had a tacit relationship – resistant and consensual – with British imperialism and its legacies.

The study of culture, canons and historical contexts – important issues in the works mentioned above – in different sites of English literary study demonstrate a concern with articulating larger social and national goals even when these are hidden under immediate debates within universities and departments over curricula, recruitments, financial support and other institutional matters.

In an essay on the relation between English, citizenship and national identity, Ingrid Johnston makes a similar point:

As an inherently political enterprise, 'English' is concerned with issues of representation of the world outside the classroom, dealing with ideas about society through the study of language and of selected texts. Language and literature are inextricably linked with notions of citizenship, society and the ways we get along with one another in the world. Today's English language arts classrooms can be the sites of new discourses that question the 'taken-for-granted' views of the past and create spaces for new bodies of knowledge and social relationships alongside the old, traditional and familiar.

(Johnston n.d.: np)

English is obviously imagined to be doing or aiming to do more and beyond simply teaching a particular literature and language.

In the journey of the discipline of English in Indian higher education – and indeed the goals of liberal education in post-independence India – evidenced in vision and objectives written into syllabuses following periodic general directives from the UGC, the UGC Model Curriculum of 2001 and its most recent advice on an 'outcomes'-based approach to curricula and teaching, it is possible to discern the tacit emphasis on the creation of the ideal citizen behind statements about national relevance in study and research.

The presence of English at all levels of the education system in India and the popularity of English Literature at BA Honours and MA has meant that the English teacher finds herself invested with responsibilities as role model for career and life, and as the source of cultural knowledge about other worlds, teaching difference and otherness and empowering students with the English language. Besides Derozio or the many British English teachers in the first universities, and the early Indian teachers as examples of the English teacher who left strong impressions on many generations of students, there is another source for the image of the teacher in India's famed gurukul system that was basic to many fields of learning where the teacher gave a comprehensive education in all aspects of life even as he (and it was almost always a male guru) taught and trained students in a particular branch of knowledge. While this system itself may have been largely replaced by modern institution-based education, the idea of it has a resonance that is often now derived from literary references to famous teachers and its continuation in the teaching of classical music and dance even today. This is evident in the expectations students and their parents have of teachers or the respectability that is commonly associated with the profession itself.

So the profession of teaching in India with its dual legacy in this ancient/traditional system *and* the modern conception of the teacher–lecturer brought in by colonial education is what Derozio and many of the teachers of English who taught in the early universities and colleges represent. Today's teacher, while not consciously drawing on such sources, is situated in the midst of this confluence of ideas and collective cultural expectation, self-interpreting her role as not merely that of teaching the subject or a set of texts but also of teaching ways to deal with the challenges of contemporary India. Teachers in different disciplines may interpret this additional responsibility differently in keeping with disciplinary culture and content. It is interesting to see how the English teacher – the Indian English teacher – positioned uniquely in mediating another culture to students understands/ interprets her brief, and this volume tries to capture a sense of this understanding.

In historical studies of English the teacher is a central figure in the founding and institutionalising of the discipline, marking out territory and establishing norms of practice for the future. Adam Smith, Hugh Blair, F.D. Maurice, A.J. Scott, David Masson, Walter Raleigh (the central figures in Franklin E. Court's magisterial study of the discipline in Britain), and accompanied by lesser known though equally important individuals, all taught English Literature even as they formulated policy and engaged in interpreting, as part of the way the subject was being fashioned, "social conflicts and cultural complexities that helped shape the discipline in Britain" (Court 1992: 2). Court also frames what might be a program for the writing of the discipline's history:

> The record of the genesis of English literary study is in part a record of major institutional commitments, of the publication of definitive critical tomes, of the shaping and projection of a teachable canon of literary works, and of the vibrant and colourful personalities who left their mark on generations of highly impressionable students.
>
> (3)

These "colourful personalities" and their careers are discussed in detail by Court even as he marks significant points in this genesis. In his evaluation of the broad goals that came to increasingly mark the discipline, Court concluded that there was "one dominant and important characteristic, the belief that racial history, social evolution, and the inherent nobility of the English spirit provide the philosophical grounding for the primacy of English literary study" (137). As a natural corollary to this shared belief was the study of English sociocultural history from the 1850s – a program that was as important internally as it was for the "promotion of empire" (138).

The institutionalization of English, the individuals who established early goals and set the parameters of the discipline in close alignment with national aspirations, the decision to study social history/or the nation's history – these are issues that cut across the history of the discipline's development in various parts of the world.

Teachers of English in India have appeared in many guises in the journey of the discipline – as revered figures who influenced many generations of students in the universities, as writers/editors of studies/histories of language and literature, as the fictional figure in R.K. Narayan's novel, *The*

English Teacher, as the target of national policies, as producers of guide books and commentaries and at local levels as multitasking figures who are expected to pitch in and help in a variety of institutional activities. They have, in the process, also had to contend with what Ann Hultgren calls a "'vocationalization' of English Studies, in which its practical and utilitarian dimensions are prioritized over its intrinsic value" (2016: 120). Being asked why we do not run courses on spoken English or on the basics of writing is something that departments of English, interviewees at selection committees and individual English teachers often encounter. Additionally, the composition of the English classroom has changed dramatically with unimaginable pressures and alternative literacies at work. Alok Mukherjee notes a "shift in the student population in terms of gender, class and caste" (2013, 36), "creating pressures and demands on the institutions" (37); and over the nearly three decades that I have been teaching, the ever-increasing diversity in each new batch of students has been a fascinating phenomenon.

Rethinking English (1991) and *The Lie of the Land* (1993) are two of the early examples of books that have tried to make sense of this complicated scene by mapping and analysing what constitutes the discipline. In retrospect, these two collections of essays on crucial aspects of English in India appear particularly important because they identified several elements unique to India (like the guide books and student's reliance on them, the role of publishers and the teaching of English texts against a multilingual background. In the intervening three decades either the same issues have been reiterated or the focus of study has been the more easily discernible idea of the English language in Indian education. The areas that were identified in these books – and their place in the disciplinary history has been to indicate and point to further areas that needed to be studied rather than close the conversation – are still being discussed without much advance having been made in critical engagement or in opening up to a possibly more inclusive approach, given the magnitude of the phenomenon of English in India. Among interesting recent works that *have* taken note of the bewilderingly plural linguistic, ethnic and historical contexts against which English is read and taught are Rashmi Sadana's *English Heart, Hindi Heartland* (2012) and E.V. Ramakrishnan's *Indigenous Imaginaries* (2017) that consider ways in which these diversities impact English in different parts of the country. Ramakrishnan's book offers the idea of *kshetra*, which he defines as a "semiotic field of linguistic and cultural interrelationships woven through language, collective memory, oral narratives and performance traditions, and multiple forms of expression" (viii). While both these books concern themselves with ways in which literature in India is produced with and against these elements, they offer useful ways of thinking about context or background as cutting across commonly acknowledged divisions and taking into account prevailing linguistic cultures.

These are heartening developments especially when the conversation on English as a discipline seems so often to be confined to only some centres while others are mere consumers of incompletely mediated ideas and opinions. Suman Gupta's essay on English in India (in Hewings et al. 2016) mentions curricular revisions at Delhi University but is apparently little interested in similarly significant revisions undertaken in the early 2000s at several state universities. Gupta's essay, in a volume devoted to the global development of English Studies, is compelled to adopt one more bird's eye view of the scene.

From the time of its origins in colonial India the discipline of English has always had attached to it a larger goal than simply the teaching of a language or a literature. Its extra edge has come from the investment made in it by its practitioners and its 'users' over the reform and transformation of society, the teaching of national identity and ideas about selfhood. From the various expressions of intention and aims written tacitly in the form of histories of the discipline, it would appear that it has never been taught for its own sake but has always, in fact, been harnessed to current ideologies and accordingly given a particular kind of shape. However, it is also important to note that while the fact of ideological influence may be a common factor in the discipline's formation and internal developments, this has not happened in the same way and at the same time everywhere. For instance, however much we in India may have felt at home in English, used it as a second language or a parallel mother tongue and given it constitutional recognition as one of India's national languages, its disciplinary development in higher education has not quite followed this trajectory in familiarisation. The colonial politics of selection of texts that has been demonstrated by Gauri Viswanathan in *Masks of Conquest* was followed by a different set of ideologies that came in with Independence. The school, college and university curricula, though different in vision, complexity and volume, basically contained texts that were already present in the pre-independence curriculum, with texts and authors that the earlier era had made familiar continuing to feature in the syllabi of English at these different stages of the education system. And teaching of language, composition and grammar, with varying degrees of competence seemed to be the dominant version of the discipline. This school teaching of English (some of these continued into college and undergraduate syllabuses) actually set the ground for the way the discipline gradually began to reinvent itself. So if the shape of the discipline is discernible at the BA and MA levels, the wider scene of English – where and how students first encounter English (language, literary texts and literary forms), that first poem in school, the compulsory English in junior college studied, for many students, alongside other Indian languages (especially where the language and medium of instruction policies of states vary widely across the country) – determines what the English teacher faces when she steps into a BA Major or MA class.

Whose business is it to think about the discipline?

One of the essays in *Rethinking English* suggests that the transformation or "reconstitution" of the discipline of English is the province of "radical academics and committed publishers" (Butalia 1991: 323) summarising what appears to be the commonly held view that English is and continues to be a discipline for the elite, notwithstanding the equally common recognition (via Viswanathan's *Masks of Conquest*, especially the chapter on "Beginnings of Literary Study in India") that it was in a way a lesser discipline in comparison to the classics as taught at Oxford and Cambridge). Rajeswari Sunder Rajan called for "a radical politicization of English literary studies, both pedagogical and critical, in India" (1986: 32) but her description of the ground is despairing, perhaps because of the time in which it was written (the height of postcolonial work in the discipline) and gives a picture that the chapters in this book would counter. However, it is useful to take a look at what she has to say— given her own path-breaking volume *The Lie of the Land*, which carried some essays that actually tried to ground teaching in the historical and cultural moment— about the secondariness that the Indian reader of English texts is doomed to suffer and that is therefore its sharpest, though often unstated point of crisis:

> Having been constituted unproblematically as (lesser) members of the community of western readers of western texts, we find ourselves as critics (a) naturalised into the role of western type critics (b) but suffering from a sense of inferiority or lack of worth as second-order critics (lacking in true language facility, sufficient scholarship etc), and (c) experiencing a loss of natural identity and alienation from lived experience.
>
> (1986: 31)

This divide continues as we look at the many more fissures that have opened up amongst those who practise the discipline of English in multiple, local ways – in urban and rural sites, town and city, college and university, state and central university, the big city and the small city – a plurality of locales that scars, marks and transforms the modes of 'doing English'.

The English teacher who is at the heart of this radical or apathetic universe is the one who works at ground level, facing what Alok Rai in his rather unsympathetic essay calls the "rising tide of illiteracy" (1991: 300) and "indifference" with the only engagement possible being to resort to the role of "a performer, an entertainer" (299). Rai's essay in *Rethinking English* is titled "An English Teacher in the Provinces" and is by turns entertaining and offensive – for example in his description of students as "the effluents of the school system who wash up at the gates of the university" (298)— suggesting the despair that he himself seems to feel as he offers an overview of all the problems facing the discipline.

The Lie of the Land also contains several essays on the classroom experiences of the English teacher. These essays are preliminary examples of a genre of writing that might be seen as metacritical reflections on the many things that are at stake in the mediation of an English text in the Indian classroom.

I have used the term 'profession' above. But is the teaching of English professional? Is the teacher a professional in the sense that we use the word? A dictionary definition does not quite capture what is at stake: "any type of work that needs special training or a particular skill, often one that is respected because it involves a high level of education" (dictionary.cambridge.org); or "an occupation in which a professed knowledge of some subject, field, or science is applied; a vocation or career, especially one that involves prolonged training and a formal qualification" (oed.com). But to profess (especially in its religious etymology) is to declare, promise or vow. In other words, it involves self-awareness and discipline, a self-awareness *of/ in* the discipline.

The UK English Subject Centre (now apparently no longer active) has over nearly two decades reflected on the teaching of literature and has "developed a unique working knowledge of the cultures and day-to-day practices of English programmes":

> 'subjects' and disciplines, while producing and resting upon bodies of knowledge, are communities of pedagogic practice. Those practices are conventionalised and habitual. They constitute the sedimented folk knowledge of teachers, their protocols buried deep in the subject unconscious. Yet it has long been evident that such tacit beliefs and habits can benefit from *being raised to consciousness, questioned, and revivified.*
>
> (Knights 2017: 2. Emphasis added)

Have we thought together, in a community, about what we do as teachers of English literature? Have we considered how, to borrow from Knights again, "the habits of the subject (if the singular even makes much sense) emerged from a contest between scholarship and transmission (on the one hand), and varieties of cultural intervention (on the other)"? (2). Have we felt the need to develop a distinct pedagogic practice that is unique to our particular geohistorical location?

Writing about oneself in the classroom

Discomfort with the many exercises seeking to make sense of the entire English Studies scene in India in one sweeping view is one reason for the piecemeal, small narrative approach of this volume. Its goal has been to capture wherever possible, practice on the ground, carefully steering clear of the temptation to give a pan Indian picture.

It came about as a result of a growing feeling about the futility of exercises in writing about the discipline in today's India as if it were a monolithic thing, done in the same way in all linguistic and cultural regions of the country, and a conviction of the impossibility of imagining a picture of English in India from above. The policy dimension is important, needs to be taken account of (and has been in many studies of the place of English in the Indian education system) and efforts to understand English as a pan Indian phenomenon usually starts from this level. In the light of the persistent resort to the postcolonial reading of the scene (with *Masks of Conquest* as its most popular reference point), the analysis of English's role in India's higher education system and its popularity as an aspirational point and vehicle as well as its appropriation as Dalit Goddess – all themes in different studies of the field – it seems that a change in approach has become necessary in order to see what is happening to/in English Studies today.

One of the areas we have not sufficiently factored in is the changing and evolving nature of the classroom especially its ethnic and linguistic diversity, varied colonial histories in different parts of the country that had inserted differences in the way English Literature and language had been mediated and learnt, urban–semi urban–rural distinctions, and the huge divergences in previously acquired knowledge and other literacies as we conceded to a rhetoric of superficial and frequently unexamined diversity. As a result, new ways of getting and keeping student attention have become imperative, involving always fresh evaluation of the class and engagement with new literacies among students so that the strange or different may be reached through the familiar. This might have many dimensions. The English text itself could be familiar in unexpected ways, especially through translated versions, cinematic adaptations or in some other forms to which the students may have had prior access. A particular English author may have become so much a part of the literary culture of a region – and the huge influence of T.S. Eliot on Assamese poetry (as also in literatures in many other Indian languages) is one such example – that students feel at home with his works. The teaching of a different culture by developing connections with the student's own knowledge establishes a comfort zone within which students are enabled to internalize social and ethical positions even as they understand otherness.

Beginning a conversation that unthreateningly leads into the unfamiliar also perhaps makes it easier to eventually teach the kind of emotional intelligence that is able to empathise more easily with otherness and difference. This is not to say that students will not learn the unfamiliar without this kind of mediation and aid. Many will and do. But given the changed profile of the classroom and very different early training from that which previous generations of students had, these are necessary ways of bringing home the relevance of the literary text that might at first glance look to them quite uninteresting, difficult and alien to their lives.

At the same time there is no substitute for close and attentive reading of a text. Whatever the intention and ideological imperative, the engagement with the text, the slow and reflective approach, spending time with the text is the foundation for exploration of the text in its reading location. In "Ecocriticism and the Mission of English" (2012), Richard Kerridge considers the distinction between "the aspiration to scholarly impersonality in reading, and the contrary recognition that reading is 'situated' and 'embodied', always taking place at a moment in someone's life and somewhere in physical space" (Kerridge 2012: 20). Garrard, citing both Kerridge and Timothy Morton (2012) takes this up as a simultaneity: "a necessary sense of urgency" along with "a countervailing sense of the value of slowness and acceptance of unprecedented emergence" (2012: 202). These are works of ecocriticism and the practice they advise is a key part of what is done or could be done in the literary studies classroom. Kerridge indeed sees close reading as:

> an alternative to the rapid consumption of the text, or its oppor-
> tunistic utilisation and reduction to commodity-value. As a teach-
> ing practice, what this idea aspires to encourage in students is the
> explicit aim of a lifelong relationship with literary texts—rereading
> and revisiting rather than discarding or obsolescence.
>
> (Kerridge 2012: 21)

Garrard elaborates: "teaching must also encourage reflection on the *difference* between such slowness and the goal-orientated, accelerated culture that prevails both within and without the university" (202).

Several chapters in this volume deal with the other, with difficult ideas and with the existence of alternative lives, of different and often less privileged lives in efforts to address the complexity they face in the classroom.

Teaching new literacies is a crucial concern with many of the writers – using the English text to educate students in the urgent issues of contemporary life, of how to live with the other not in mere tolerance but by knowing and understanding. Given the diversity and unevenness of the Indian nation such teaching is perceived by most of the contributors to be the only option available for them. So the classroom becomes a place where critical questions are presented – where we can still speak of class and caste and group relationships – a place where a certain subversive will is at work in teaching a story of the nation as plurality.

Bibliotherapy where reading literature becomes a way to help regain mental equilibrium (for instance, McCulliss 2012) is a useful way of thinking about what is sought to be achieved in several of the chapters especially in using literature to teach emotions, to teach young students to be sensitive to the trauma of their times.

In responses to that ubiquitous essay topic we were given as we entered into BA Honours in English in the 1980s – Why do you want to study

English – was embedded the expectation that it would give us something more than a knowledge of English Literature and culture and in our callow ways most of us came up with the same set of aspirations: learning life skills, increasing our knowledge about the world and avoiding insularity. The teachers who wrote for this volume, in their accounts of classroom practices seem to have had these very same aspirations as evidenced by the strategies they used and the ideas with which they entered classrooms.

In the process what they have all contributed to is a genre of writing uniquely fitted to capture a sense of the shifts and emerging concerns in the discipline particularly because these pieces all variously take account of the policies that undergird the discipline, the requirements of a teacher, the uniqueness of each classroom and the culture alongside which the English text is read. The styles adopted in these chapters, anecdotal and reflective, urgent and scholarly, are nicely suited to recording and capturing a variety of classrooms and teaching strategies. They are personal accounts, embedded in the individual teacher's reading, temperament and persona, engagement with her time and sense of responsibility to the students. Varying perceptions and understanding of the profession and evaluation of the present are at work in them. Along with the narration of personal experience and of the strategies employed are also offered brief interpretations of individual texts in unique reading contexts, especially the two-way process at work when the text is brought out of its original location and read again in another place. The anecdotal style and the choice of the little narrative is also critical for representing the many regions where English is taught and studied against a variety of socio-cultural conditions. Through the anecdotal mode these chapters avoid the temptation to get the big picture or suggest typical situations. They are 'reports from the field' – institutionally situated certainly but offering pictures of the specific and the local. At the same time they are built on practices of close reading (still taught in most English Literature courses in India), which allow for detailed engagement with the selected texts that is a necessary precondition to the contextualisation that defines the local practice.

The chapters that might have been are quite as many as the ones that finally got written. The variety of contexts that several young teachers considered were exciting and perhaps these will get done in the future. One young teacher proposed a reading of Shelley's "Ozymandias of Egypt" – a much anthologized poem read at many levels of the education system – in the backdrop of the 240 metre tall Statue of Unity (of Vallabbhai Patel) recently put up in Gujarat, as well as statues in the political culture of Modern India. Another, with fair knowledge of Sanskrit, gave himself the challenge of addressing the teaching of Indian classics as an introductory paper in a college in West Bengal: what would it mean for an English teacher to teach Kalidasa's *Shakuntala* (prescribed as part of a paper on Indian classics in the UGCs newest contribution to the undergraduate English syllabus)? These and similar challenges are aspects of the ongoing culture of English in India.

The invitation to English teachers from university and college departments to think about their practice was something that required a shift in orientation. It is not often that the English teacher in India has the opportunity to do this, especially in the heavy and unimaginative workload at the undergraduate levels, and in the rush to 'finish' courses in unbelievably truncated semesters in many universities. This is one reason why I retained the somewhat elaborate and lengthy discussions of teaching individual texts offered by some of the contributors – giving a sense of time spent lovingly with the text and therefore enthusing students in a very special way. Many of the chapters in the volume have drawn on what they have interpreted as knowledge already existing in the student individually and in the classroom collectively in a way that we have begun to see in the field of new literacy studies. In an essay on "Englishes and digital literacy practices", Colin Lankshear and Michele Knobel present the "language variety and the sheer plurality and diversity of 'Englishes'" and "the empirical reality of the 'multilingual internet'", particularly the fact that "many millions of non-native English-speakers are active participants in online cultural affinities within English-dominant contexts" (2014: 451).

This is an example of the existence of literacies other than those presumed to circulate in an English classroom and the writers in this volume have tacitly drawn on or responded to these unexpected literacies and shared areas of concern among students. Other elements that might be glimpsed in the chapters are the character of the profession and the education of the English teacher. The fact that there is no training available for the teacher in the higher education system and only the examples of their own teachers and strategies learnt by hit-and-miss methods has to be a factor in the way teachers fall back on their individual perceptions about students and their needs in the times for which they feel they have to equip them.

The editors of *The Routledge Companion to English Studies* perhaps have it right when, citing some of the essays in their volume, they declare:

> If we can no longer think only of 'English' as a single, standardized 'language, or of literature as a single, hierarchical or aesthetic privilege, but as 'open to discourses across a range of fields and approaches', then English studies have to take account of Englishes and of such discourses in the wider world and be ready to take account of new and sometimes unpredictable cultural, political, social and technological shifts in that global context.
>
> (Leung and Street 2014: xxx)

A range of historical and social realities, frequently the site of such shifts, are referred to in the teaching accounts presented here. The texts chosen for these exercises offer diverse opportunities for evoking the present even as they familiarise students with the milieu and culture represented. They enable reading of the contemporary and the processes of teaching show different concerns that teachers carry with them into the classroom even as they perform the duty of teaching prescribed texts. While some of the writers give elaborate accounts of the teaching of specific texts (Roy, Ashraf), others take individual texts as occasions for discussing issues of current interest and return to the text with renewed understanding (Kurian, Jain, Sharma), and a couple of essays discuss the challenges of teaching theory (Bhattacharjee, Gogoi). Bhattacharjee's essay, in fact, is an interesting exercise in creatively using the distance between the local and the global: "This distance is intersubjective as it works like a norm othering the English while appropriating it in a variety of indigenous and local contexts of life" – something that evokes her particular teaching context in Meghalaya with its rich Khasi oral culture and its use of English to express the indigenous and create its own body of English writing.

Nayar's chapter suggests that to read the literary text anew non-literary texts are essential – not only as information and background but to be read alongside as parallel texts – establishing familiarity with the debates around Human Rights (specifically the Universal Declaration of Human Rights document) and noting how HR is discursively represented, before going on to the literary texts themselves. Teaching the language of global Human Rights is seen as a way to introduce students to the possibility of looking at questions of representation anew. In that sense the essay reflects on the pedagogic aims and outcome of teaching HR as a sub discipline of English Studies. Its point about reference to one context and evocation of another – "We may seek verisimilitude but not exact correspondence. To word it differently, one can see the Dalit in the process of excavating the victimhood of the Jew, the refugee and the injured" – is what most of these essays seek to express as their own different teaching challenges.

While one of the aims of this volume was to track the uniqueness of the classroom, and several essays did attempt evaluations of the nature and interests of students in specific classrooms, this is an area that deserves more detailed attention. Even though we have informally been discussing the composition of classrooms and the possible predilections of students in and across English departments, this is still a relatively new idea. While the fact that differences amongst students, and especially the profile of the classroom, should matter and can, in fact, be enabling is acknowledged, taking account of it in curricular reform and teaching plans remains a challenge for Indian higher education and the specific practice of discipline.

Nevertheless, at least one essay in the volume articulates a sense of the classroom somewhat differently from the others. K. Narayana Chandran speaks of the "sociality of reading that only classrooms afford" and in the idea of hauntings he suggests the presence in the classroom of "collective and circular memory". His many essays on English in India like the one he has written for this volume, show a deeply felt sense of classrooms and the linguistic and cultural traditions that surround them, but it his reference to allusions that 'haunt' that makes one think of the ideal (and quite rare) English teacher who carries so much around in his head that he cannot but be haunted and be able to call upon this at will.

Most of the chapters have undertaken close readings of their selected texts but two have especially carefully detailed the painstaking effort with which they have lead their students through the potential uncertainties in Joyce and Forster.

Jinan Ashraf's chapter on *A Portrait of the Artist as a Young Man* – is one example of the meticulous preparation undertaken in order to bring home a difficult text to the reader. While she does not directly refer to the cultural distinctiveness of her classroom, the exhaustive process she describes tacitly refers to the difficulties a young Indian reader is likely to face with the style and context of the novel.

Binayak Roy's essay, almost like Jinan's in its detail, is a comprehensive reading with students of Forster's novel, *A Passage to India* and shows how the English classroom in India might work out its dynamic of the familiar and the strange. His use of the *adda*, a Bangla word that describes freewheeling, informal interactions among individuals who might gather at a street corner or a tea shop, on topics that might range from philosophy to food, as a notion and practice familiar to the students of eastern India and specifically Bengal, adds a dimension to the exchange of ideas that can be enabled in the classroom.

Johnston, cited above, suggests that a common investment is made in English wherever it is taught: "Historically, 'English' as a discipline is steeped in concerns about national identity and culture and about shifting notions of national communities" (Johnston n.d.). Similar claims are made by many historians of the discipline. For this volume this is particularly interesting because in many of the essays writers are tacitly addressing the diversity of India's social fabric in attempting to draw on local knowledge and practices and also taking cognizance of the unevenness in awareness about current events or concerns of the nation, ideas about which are variously processed and understood in different parts of the country.

Making connections between events and texts, teaching/awakening emotion, activating the local (as Namrata Pathak recounts in her chapter) – these are some of the things that writers have done in this volume. The regional life of the English text (in English or in translation and sometimes as abridged versions) and how this influences thinking and writing about other texts and authors is perhaps what the chapters also tacitly recognise in such efforts.

As Jeetumoni Basumatary shows, the question of discomfort at suggestive and sexually explicit language has been an issue for many English teachers – possibly all over the country. It is likely to be a general problem in societies like ours where, even as classical art forms – dance, music, and sculpture – have represented the body on the one hand, and there is now increasing freedom of language and imagination, with popular cultures around us replete with overt references to the body, sexuality and gender (in films, books, rape protests and rape reporting, for instance), repression and shaming practices derived from the ordering impulses of a hierarchical society continue. And yet we also have the experience of teaching works like *Measure for Measure*, *The Alchemist*, *Volpone* or the poetry of John Donne, where the sexual innuendoes are such an integral part of the text that they cannot be elided over. It might therefore be interesting to study in greater detail whether there is a change in the way students receive these texts in today's classroom and how such texts and classroom discussions in fact aid understanding and evaluation of the present. This chapter suggests several issues that might be at work in the atmosphere of the classroom.

Jeetumoni also makes a comparison between Guwahati and Delhi that enables her to discuss the very different challenge faced by the teacher in the smaller city. However, this and other essays that are distinctly limited by the region they refer to encourage me to think that the study of the classroom and its diversity might need examination of the milieu of the urban/semi-urban and rural and its impact on the kind of students who appear in the English Literature classroom. Ethnography might need to be accompanied by psychology – as we explore the greater 'canniness' of the student who arrives in the big city from smaller places – a quality acquired because of this milieu, the struggle to make it, learn to cope without home support and generally 'keep up'. The other is, of course, the case of the more advantaged student whose upbringing in wealth and comfort gives her a certain kind of confidence and even sense of entitlement, as well as a vastly different exposure to the world (which might include travel abroad, foreigners as friends and intimates and a different idea of 'liberation'). Obviously, for a class that hosts both these kinds of students, a problem like homosexuality would be received without the uncomfortable giggles or the uneasy silence mentioned by the writer because if one section of the class would have encountered it at least discursively in the society they moved in, the other section would endeavour to take it with composure in order to appear to be 'with it' and 'cool' and urban. This is an interesting aspect of how classrooms differ in that it is not necessarily always a factor of the ethnic-cultural or local-political.

Understanding how students get used to or acquire ideas, opinions and styles of response, which in turn influence classroom behaviour are equally important factors to take into account. If discomfiture is common, this obviously differs from class to class even in the same region and might well be a reflection of a teacher's own discomfort with discussing certain kinds of ideas, especially relating to sexuality, because she might share the same social world that her students come from. The argument for regional variation is strengthened because of these ground experiences, which are also necessary to take on board in discussing what happens in the English Literature classroom. Regional variation is very much about language cultures – the habits of thought, existence of words that are fully or only partially equivalent to English words and the ideas carried by them, conversational taboos etc. – but it is also about the relationship of the region to the centres where English lives differently.

One of the writers (Sukalpa Bhattacharjee) mentions 'unlearning' as a necessary strategy for her particular classroom which she finds has a shared ethnic life world while others suggest going with this kind of 'preparation' that students might come with or catch from the circulating national discourse. It is noticeable that the distinction among the kinds of strategies used is on this level: the smaller places, those that are distant from the centre, have different compulsions from the bigger ones, with the region caught more deeply in the local, while the big city is attuned to the national, so that the situations for interfering with/adulterating/transforming texts – the sites of reception – are varied.

What teaching achievement do the essays indicate? Helping students reach some degree of comfort with the strange, the discomfiting, the silenced and the invisible in society and literature are concerns that the writers of the essays variously articulate, doing this against a complex sense of the place of English in India, and for all of these teachers in college and university departments of English, with the place of English *Literature* in India. Claire Westall in the suggestively titled "The New Rise and Fall of English Literature" declares, only half humorously: "English Literature does not know what the 'English' of its own disciplinary label refers to – as language, as population, as of England" (2013: 218). A similar confusion exists in India on what is meant by the term English. In common conception it refers mostly to the English language and only rarely to English Literature. This is why most studies of English speak about the place of the language in higher education, in society, in professions and in government, and endlessly debate whether it empowers or divides an already divided and uneven society.

The editors of *The Routledge Companion to English Studies* declare that

> [A] significant proportion of the volume focuses on studies of English as a 'language' – with all the qualifications this term now signifies ... – but we also acknowledge that the term 'English' for many people can indicate literary practices, for instance creative writing, poetry and drama, but also the kinds of literary criticism entailed in addressing these scholarly endeavours.
>
> (Leung and Street 2014: xxi)

'Literary practices' is clearly an also-ran. In a work largely devoted to language there is a sideways glance at literary criticism: "there is *also another strand* to the study of English that is associated with literature and is often defined in terms of the concept of 'literary criticism'" (xxiii. Emphasis added). This appears in a solitary chapter in Part 1 of the volume. The book, however, represents the huge diversity in the field with English

17

being recognised in education and in new technologies (embracing digital literacies as a key aspect of its expansion) even as the influence of national policies and its role as a global language are seen as key aspects of its development.

The expansion marked by several of these volumes (Hewings et al. 2016; Leung and Street 2014; Westall 2013) suggest newer fields, newer uses to which English is put and newer conceptions of what constitutes English Studies. In this fertile ground there is really no limit to the ways of doing English. What this volume attempts through its teacher-accounts is a small step in representing the challenges faced by teachers in today's English classroom in India and the strategies evolving to bring the English text closer to the Indian student for whom colonial politics and even postcolonial inability to shake off its legacy have little meaning.

Works cited

Butalia, Urvashi. "English Textbook, Indian Publisher," in Svati Joshi Ed., *Rethinking English*. New Delhi: Trianka, 1991, 321–345. Print.

Chaudhuri, Rosinka. Ed. *Derozio, Poet of India: The Definitive Edition*. New Delhi: Oxford University Press, 2008. Print.

Court, Franklin E. *Institutionalizing English Literature: The Culture and Politics of English Literary Study*. Stanford, California: Stanford University Press, 1992. Print.

Dale, Leigh. *The Enchantment of English: Professing English Literatures in Australian Universities*. Sydney: Sydney University Press, 2012. Print.

Edwards, Thomas. *Henry Derozio, the Eurasian Poet, Teacher and Journalist*. Calcutta: W. Newman, (1884) Project Gutenberg EBook.

Fish, Stanley E. "Being Interdisciplinary Is so Very Hard to be", *Profession* (1989). 15–22. www.jstor.org/stable/25595433 Accessed 18 January 2021

Garrard, Greg. "Towards an Unprecedented Ecocritical Pedagogy" in Ben Knights Ed. *Teaching Literature*. Basingstoke: Palgrave Macmillan, 2017, 189–207. EBook.

Graff, Gerald. *Professing Literature: An Institutional History*. 1987. New York: University of Chicago Press, 2008. Print.

Guillory, John. *Cultural Capital: The Problem of Literary Canon Formation*. Chicago and London: University of Chicago Press, 1993. EBook

Gupta, Suman. "English Studies in Indian Higher Education" in Ann Hewings et al. Ed. *Futures for English Studies*. London: Palgrave Macmillan, 2016, 99–119. EBook.

Hewings, Ann, Lynda Prescott and Philip Seargeant Eds. *Futures for English Studies: Teaching Language, Literature and Creative Writing in Higher Education*. Houndmills, Basingstoke: Palgrave Macmillan, 2016. EBook.

Hultgren, Anna Kristina "The Role of Policy in Shaping English as a University Subject in Denmark" in Ann Hewings et al. Eds. *Futures for English Studies*. London: Palgrave Macmillan, 2016, 120–138. EBook.

Johnston, Ingrid. "English Language Arts, Citizenship and National Identity" (n.d.). www2.education.ualberta.ca/css/css_35_3/arenglish_language_arts.htm Accessed 21 August 2017.

Joshi, Svati. Ed. *Rethinking English: Essays in Literature, Language, History*. New Delhi: Trianka, 1991. Print.

Kerridge, R. "Ecocriticism and the Mission of 'English'" in Greg Garrard. Ed. *Teaching Ecocriticism and Green Cultural Studies*. Basingstoke: Palgrave Macmillan, 2012. Print.

Knights, Ben Ed. *Teaching Literature: Text and Dialogue in the English Classroom*. London: Palgrave Macmillan, 2017. EBook.

Lankshear, Colin and Michele Knobel, "Englishes and Digital Literacy Practices" in Constant Leung and Brain V. Street, *The Routledge Companion to English Studies*. London: Routledge, 2014, 451–463. EBook.

Leung, Constant and Brian V. Street Eds. *The Routledge Companion to English Studies*. Oxon and New York: Routledge, 2014. EBook.

McCulliss, Debbie "Bibliotherapy: Historical and Research Perspectives," *Journal of Poetry Therapy*, 25(1), (2012): 23–38, doi:10.1080/08893675.2012.654944, Accessed 21 July 2018.

Morton, T. "Practising Deconstruction in an Age of Ecological Emergency." in G. Garrard Ed. *Teaching Ecocriticism and Green Cultural Studies*, Basingstoke: Palgrave Macmillan, 2012. Print.

Mukherjee, Alok. *The Gift of English: English Education and the Formation of Alternative Hegemonies in India*. Hyderabad: Orient Blackswan, 2013 (1st edn. 2009). Print.

Rai, Alok. "An English Teacher in the Provinces" in Svati Joshi, Ed. *Rethinking English*. New Delhi: Trianka, 1991, 298–320. Print.

Ramakrishnan, E.V. *Indigenous Imaginaries: Literature, Region, Modernity*. Hyderabad: Orient Blackswan, 2017. Print.

Sadana, Rashmi. *English Heart, Hindi Heartland: The Political Life of Literature in India*. Berkeley, Los Angeles, London: University of California Press, 2012. Kindle.

Sunder Rajan, Rajeswari. "After 'Orientalism': Colonialism and English Literary Studies in India" *Social Scientist*, 14(7) (July 1986): 23–35. www.jstor.org/stable/3517248 Accessed 18 January 2021.

_____. *The Lie of the Land: English Literary Studies in India*. Delhi: OUP, 1993. Print.

Viswanathan, Gauri. *Masks of Conquest: Literary Study and British Rule in India*. New York: Columbia University Press, 1989. Print.

Westall, Claire. "The New Rise and Fall of English Literature" in Claire Westall and Michael Gardiner Eds. *Literature of an Independent England: Revisions of England, Englishness, and English Literature*. Houndmills, Basingstoke: Palgrave Macmillan, 2013. 218–233. EBook.

THE HAUNTED CLASSROOM

The afterlife of allusions

K. Narayana Chandran

Those of us who move in and out of classrooms have felt them to be delectably haunted and haunting. Teaching *The Family Reunion* some years ago, I stumbled upon the following, spoken by its Chorus:

> ...an old house [where] there is always listening, and more is heard than is spoken.
> And what is spoken remains in the room, waiting for the future to hear it.
> And whatever happens began in the past, and presses hard on the future.
> [...]
> There is no avoiding these things
> And we know nothing of exorcism
> [...]
> There is nothing at all to be done about it...
>
> (Eliot 1962, 101)

This old house, I told myself then, bears the closest resemblance to what we might fancy our classrooms to be. They sometimes have an air of the Monchensey house where words long for auditors and responders who, alas, have long left, leaving no addresses. The classrooms where I read the very first samples of 'English Literature' were such haunted sites, where classic memories and exegetical desires often met and exchanged vows. Voices and visions (rather than texts, interpretations, and commentaries in tandem) seemed to arrive and depart there, trailing clouds of their canonical glory. Reading English in our classrooms of the mid-to the late-1960s, the blessed pre-*Norton Anthology* days, have always struck me as deeply resonant and reflexive of crowded conclaves from the near and the far, now gathered in one Indian school, the voices of earlier generations of pundits on parade, of our Indian teachers and batches of earlier students—all of them jostled in reading, debating, and commenting upon verse and prose passages. Where then was the fabled common reader? Nothing, as far as I

DOI: 10.4324/9781003146209-2

recall, stood alone. Every minute detail in texts seemed hitched tangentially, cross-referentially, to every other hoary detail. Reading Shakespeare for B.A. English, for example, was not complete unless we read Johnson's *Preface* as well. Reading Milton's shorter pieces and Books I and II of *Paradise Lost* invariably meant the Milton, primarily, of *The Lives of the Poets*. Did Milton have other lives? We hardly knew or cared. Where there was leisure for fiction, why would there be grief?[1] Upon getting past my first *post* in graduation, how flattering it was to write *Faerie Queene* on answer sheets while annotating learned allusions to its eternal tropical tangle only to safely enter those sparse radiant sunlit clearings. Those of us who did not notice that Gray's "The Progress of Poesy" was virtually charting the *regress* of Poesy all through its reticulated allusions scored a poor 50 per cent and still felt grateful, like the poet: "Beneath the good how far—but far above the great."

Our questions for the university's public exams were thus safely guessed. I do not know anyone of those years who passed English exams by reading only the texts. Annotators, editors, and emendators alerted us to innumerable passages that rang somewhat loud reminiscent bells for *them* and perhaps for some of our revered teachers, albeit most of them were quite faint for us! Echoic if choric voices of literary forbears on such perennial pairs as death–life, light–darkness, earth–heaven seemed almost natural and hard to miss what with such benign spectral emanations from splendidly annotated editions of classics. I have often marvelled at the ironic pun on an old classic editor's name—A. W. Verity. This sometime Cambridge scholar's English texts, read intensively by Indian undergraduate students of at least six generations, had something of a phantom-like verity in our classrooms because our gut reactions to a passage, our half-formed thoughts of its meaning (or its refusal to mean anything at all for us) in Shakespeare or Bacon were finally settled by looking up Verity's crisp notes often cross-referred to another revered scholar. *Standard* editions, such as the Macmillan Classics, of canonical English authors had not only a wide circulation in Indian metropolitan colleges but in mofussil libraries where they occupied the most exalted 'Reference' shelves alongside a complete set of *Scrutiny*. Since our English authors were all dead, the Standard Editions of English Classics ensured eternal lives for their texts. Eliot's remark on the dead in *Little Gidding* comes to mind; they begin to speak, not when they were alive, but once they are dead.

The routine of our classrooms was so inured therefore to their strange spectrality. While the spectrality of reading may now be somewhat commonplace thanks to Derrida's *Specters of Marx*, I have often been fascinated by certain other forms of the *spectral* involving readers and texts, rather the dynamics of classroom intertextualities of the kind we have not quite registered when passages are negotiated among students in their open discussions.

Young adults seem easily drawn towards gothic fiction, especially stories centred on mentally distraught women or children confined to desolate chambers and attics; tales featuring a protagonist's occasional brushes with ghosts or medicine men. The courses I offer postgraduate students invariably list some such texts. The tales of Edgar Allan Poe involving lovers and quests, adventure, mystery, and romance are a safe bet, but a few other texts (Henry James's *Turn of the Screw*, W. W. Jacob's classic "The Monkey's Paw" …) are equally well-received. While reading such texts with a class, the spooky details in them (combined with the paraphernalia of love's intrigue, nightmare and reverie, obsessive rumination and melancholy …) never leave the minds of readers. Long after the class has moved on, the details from these texts haunt subsequent reading and readers. I consider myself fulfilled as a teacher when I begin to sense that my class and I maintain a fairly decent portable library of resources for the study of texts at hand. "We return to texts," John Taggart once remarked, "because something cannot be forgotten or because something has, indeed, been forgotten" (155).

One poem, with which successive batches of our senior MA have found enormous favour, in contexts of guilt and suffering in a woman-centred narrative like *The Yellow Wallpaper*, is Emily Dickinson's "One need not be a Chamber—to be Haunted –" (# 670). It is difficult to say why these texts haunt each other every time our students read them in tandem; or whether the texts continue to haunt their fancy ever afterwards, but the classroom seldom frees itself from this haunting when such sensory details of the Dickinson poem as the following animate our discussion: The Brain's Corridors, Midnight Meeting, External Ghost, Ourself behind Ourself, Assassin Bolting the Door, and a Superior Spectre. Surely, neither Emily Dickinson nor Charlotte Perkins Gilman had known Freud's *Das Unheimlich* essay. Neither would have been therefore able to theorize the difference between the *uncanny* in real life and its reflection in literature. The students, however, are struck by the imagery of the Haunted Chamber and the distraught female selves having to negotiate real and imagined fears through corridors, both near and far, contrived so cunningly by men, where the women must confront disasters all by themselves. Through the mid- to the late-nineteenth century, narratives portraying the lives of Anglo-American women confined to attics, formerly untenanted houses, locked-up rooms, garrets, etc. have received close studies; their triadic commonplaces of marital mismatch, misogyny, and madness are the stuff of most fiction of the period. No wonder such commonplaces haunt readers' imagination from text to text. I was impressed that in a couple of minutes, a 'poet' in our class once composed a parody of Dickinson by splicing syntactic bits from *The Yellow Wallpaper*:

A Colonial Mansion—so long Untenanted?
The Place empty for years—
That spoils my Ghostliness—but I don't care
Something strange about the House …

A recurrent spot where the Pattern lolls—
A broken neck and two Bulbous Eyes
Up and down and sideways
They crawl— Unblinking Eyes everywhere ...

This Great Immovable Bed
It's nail'd down I believe—
The Pattern—always the same shape,
Only very numerous.

A Woman stooping down and creeping about
Behind that Pattern—
Something else about that Paper—
The smell!

A great many women behind?
And sometimes only One,—
Those Creeping Women, and the creep so fast—
They all come out of that Wall-paper—

As I did?

Not bad at all for a budding poet who had since confessed to the class that her notebook of poems after Dickinson was titled *Stairway of Surprise*. She gave us indeed the gist and pith of the Gilman classic besides showing us how hauntingly creative such devotion as hers might be. None of the lines in this parodic exercise is hers. The lines are all from the Gilman text but the parody occasionally deploys Emily Dickinson's trademark dashes and odd capitals for stresses with great stylistic aplomb.

This versified gist of *The Yellow Wallpaper*, however fascinating at first flush, had had its detractors among the parodist's peer-group. One of them pointed out that her classmate had completely omitted the most crucial passages in Gilman where the *yellow* seemed to compel both literal and symbolic attention. She cited the following passages for example:

> I caught Jennie with her hand on [the wall-paper] once. [...] I asked her [...] what she was doing with the paper— [...] Then she said that the paper stained everything it touched, that she had found yellow smooches on all my clothes and John's, and she wished we would be more careful!
> [...]
> There are always new shoots on the fungus, and new shades of yellow all over it. I cannot keep count of them, though I have tried conscientiously.

> It is the strangest yellow, that wall-paper! It makes me think of all the yellow things I ever saw— not beautiful ones like butter-cups, but old foul, bad yellow things.
>
> But there is something else about that paper— the smell! [...] Now we have had a week of fog and rain, and whether the windows reopen or not, the smell is here.
>
> (*YWP*, 27–28)

Very true, we agreed. Flashes of memory, the immediate association that such flashes sometimes trigger, in a reading group are the surest evidence that: (1) allusions are happenstance, and they cannot be forced; and (2) allusive fragments are better gathered and preferably sorted out among a community of readers, willing to share and 'see' their significance. In other words, the dynamics of the classroom is not to be replicated elsewhere. A student who had until then shown no particular interest in the discussion or had added anything memorable thus far suddenly raised her hand to check whether the class was familiar with Manjula Padmanabhan's "Stains." (Cross-registration of courses in our Department often aligns and re-aligns the same class of students—one group registered for the "Classics in Translation" are not familiar at all with the texts discussed in, say, "Literature of the Diaspora.") This intervention was from a student of the literary diaspora. Another day we all returned to class reading "Stains." Padmanabhan's is a story of cross-racial travails of cultural adjustment among diverse ethnic minorities (especially the South Asians) settled in the US and other foreign countries. The immediate link this student was keen to suggest was to the peculiar embarrassment an American black woman called Sarah faces during her visit to a house where she meets and stays overnight with Deep, her Indian lover (and possibly her future husband), and his old mother, Mrs Kumar. Sarah cannot quite get over the circumstances (or their cultural logic, so to speak) of her having had to clean up a stained bed sheet on which she had slept the night because Mrs Kumar spots blood stains on it. Her obsession with the blood stain, this student found, was quite of a piece with the Gilman-narrator's obsession with blotches and patterns of the yellow that repels and revolts her. Shades of Mary Douglas, added an alert reader of anthropological literature, *purity*, *danger* …

The portable library a class harnesses sometimes grows rather unwieldy for discussion when students generously contribute to its collection, some of its leads surely wide of the mark or unsustainable owing to certain dubious readings of the texts at hand. Myths thrive on memory, both collective and individual, but their unique capacity for transformation and adaptation to contexts has been noted by critics such as Harold Fisch. Speaking of the Wandering Jew, Fisch observes that spectral forms and figures of Faust, Shylock, or Christ in literature and art do not conform to a singular pattern or uniform effect whenever or wherever they appear. Successive generations treat the ghostly avatars of these personae best suited to their belief systems, contingent values or circumstances. These mythical figures therefore alternatively represent retribution or rebellion, appear as saviours and sages, or act simply as agents of the devil. What haunts readers as something fixed and integrated (a *house* or *chamber*) is subject always to narrative manipulation by newer generations of readers. In short, we do not seem to 'see' the same spectres as readers, if only because *we* are not the same readers always, either by happenstance or by volition.[2] "Just as the plot or 'fable' of the Wandering Jew has no real shape, no *telos*, so his identity merges with that of many others," observes Fisch. "The formlessness of the myth, its tendency to lose its shape and to be displaced by other myths," he adds, "is of its essence" (65). The classroom, to my mind, is possibly the best site where transformations of the kind and scope Fisch suggests might be perceived every time a teacher discusses the topos of the Haunted Chamber.[3] The mythical object itself shares with the spectral the latter's protean dimensions. As Fisch quite succinctly puts it *a propos* the many lives of the Wandering Jew:

> The myth itself wanders and changes in the course of time; it goes underground and comes back to the surface revealing each time a different aspect because that is the way that history is apprehended. The Wanderer expresses the dialectic of time itself; its predetermined form and yet its lack of determination.
>
> (66)

The spectral emanations in a classroom seem somewhat steady and endless, not least because the liberal arts students are averse to the idea that a text is finished and done with (in contradistinction to the STEM students for whom 'progress' would mean only when the *end* is foreseeable, from the 'finished' to the 'unfinished'). One of the easy ways of broaching a new topic/ text in literary studies is by resorting to a familiar opening like: *the story so far....* By calling up a suggestive parallel, by citing an analogy, or quite simply by adverting to a sign or a voice that might guide us through new textual corridors, we begin afresh. Prospective links are indeed retrospective, and are seen as such. They are pretty much like some signpost we look for when we navigate completely unknown waters. Once set on a reading course, recalling echoic tributes or parodic riffs in a disorienting procession of genres is a collective effort by the class. Some clues admittedly are misses rather than hits, but the effort is certainly commendable when such clues help forego young readers' plodding, stumbling entry into unknown textual or topical terrains.

Few poems illustrate this spectrality of reading more readily than *The Waste Land*. Its "voices" emanate more from the dead or the dying than the living. Perhaps the lines referring to a perennial 'third' presence – (ll.359, 362, 364–365) – in "What the Thunder Said" are most exemplary in showing the poet's allusion *as* illusional or delusional, especially of the texts sensing their own spectrality. If we discount for the nonce that the poet's allusions are indeed to the Antarctic explorers as well as to Christ as "the third" who accompanied, unrecognized, his two disciples to Emmaus, we shall see texts themselves (initially seen and counted as two) sensing yet another, "that on the other side," creating a misapprehension of being stalked. Perhaps this one example from *The Waste Land* will also serve to help young readers *see* allusion in better light: as *illusion*, *delusion*, and in rare cases, as *hallucination*. In short, the inherently unfinished nature of allusion needs no better example than when readers imagine the passage they are reading looking askance, as it were, at other passages.

T. S. Eliot's own quotes, mostly fractured and fragmented from his "dead masters" such as Andrew Marvell—"But at my back ... I hear" (l.185)—however, act at once as certain assurance and suggestion directed at the fumbling reader. Besides such oblique hints, readers are directly addressed (ll. 20–22, 27, 76) in order to reassure them that *this* poem at least breaks down the usual barriers between readers and their writer, and that what they *together* make of the passages is the poem. Of course the poet's "Notes" are meant to offer additional help. *But at my back .... I hear* in particular seemed to run almost like a mnemonic refrain when the class got round to reading *The Waste Land* a few weeks after sampling the British poets of the First World War. What worked for us was not so much Eliot's putative allusion to the line from Marvell's "To His Coy Mistress," but the "cold blast," the rattling bones and the chuckle in ll. 185 and 186.

First of all, it doesn't take long for the class to notice the *waste* of war (of youth, love, hopes, aspiration, material investments in grooming the young ...) in a poem that breathes the air of a long-drawn-out elegy composed under the shadow of the Great War (1914–1918) and the Spanish Plague (1918). Students associate death in war poetry with expense and entropy—whether it be "The unreturning army that was youth" in Siegfried Sassoon's "The Troops" (Church and Bozman, 100) or the young soldier, "the clay [that] grew tall" for death in Wilfred Owen's "Futility" (Ridler, 77). Other echoes, shockingly louder, from the war-torn world; and shadows, uncannily resembling prowling beasts and wounded combatants seeking care and shelter fill *The Waste Land* air when we read, "I had not thought death had undone so many" (l.63). Recall "The Death-bed" by Sassoon where we read that "the pain/ Leaped like a prowling beast" in the dying man while "Death, who'd stepped toward him, paused and stared" (Church and Bozman, 102). Clumsily moving among corpses, lumbering along death's alleys where a rat creeps by "Dragging its slimy belly" (l.188), Eliot's persona notices naked white bodies, and bones "[r]attled by the rat's foot only" (ll.193–95). "The restlessness of sleepless nights digs trenches," muses E. M. Cioran in one of his fragments, "where the corpses of memory are rotting" (113). Sassoon's persona in "The Rear-Guard" "stagger[s] on until he [finds] "Dawn's ghost," but not before noticing "muttering creatures underground/ Who hear the boom of shells in muffled sound" (Reidhead, 2024). And where have we heard "The rattle of the bones" before we began Eliot's "Fire Sermon"? Perhaps in Isaac Rosenberg's "Dead Man's Dump" that begins with the racket of "The plunging limbers" that run "over the sprawled dead ..." crunching their bones while "Their shut mouths made no moan" (Reidhead, 2032). Also, perhaps, in the third line of Owen's "Anthem for Doomed Youth:" "the stuttering rifles' rapid rattle ..." (Reidhead, 2034).

I have wondered to myself what makes some texts continue to haunt classes, long after their passages, like the Solitary Reaper's song, are heard no more. Most devoted readers carry whole anthologies in their heads. At least a few of my generation fondly do. Allusions, alas, have yet to secure a ready-reckoner but the joy of spotting them in élite conversations or books (and having spotted them, reflecting on their extended appeal and appropriate timing) was once an *art*. Stephen Greenblatt's *Culture in Mobility* would need no further proof if one knew *how* allusions work in our everyday lives. The shared cultural capital of allusion is nearly always an institutionalized *répertoire* upon which a class draws. I suspect, however, that *that* class has either withered away like the State in Marxian thought, or perhaps our students these days are wired differently from us. When they miss a crucial narrative beat in our conversation with them or when I see no glimmering recognition of a famous textual episode to which some occasion adverts, I pause. Do they feel perplexed by the variegated practice of the writers of this century who still recall their Testaments of Faith by chapter and verse, their home-grown myths and legends, local languages, and the innumerable folkloric motifs as yet unindexed in Stith Thompson? Perhaps our students no longer relish the beauty of inflections in literary allusions as their parents and teachers used to. With larger and mightier storage and retrieval devices at hand, our young Axels seem to have left their living to such e-servants.

Perhaps teachers of languages and literatures need to take *passages* more in their multidimensional senses than they have. A *passage* is not merely an organizational unit of text or image, or a printed paragraph of prose or verse. It is also a *movement*, and a *way* the movement records in its progress or regress, marking the corridors of its politics and history through which it reaches us from afar. Texts do not 'happen' at once or 'occur' one after another in our reading, but they *pass*. They pass among, between, and across one another. Allusion alerts us to such 'passages' by their *textural* rather than textual alliances and alignments, a phenomenon *The Eye in the Text* prefers to call "intertexturality" (Caws, 11).

If only to reassure myself that my classrooms are not lost in theoretical ether but do remember some of what they have read and that they could connect with and comment on styles of thought they have discerned earlier, I list among texts for intensive reading selections from Cynthia Ozick's *Art & Ardor,* or such essays as Toni Morrison's "Rootedness: The Ancestor as Foundation," Hanif Kureishi's "Loose Tongues," Salman Rushdie's "Step across This Line," and Seamus Heaney's *Government of the Tongue.* Now a caveat: I do not for a moment believe that such allusive significance as *I* see in reading texts can be hammered home. Nor is it prudent for a teacher to assume that an inherently haunted piece, regardless of its classic status, will haunt *all* its readers. I cite Heaney's *Government of the Tongue* as an example here of a text that evoked absolutely no spectral appeal in my classes despite my valiant efforts to canvass some sympathetic response from my students. (There is, by the way, no theory known to me that asks why readers do *not* respond to textual events.) While I vouch for the hauntedness of Heaney's richly allusive reflections, my students often seem rather unimpressed if dismayed by his welter of references, nearly all of them quite foreign to them. How could I be blind not to recognize that the tides of fashion in literary conversation have turned radically, and probably even the poets with whom our young readers must have been somewhat familiar now seem rather invested with some mysterious spectral aura *Heaney* vouchsafed to them? Here's one such, whose salience I have had to *explain* to my class at length:

> [T]he example of Dante was [...] important, although his import was significantly different for Eliot than for Mandelstam. Both men, interestingly enough, were turning to the great Florentine at a moment of mid-life crisis .... What obsessed Mandelstam and shook him into heady critical song—namely, the sensuous forag-ings and transports of the body of poetic language—hardly seems to interest Eliot at all. He is much more preoccupied with the philo-sophical and religious significances which can be drawn from a work of art, its truth quotient rather than its technique/ beauty quotient, its aura of cultural and spiritual force. There is a stern and didactic profile to the Dante whom Eliot conjures up and, as he embraces religious faith, it is to this profile he would submit in order that it be re-created in his own work.
>
> (Heaney, 98)

The class was most dutiful in reading Heaney but never felt *haunted* as the Irish poet had evidently been when he lectured to his scholarly audience at the University of Kent in 1986. Let me just add that Heaney's might still prove to be a piece that passeth all understanding in any Indian classroom except for its thesis that totalitarian regimes and the poets run parallel governments. "A population of ghosts speaks through us [,]" admits Paul Zweig while speaking for all writers. "This may be what the Sufis mean," he continues, "by 'the friend:' the layered otherness which inhabits us, and is ourselves" (285).

Let us now turn to yet another experience, varieties of which are not unknown to readers generally but to teachers in particular. Perhaps we could call the basis of such experience a "ghostly paradigm of things," a phrase I borrow from W. B. Yeats's "Among School Children" where the poet observes rather gnomically that "Plato thought nature but a spume that plays/ Upon a ghostly paradigm of things …" and alludes in rapid row to Aristotle, Alexander the Great, and Pythagoras, all of them life-long learners who, sadly, look rather pathetic in old age: "Old clothes upon old sticks to scare a bird" (Yeats, 129). Even as such allusions might seem dubious, and perhaps far too abstruse to qualify as pointed references to anything that one reads at hand, the "ghostly paradigm" nonetheless is most apposite (and answer) to the readers' private sense or mood. The line that inevitably cheers me up on such quaint occasions is W. H. Auden's: "The blessed will not care what angle they are regarded from, / Having nothing to hide" (242). Since students will hardly see *our* point if they haven't read or seen a passage we cherish, there is little chance of our sharing this *secret* intertextuality with anyone at all. Philip Davis has remarked on this phenomenon most tellingly in his *Reading and the Reader*. He believes that readers often respond to an "inner speech" that they hear apart from a text's voice, "an electric association of feeling or a pang of memory." Such textual fragments gather within readers unbidden, and they suggest certain directions if only to suggest that the readers' errancy has not altogether been pointless. Davis goes on to suggest that

> These memorable fragments serve as metaphors for what readers [...] may or may not quite recall. [...] This idea that the text contains within it a niche for its secret personal meaning to the reader, thinking off the back of the text, also is itself one of the secrets of reading.
>
> (129–130)

In such cases, we are not sure whether the text reflects on itself when it begins to see its likeness in another text. What we do know, nonetheless, is that this is uncanny, and it does open within the text that space where we sense it at once as the *written*, and the written *upon*. If we cannot distinguish within this "ghostly paradigm of things" a *writing* effect and a *reading* effect, we might be none the worse for it. Such allusive effects, so common in reading, do not fit neatly into any known narrative theory. Nor are their jagged edges blunted by explicatory or exculpatory denials.[4]

I have no other means here to illustrate this haunting, this strange "logic of spectrality" as Derrida calls it (178 n.3); one's listening to some ghostly double as it were, except by reading two poems, both *secrets* that poets sometimes feel rather privileged to share with their readers.[5] Not only are they secrets of the trade but a deeper *sense* of secrecy that attends all creation. The first, "The Child on the Stairs," is a poem by Jules Supervielle, a Franco-Uruguayan poet (1884–1960) who captures memory infolded in an experience of his "childhood/ haunting a favourite place." The visitant here is not a child, but *Childhood* that baulks at commitment or confrontation:

29

You prowl around me when no one's looking,
   and hurry away, as from an illicit meeting.

                                                  (Supervielle/ Alvi, 296)

This short poem ends on a deal the poet offers Childhood. He wouldn't tell anyone of this visitation but Childhood "must also keep our secret" (Supervielle/ Alvi, 296). Another explicit line following this would certainly diminish the charm of this half-way deal between barter and offering, a gift promised in winks.

The second poem, Denis Levertov's "The Secret," is very much within the haunted precincts of a classroom, the more we reflect on the exquisite mysteries of reading poetry and poets. Perhaps what this poet suggests is the afterlife of allusions that tantalizes readers who seem challenged by textual remnants/ revenants traversing their minds that elude their distinct grasp. The narrative voice here cannot but be Levertov's. It evidently poses a puzzle involving "Two girls" who discover "the secret of life" in a poem of hers. The poet is intrigued. She does not know the secret. The news of the girls' discovery of it is conveyed to her by "a third person." The gist of it all is that the girls had found it, but they are at a loss to say what they had found. Was it not, as we recall, in "a *sudden* line/ of poetry" they found it (my emphasis)? More than a week gone by, the girls have forgotten *it*—"the secret, / the line, the name of / the poem" (Levertov, 33–34).

Isn't all this simple, quite natural, as one would expect in reading poems in circumstances like this? How many of us remember exactly such "secret[s] of life" we might have intuited in the poems we have read? What, in any case, makes this narrative a *poem*? Exactly halfway through her lyric narrative, Levertov seems rather troubled by this "secret," not quite the secret the girls have since forgotten, but the *poet*'s furtive fascination with "the secret of life" someone else claims to have found in her poem (Levertov, 33–34). As we read the lines over and over again, we see how the poet's fascination with the "secret" has now begun to haunt her; its pleasant curiosity and self-awareness now, a "secret" of another kind, somewhat of a magnificent obsession. It has slowly transformed itself from the girls' "secret" into a rather cute puzzlement over *their* "finding" what the poet cannot find, to their loving her for the line she wrote, and then their forgetting of it. Lessons in the phenomenology of reading now begin to haunt us as well when the poet recognizes, first, that a poem's ultimate fulfilment is in its *performance* elsewhere, among its readers. It does not matter who 'performs' the poem as long as the poem fulfils its dharma. Now *this* secret, what a poem *for* a reader might be, will hardly ever be known to the poet, not even when the best commentaries on it salute its maker's prodigious art. What the poem has since meant for every other of its possibly thousand readers will, of course, remain a riddle, especially for the poet who has made the poem and would love to solve it. Again, at every reading, the 'performance' is not the same, assuming that the same person were to read it over and over again.

Now, what is it precisely the two girls have *forgotten*— the details, so to speak, of their first 'performance': who read it first, and who, after; whether they read loudly; silently; or, one just listened as the other read; or whether they went over the lines together by turns …? Since no one reads the same poem twice (*pace* Heraclitus's river metaphor), how crucial would the loss of *that* "secret," at first flush, be? All these are riddling, fun to ponder when the poem prompts them, but finally, is the "secret" then, not so much the "secret" *in* the poem as that *of* its 'performance'? The poem's last lines swell the poet's mysterious fascination for the most difficult of all secrets—"most of all" the fact of their assumption of there being such a secret (Levertov, 34).

That *most of all* has a lot of work to do. Most of all now, it binds readers and the poet ineluctably in a relationship. Why? It is this *assumption* that keeps all writers going, and puts their readers on an allusive trail, as it were. It is not as though one has *a* secret of which the other knows nothing. The poem now haunts for its *shared* secret, at least for the assumption that if the secret is worth keeping, it is because it can be, some day *will* be, shared. A related thought: who might call anything a *secret* and still not feel specially privileged that they (alone) hold it? The magic of poetry, the art's ardour, has seldom been caught so brilliantly as here.

We are not yet done with such paradoxes when, as a community of readers, the class always begins to relish the fruits of a hermeneutic bid founded on a suspicion that the texts it reads surely bury more secrets than others (especially our revered critics) have unearthed in their readings. Again, that Poe story comes to mind, unbidden—"The Premature Burial," but I shall recommend to all young researchers instead Frank Kermode's *Genesis of Secrecy*. Kermode makes compelling reading when we realize that texts of authority, especially the Biblical parables, invite what he calls *divination* that affords them insights into the secret worlds of text-building, a hoary tradition still celebrated or revered in all cultures:

> What is the interpreter to make of secrecy considered as a property of all narrative, provided it is suitably attended to? Outsiders see but do not perceive. Insiders read and perceive, but always in a different sense. We glimpse the secrecy through the meshes of a text; this is divination, but what is divined is what is visible from our angle. It is a momentary radiance, delusive or not … When we come to relate that part to the whole, the divined glimmer to the fire we suppose to be its source, we see why Hermes is the patron of so many other trades besides interpretation. There has to be trickery. And we interpret always as transients—of whom he is also patron—both in the book and in the world which resembles the book.
>
> (Kermode, 144–145)

No harm either when we entertain, as a *haunted* community, the basic paradox that a secret is hardly one unless you secretly share its capital with someone, besides the more ethico-aesthetic challenge it poses. Held purely as an aesthetic object (like Levertov's poem), the secret is tantalizing and seductive at once. Translated and verbalized, shared and explicated, unriddled like the Sphinxian, where is the secret?[6] When Jonathan Culler, for example, wonders *who* speaks Robert Frost's "The Secret Sits" (278–279), the haunting begins yet again in a classroom while, as Frost puts it, "the Secret sits in the middle and knows." Culler gets this much right: what the Secret knows, alas, is what we would always want to know. Will anyone ever know what *Maisie* knew? What really happened in the Marabar Caves? What story *Bartleby* might have told us? Or who indeed sat down to write "Borges & I"? The Secret sits in the middle and smiles.

All that said however, one student brought this up once for discussion: Would Page duBois's observation add or subtract from such knowledge, she asked, that in Greek thought truth is supposedly hidden in the female body, and that its mysterious powers draw men to seek it often by violent means of intrusion and extortion. Absolutely appropriate and most pertinent I thought if the class was, as it seemed, still haunted by Margaret Atwood's brilliant memoirist assay called "The Female Body." (We had of course discussed the Atwood piece a couple of weeks ago, but what haunted *me* personally was Atwood's epigraph which read: "entirely devoted to the subject of 'The Female Body.' Knowing how well you have written on this topic ... this capacious topic" (343), which indeed sounded like the ghostly voice of an editor at the *Michigan Quarterly Review* where her article had first appeared.) The class seemed, however, to recall DuBois's observation that Truth's "hiddenness, secrecy, female potentiality, the tempting enclosed interiority of the human body, [its] links with both treasure and death, with the mysteries of the other" align it with the most vulnerable of the species, women and slaves (DuBois, 91).

Some Levertov poems are quite those mysteriously mythic corners, like Rukeyser's, into which no one looks. To my mind, however, "The Secret" is that one poem that haunts me still for the difficulty of getting its sonorous power into discursive focus. This again ought not in fact to strike anyone as exceptional or unprecedented since Derrida's reminder that 'seeing' ghosts is the most *theatrical* of textual events. And that gladdens teachers who have always valued academic orality on par with rich *dramatic* performance. The logic of aligning the *spectral* with *specular* derives from Derrida's remark in *Specters of Marx* that "A spectral asymmetry interrupts here all specularity. It de-synchronizes, it recalls us to anachrony" (6). Class and clowns are old bedfellows; they feel themselves pushed toward edges of certain errata of conscience. No one *sees* a ghost in printed matter. When haunted, the classroom is *ersatz theatre*.

Notes

1 And this, despite Johnson's "Notes are often necessary, but they are necessary evils" in *Preface* to his edition of Shakespeare, 1765.
2 The classic instance of such an apparitional traversal is, of course, Eliot's "familiar compound ghost" of *Little Gidding*. Many readers have glanced at "ghosts," all familiar and compounded as Eliot would have wished, given the textual warrant of such recognitions as happening "In the uncertain hour before the morning ..." (*Collected Poems*, 216).
3 For an example of such unusual if unsuspected haunting, see A. K. Ramanujan's titular poem of his posthumous volume called *The Black Hen* and my note, "A Source in Sorcery: *The Black Hen* and the Posthumous Poet."
4 On writing and the uncanny I have consulted Alan G. Lloyd-Smith's "Preface" to *Uncanny American Fiction: Medusa's Face*, ix–xii. Some of the material that follows has appeared in my essay "Invisible Poetry: Secret-sharing Classrooms" of the *Comparative Media Arts Journal*, # 8 (2020). www.sfu.ca/cmajournal/issues/issue-eight--invisibility--escaping-notice-.html
5 Writers do not always share such secrets of their reading with us. They would rather, like T. S. Eliot, cross textual borders, and close contextual gaps with such impunity that the best critics manage to alert their readers with "hints and guesses, hints followed by guesses." For an example of this arduous exercise and the enormous pleasure the critic derives from it, see my "Phantoms of the Mind: T. S. Eliot's 'To Walter de la Mare" (1997).
6 Perhaps it is too early to solve the complex Oedipus riddle, if one reads the famous "Myth" by Muriel Rukeyser and its brilliant discussion in Cavarero (2000, 49 ff).

Works cited

Atwood, Margaret. "The Female Body." *The Fields of Reading: Motives for Writing*. Ed. Nancy R. Comley et al. New York: St Martin's Press, 1998. 343–355. Print.

Cavarero, Adriana. *Relating Narratives: Storytelling and Selfhood*. Trans. Paul A. Kottman. London and New York: Routledge, 2000. Print.

Caws, Mary Ann. *The Eye in the Text*. Princeton: Princeton UP, 1981. Print.

Chandran, K. Narayana. "Phantoms of the Mind: T. S. Eliot's 'To Walter de la Mare'." *Papers on Language and Literature*, 33. 2 (1997): 213–219.

———. "A Source in Sorcery: The Black Hen and the Posthumous Poet." *A R I E L: A Review of International English Literatures*, 40. 4 (October 2009): 143–150.

Church, Richard and Mildred Bozman. Ed. *Poems of Our Time*. London: J. M. Dent, 1945. Print.

Cioran, E. M. *Tears and Saints*. Trans. Ilinca Zarifopol-Johnston. Chicago and London: U Chicago P, 1995. Print.

Culler, Jonathan. "The Literary in Theory." *What Is Left of Theory?: New Work on the Politics of Literary Theory*. Ed. Judith Butler, John Guillory, and Kendall Thomas. London & NY: Routledge, 2000. 272–292. Print.

Davis, Philip. *Reading and the Reader*. Oxford: Oxford UP, 2013. Print.

Derrida, Jacques. *Spectres of Marx: The State of the Debt, the Work of Mourning, and the New International*. Trans. Peggy Kamuf. London: Routledge, 1994. Print.

duBois, Page. *Sowing the Body: Psychoanalysis and Ancient Representations of Women*. Chicago: U Chicago P, 1988. Print.

———. *Torture and Truth*. New York and London: Routledge, 1991. Print.

Eliot, T.S. *Collected Plays*. London: Faber, 1962. Print.

———. *Collected Poems 1909–1962*. London: Faber, 1963. Print.

Fisch, Harold. *A Remembered Future: A Study in Literary Mythology*. Bloomington: Indiana UP, 1984. Print.

Gilman, Charlotte Perkins. *The Yellow Wallpaper*. New York: The Feminist Press, 1973. Print.

Heaney, Seamus. *The Government of the Tongue: The 1986 T. S. Eliot Memorial Lectures and Other Critical Writing*. London: Faber, 1988. Print.

Kermode, Frank. *Genesis of Secrecy: On the Interpretation of Narrative*. Cambridge, MA: Harvard UP, 1979. Print.

Levertov, Denis. *Selected Poems [O Taste and See, 1964]*. Ed. Paul A Lacey. New York: New Directions, 2002. Print.

Lloyd-Smith, Allan Gardner. *Uncanny American Fiction: Medusa's Face*. New York: St Martin's Press, 1989. Print.

Padmanabhan, Manjula. "Stains." *Written for Ever: The Best of Civil Lines*. Ed. Rukun Advani. New Delhi: Viking/Penguin, 2009. Print.

Reidhead, Julia. Ed. *The Norton Anthology of English Literature. The Twentieth Century and After*. Volume F. New York and London: Norton, 2012. Print.

Ridler, Anne. *A Little Book of Modern Verse*. London: Faber, 1941. Print.

Supervielle, Jules. "The Child on the Stairs." Trans. Moniza Alvi, *Split World: Poems 1990–2005*. Northumberland: Bloodaxe, 2008. 296. Print.

Taggart, John. "Come Shadow Come and Pick This Shadow Up." *Artifice and Indeterminacy: An Anthology of New Poetics*. Ed. Christopher Beach. Tuscaloosa and London: The University of Alabama Press, 1998. 155–182. Print.

Yeats, W. B. "Among School Children." *Selected Poetry*. Ed. A. Norman Jeffares. London: Macmillan, 1974. 127–130. Print.

Zweig, Paul. "A Voice Speaking to No One." *Praise of What Persists*. Ed. Stephen Berg. New York: Harper & Row, 1983. 281–289. Print.

2

TEACHING *CYMBELINE* DURING INDIA'S #METOO MOMENT

Anna Kurian

The elective course on Shakespeare's Genres that I was teaching to an MA class at the University of Hyderabad was drawing to an end, with only two genres left to study: the Shakespearean romance or tragicomedy, to be exemplified by *Cymbeline* and Shakespeare's non-dramatic verse under which we were to examine *The Rape of Lucrece* and select sonnets. While the keener students were still focussed on learning as much as they could, several others had lost steam and were disinterested in these texts, surfeited with analyses of state and gender politics via the tragedies, comedies and history plays. They had also gained some understanding of the politics and conventions by which these forms and genres were sorted and classified. It was in this somewhat lackadaisical mood that we began talking about *Cymbeline*. Apart from one student who enjoyed the play for its British-Roman politics, most found it involved and rambling, and could see the truth in Jennifer Forsyth's pronouncements about the play: that it was about the "bafflement of expectations", that its themes reinforced the "pattern of ambiguity", the strange silences lead to confusions and eventually resulted in an "inability to interpret the play unambiguously" (Forsyth 2014, np).

The students' disdain for the text was quite apparent (there was the frank question from one of the students: what is the point of studying this involved and silly play, which has no relevance to our lives?) and it was with this attitude that we began studying the play. However, as I hope to demonstrate, reading any Shakespeare or Early Modern play in contemporary India makes perfect sense if it is read paying close attention to features that link it contextually to the present, rather than by limiting it to its historical and temporal location. This, of course, does require the teacher and the students to be constantly alert to the presentist values that they bring to the text, but at the same time it helps the learners to see continuities between Shakespeare's plays and our times. This approach works well with the gender politics within the plays, but it can also be used to read state politics and questions of governance and tyranny. In what follows I show how students can learn to see continuities and discern differences within ideological issues related to

DOI: 10.4324/9781003146209-3

family, patriarchy, gender roles, and male solidarity, by making connections between *Cymbeline* and India during its #MeToo moment in October 2020.

When women choose

A remark about parental control of daughters brought some of them awake, enough to remark the similarity between Cymbeline and Polonius, but also Cymbeline and King Lear, as also Cymbeline and Capulet: each male parent trying to control his daughter and her choice of husband. The women students were especially invested in exploring this connection, remarking the affection that tied fathers such as Lear and Capulet to Cordelia and Juliet, an affection that disintegrated quickly when the daughters failed to fall in line with the plans their fathers had made for them. Students who had struggled with *King Lear* in their first semester were quick to point out the likeness between Lear saying, "I loved her most, and thought to set my rest/On her kind nursery" (I.i. 123–124) and Cymbeline saying of Imogen, "O disloyal thing/That shouldst repair my youth, thou heapst/A year's age on me" (I.i. 132–134).

The easy conflation of disloyalty and treachery with the daughter's assertion of her own choice and identity, and the refusal to accept the daughter's choice was something that many students connected to incidents that had occurred in the previous month in and around Hyderabad. In one case an upper caste man, enraged by his daughter's marriage to a lower caste youth, hired a hitman who hacked the young man to death. The upper-caste wife whose father had masterminded the killing was a witness to the horror (see "Pranay's fears came true"). In another case, again involving an upper caste girl marrying a lower caste man, the girl's father himself attacked the couple causing grievous physical harm, to his daughter primarily, but also to his son-in-law (see Mallick 2018). In both cases the daughters repudiated their fathers and refused to return to their natal homes, preferring to assert their right to choose, and their conviction about their marital choice. Imogen's loyalty to Posthumous, her defiance of Cymbeline and the consequences she suffers, even as she was forced to stay on in her natal house after Posthumous's banishment was read by a student as "custodial harassment" extending Pratiksha Baxi's use of the terms "custodial death" and "custodial violence" to describe what is more often called "honour killing" by the media or violence perpetrated by the natal family against daughters and sons who marry against their family's dicta (quoted in Menon: 2012: 8). The student pointed out that Cymbeline raging against his daughter, asking his wife to keep a careful watch over her and trying to force Imogen to marry Cloten could collectively be read as custodial harassment: "The methods employed by Cymbeline, much like an Indian parent in this context, are very similar" was how she phrased it.[1]

Parental deception and intimidation and the ways in which the daughters are conditioned to respond to it was immediately seen as valid and pertinent in today's India too. Thus, in the incident in which the father attacked his son-in-law and daughter, it was clearly stated by news reports that the father made overtures to make it appear that he was interested in arranging a reconciliation and that they were meeting to further that purpose (Mallick 2018). Similarly, in the case where a killer was hired by the girl's father to eliminate her husband, the girl's parents, especially her mother, called them repeatedly to gather information as to their whereabouts ("Pranay's Fears Came True"). In *Cymbeline* the Queen plays the 'good cop' to Cymbeline's 'bad cop' and this routine was something that the students recognized as a parental gambit still in operation today in many households where the parents seek to control their children and their children's choices. That Imogen recognizes this is apparent (She says of the Queen: "O dissembling courtesy! How fine this tyrant can tickle where she wounds!" (I. i. 85–6) but it does not prevent her from resorting to using her father as her protector when Giacomo suggests that she should revenge herself on the supposedly straying Posthumous by engaging in a sexual liaison with him:

> The king my father shall be made acquainted
> Of thy assault: if he shall think it fit,
> A saucy stranger in his court to mart
> As in a Romish stew and to expound
> His beastly mind to us, he hath a court
> He little cares for and a daughter who
> He not respects at all.
>
> (I. vi. 150–156)

That Imogen believes her father to be her protector despite his ill-treatment of her and that she speaks of him as "the King my father" clearly demonstrates her belief in patriarchal systems of family organization which align the king with the father, and in Imogen's case clearly the alignment fits perfectly. She is even concerned with how her father's court will appear akin to an Italian brothel and she draws an equivalence between the court and herself, and Cymbeline's lack of care or respect for each. The class considered this evidence of a deeply indoctrinated mindset on Imogen's part and that resulted in her inability to see herself as other than her father's daughter, so that it became his duty to avenge Giacomo's insults to her. But the students were also alert to how the women who asserted their choice in marriage in India now were often steadfast in their determination to stand with their marital families, even when the natal families offered far more material security and comfort. This was traced by the class in various real-life incidents including the two referenced above. The students who had studied *Othello* were also quick to point out the similarity between contemporary Indian women and Desdemona who asserted in the Venetian senate that:

> I am hitherto your daughter: but here's my husband,
> And so much duty as my mother show'd

To you, preferring you before her father,
So much I challenge that I may profess
Due to the Moor my lord.

                                    (I. iii. 184–188)

The general conclusion was that the transference of duty from one male to another, both legitimized by patriarchal structures and codes, was as far as the assertion of women's choices and identities went. They additionally cited the Hadiya case where the marriage was annulled by the Kerala High Court due to the parents objecting (the girl, a Hindu, married a Muslim and converted to Islam) but when it was taken up by the Supreme Court, the woman's freedom to choose was upheld and she asserted, much like Desdemona (I. iii. 247–258), that she wanted to live with her husband ("'Personal relationships …'"). Within the context of women's rights to choose, and their guardians' reactions to those choices, the class could see similarities proliferating across the plays they had read and contemporary news accounts and stories across India.

When men talk …

The second moment that energized the class was to do with the early scene in *Cymbeline*, set in Rome, wherein the wager between Posthumous and Giacomo is first set in motion (I. iv.). This discussion began in the *Cymbeline* classes and was revisited when we studied *The Rape of Lucrece* in our final genre, Shakespeare's non-dramatic verse. Accounts of conversations among men, at men-only banquets and gatherings, which then threatened women, brought about lively but fractured discussions as the split along gender lines created some tensions and annoyances.

The conversation at Philario's house in Rome which begins with men assessing each other (I. iv. 1–20), proceeds to reminiscences about duels and contests, and leads, via contests and competitions among men to a discussion in which the competing merits of women of various nationalities are evaluated. The cosmopolitan nature of the gathering at Philario's (the stage direction at I. iv. speaks of "a Frenchman, a Dutchman and a Spaniard" in addition to the Briton, Posthumous and the Italians Giacomo and Philario, though neither the Dutchman nor the Spaniard speak) generalizes what might otherwise be seen as a preoccupation of particular people groups. In contrast, in *The Rape of Lucrece* (hereafter *RoL*), we are given two versions of the conversation that leads to the rape and suicide of Lucrece: in the Argument that prefaces the poem we are told that:

the principal men of the Army meeting one evening at the tent of Sextus Tarquinius, the King's son, in their discourses after supper everyone commended the virtues of his own wife; among whom Collatinus extolled the incomparable chastity of his wife Lucretia.

38

In that pleasant humor, they all posted to Rome; and intending by their secret and sudden arrival to make trial of that which everyone had before avouched, only Collatinus finds his wife, though it were late in the night, spinning amongst her maids; the other ladies were all found dancing and reveling, or in several disports. Whereupon the noblemen yielded Collatinus the victory and his wife the fame.

(*RoL* 669)

In the poem's third stanza we are told of a conversation between Collatine and Tarquin, in the latter's tent, wherein he extols the peerlessness and virtue of his "beauteous mate" (18) and boasts of her "sov'reignty" (36). However, whether we accept the version from the Argument or from the poem proper there can be no doubt that Lucrece's rape is set in motion by a conversation amongst men, in a similarly competitive framework as that in *Cymbeline*. The bleak mood in the classroom was palpable as I introduced this aspect of *RoL* and reminded them of *Cymbeline*'s similar trajectory.

To add a comparable but contemporary take on these Shakespearean incidents, I mentioned Donald Trump's easy dismissal of his comments about grabbing women's genitals as "locker room talk"[2] ("Donald Trump Apology ...") and asked the class whether the two conversations in these Shakespeare texts could be seen as the Early Modern equivalent of Trump's conversational descriptor. Initially, silence reigned and then hesitantly the women students began thinking aloud: is that how men talk when there are no women around? The men in the class refused to answer this question but one did say that women were not the only subject of men's conversations when they were in their same-gendered peer groups. Cutting short this potentially explosive route, I instead asked the class to consider what these conversations can be characterized as. Immediately, some of the students who were more familiar with the text spoke of the strongly competitive streak that was apparent among the men. This fed into accepted stereotypical notions about men's conversations when they are in a same-sex group: which are "commonly organized around a series of global oppositions, e.g., men's talk is 'competitive' whereas women's is 'cooperative'; men talk to gain 'status', whereas women talk to forge 'intimacy' and 'connection' ..." (Cameron 1997: 55). It was clear to the class that the men spoke of themselves and each other in ways that could be seen as competing for status, and Posthumous is not liked by Giacomo ("But I could then have looked on him without the help of admiration", I. iv. 3–4). The Frenchman further demonstrates this competitive streak as he claims that when he had earlier met Posthumous in France "We had very many there could behold the sun with as firm eyes as he" (I. iv. 10–11). While courtesy rules their exchanges once Posthumous enters at line 24, the underlying tone of competition continues with the anecdote of the near-duel in France which was averted by the Frenchman. The reason for that duel was the praise of Posthumous's mistress, and we are also told by the Frenchman that "it was much like an argument that fell out last night, where each of us fell in praise of our country's mistresses" (I. iv. 47–49). At this juncture several students remarked on the fact that this appeared to be an on-going theme in men's conversations, especially when read alongside the Argument in *RoL*. At the same time, one student noted the distinction between *Cymbeline* and *RoL*: in the former nationality plays a part and each country's representative valorises his mistress, in his particular country, while in the more homogenized society of *RoL*, they each commend the virtue of their "own wife". She went on to remark that the woman as possession and valued object to her husband is made explicit in *RoL* when the narrator asks, "Or why is Collatine the publisher/Of that rich jewel he should keep unknown/From thievish ears, because it is his own?" (*RoL* 33–35). The discussion centred on the idea of woman as object and valued possession, an idea that is repeated in *Cymbeline* where the wager between Giacomo and Posthumous involves both Imogen's chastity and also the ring that was a gift from Imogen to Posthumous: if Giacomo can successfully seduce Imogen, Posthumous must then give him the ring as well. From line 62 till the end of I. iv. Giacomo and Posthumous speak of Imogen and the ring as interchangeable and both her chastity and the ring as easily stolen. As Giacomo says:

> You may wear her in title yours: but, you know, strange fowl light upon neighbouring ponds. Your ring may be stolen too: so your brace of unprizable estimations; the one is but frail and the other casual; a cunning thief, or a that way accomplished courtier, would hazard the winning both of first and last.
>
> (I. iv.77–82)

The misogyny and the quick belief in women's frailty was something that resonated with the students as they had just finished *Hamlet* a month earlier and could see recurrent patterns. The idea of competition and of the status that accrues to the man from his possession of a beautiful and chaste mistress was comparable to his possession of material wealth, as the class saw clearly. This was understood by the class, but it was, as I discovered, an anterior moment to what was to come.

The wager scene in Cymbeline continued to puzzle several of the women students and finally one asked the men: why would you bet on the chastity or faithfulness of your lover? Some of the men looked distinctly uncomfortable and were quick to repudiate any such possibilities in today's world but some of the others could see nothing troubling and one of them finally said: in a long-distance relationship one does doubt these things and it is possibly why Posthumous agreed to the wager. The uproar that resulted was only quelled by my stepping in to speak of how storytelling about women was a traditional mode of forging and establishing bonds between men. Stories that rehearse stereotypes and 'common knowledge', such as those that Giacomo tells, work to build men's communities and though initially Posthumous rages, eventually he agrees to the wager, and goes so far as to say, "if you make your voyage upon her and give me directly to understand you have prevailed, I am no further your enemy; she is not worth our debate" (I. iv. 138–141). Indeed Giacomo has previously demanded that if he should prove unsuccessful in his assault upon Imogen's chastity he should then have Posthumous's "commendation for my more free entertainment" (I. iv. 136), but this Posthumous refuses, reserving the right to challenge Giacomo to a duel if Imogen should prove true.

The building of bonds on the basis of 'locker-room talk' is also predicated on a particular view of women and this is a perspective common to all the men within the play: Philario intercedes thrice to ask Posthumous and Giacomo to desist but his objections are brushed aside and eventually the wager is made and "set down by lawful counsel" (I. iv. 145). That these bonds between men are privileged above the relationship with his wife is brought home to the reader/viewer with the return of Giacomo, with his false story of Imogen's seduction in II. iv. And when Posthumous hopes that they are not to "continue friends" Giacomo assures him "we must/if you keep covenant" (49–50). Thus reminded of the covenant, Posthumous assures him: "If you can make't apparent/That you have tasted her in bed, my hand /and ring is yours" (56–58). The devastating clarity of that pronouncement underscores the lowly worth of women as well as elevating the "covenant" and bonds which men must honour, and which they do, even at the cost of their marital or other relationships. This elevation of male friendships and bonds above heterosexual (even marital) relationships was not a feature that the class found relevant in the contemporary context until one student remembered and spoke about a news item that had appeared a few days earlier in the newspapers, about a woman who committed suicide at her parents' home in Hyderabad because her husband expected her to dance, drink alcohol and gamble with his friends ("Hyderabad: NRI Woman ..."). The assertion of patriarchal rights over the wife, subduing her agency and her will, in the pursuit of male friendships and bonds may not be as prevalent today as it appeared to be earlier but nor was it completely eradicated, was the conclusion the students arrived at.

Returning to the all-male conversations, which fuelled desire in both Giacomo and Tarquin, a woman student raised the point that the idea of virtuous and chaste womanhood is itself seen as an affront by some of the misogynist men in these texts: that by their chastity they demolish the stereotypes that are prevalent regarding the frailty of women and this cuts away at the common narratives which circulate regarding women. In addition, a chaste woman/wife is seen as a challenge to be vanquished so that she can be judged promiscuous and fallen, just like all women. This self-validating narrative is rehearsed in *Cymbeline* in I. iv. and the threat to Imogen is within the conversation itself, in which her husband is an active participant. It is *in the conversations between and among men that patriarchal violence is first initiated*—this was the key argument that this student made, thereby indicating also the culpability of the husband, a participant in such a conversation, in what befalls his wife.

The importance of male friendships is also underscored via notions of hospitality within these texts and students were quick to point out that both Giacomo and Tarquin were offered hospitality by Imogen and Lucrece, because of their (supposedly) close friendships with their absent, much loved husbands. In *Cymbeline*, Imogen does not offer hospitality to Giacomo but a subterfuge on his part leads to her keeping a trunk safe for him:

> Giacomo: Some dozen Romans of us and your lord—
> The best feather of our wing—have mingled sums
> To buy a present for the emperor
> Which I, the factor for the rest, have done
> In France: 'tis plate of rare device, and jewels
> Of rich and exquisite form; their values great;
> And I am something curious, being strange,
> To have them in safe stowage: may it please you
> To take them in protection?
>
> Imogen: Willingly;
> And pawn mine honour for their safety: since
> My lord hath interest in them, I will keep them
> In my bedchamber.
>
> (I. vi. 186–197)

That Imogen should be willing to "pawn (her) honour" for some material possessions led the class to consider how women had so internalised the codes of masculine honour that they were willing to give up their honour for that of their spouses.

Interim

During the *Cymbeline* classes India was experiencing its own #MeToo moment, with charges of sexual harassment being made by women against many stars in the entertainment and advertising industry. The class found it an easy matter to read Cloten's and Giacomo's pursuit of Imogen in this light, especially the latter who propositions her and then violates her privacy, symbolically violating her with his presence in her room and his gaze. In Cloten's case, his unwanted advances initially, and later, his decision to rape Imogen, taken with the purpose of subduing her to his will, were both read as customary male stratagems, occasionally seen in today's India as well, where one hears of parents willing to marry off a raped daughter to the rapist. Cloten is positive that Cymbeline "may haply be a little angry with my so rough usage; but my mother, having power of his testiness, shall turn all into my commendations" (IV. i. 16–18) and that conviction, that marriage legitimises the earlier crime is sometimes reported in news accounts of rapists who offer to marry the survivor in the certainty that thus their crimes are, or will be, rendered null and void (Chatterjee 2007, Kokra 2017). Judges have also been known to encourage such ideas as seen in a case that was written about in 2015 (Karat 2015).

And we all live happily ever after

By this time the class was deeply disturbed, unable to see any hope for Imogen in the bleak scenario that prevailed in *Cymbeline*. This was worsened with the death of the nameless Queen, her wickedness laid bare for everyone to wonder at and Cymbeline exonerating himself of all blame for his folly:

> Mine eyes
> Were not in fault, for she was beautiful;
> Mine ears, that heard her flattery; nor my heart,
> That thought her like her seeming; it had been vicious
> To have mistrusted her: yet, O my daughter!
> That it was folly in me, thou mayst say,
> And prove it in thy feeling. Heaven mend all!
>   (V. vi. 62–68)

Students who had read *RoL* swiftly pointed out that Tarquin also lays the blame on Lucrece, saying "The fault is thine,/For those thine eyes betray thee unto mine ... Thy beauty hath ensnared thee to this night" (*RoL* 482–483, 485). This easy disavowal of all responsibility by the male of the species struck my women students as stereotypical but a common practice, as blaming the victim is also a common practice, particularly in cases of sexual violence.

However, it was in the conclusion of the Posthumous–Imogen–Giacomo plot line that all these strands came together. Once Imogen gets Giacomo to tell the truth about how he deceived Posthumous regarding her chastity and virtue, the stage is set for the reconciliation of Imogen and Posthumous. However, before this comes to pass there is the singularly startling moment when Posthumous knocks Imogen to the ground, as the stage direction at line 229 of the final scene indicates: "Striking her; she falls". Dressed as a pageboy still, Imogen might well have been unrecognisable but to strike him/her down struck the students as extreme and was possibly the result of the hierarchical social structure where Imogen as pageboy could not be treated with respect or affection by Posthumous, a nobleman. The contrast they directed me to was Posthumous's attitude to Giacomo when he finally asked his pardon and returned to Posthumous his ring and Imogen's bracelet:

> Kneel not to me:
> The power that I have on you is, to spare you;
> The malice towards you to forgive you: live,
> And deal with others better.
>
> (V. vi. 418–421)

Yes, they agreed that by this time Posthumous had discovered Imogen to be alive and well, they were reconciled to each other and had also had their stations in life rendered more equal by the discovery of Cymbeline's sons and heirs, Imogen's brothers who would inherit the throne before her, leaving her free to be a woman, primarily a daughter, sister and wife, rather than heiress, Crown princess and such. But the easy forgiveness that Posthumous demonstrated to Giacomo appeared to them to reinstate those bonds of social hierarchical positions and male solidarity that were forged between them (even) in antagonism and annoyance in I. iv. and reinforced in II. iv., when Giacomo falsely won the wager and Posthumous lived up to the ideals of male honour that the wager enforced upon him. The forgiveness that Posthumous now extended to Giacomo made Imogen's ordeal appear insignificant and also exonerated Posthumous of any responsibility for all that befell his wife. Indeed, Imogen's own forgiving of Posthumous, despite knowing that he ordered her death struck the class as unjust and trivialised the magnitude of what she had undergone. While both these acts of forgiveness are essential to the play, to retain its "happy ending" and make it fit the genre of "tragi-comedy" or "romance", they both also render a woman's suffering trivial in the larger cause of reinstating privilege based on social hierarchies, male solidarity and patriarchal power. Imogen, the only woman left standing on stage at the conclusion of the play (in her pageboy costume), is no longer even minimally agential: she is reduced to her familial roles and has no role in the state and its doings, not even nominally. The students concluded that *Cymbeline* worked to restrict women to the domestic sphere even as it gave male bonds pride of place. When we added *RoL* to the discussion the conclusion was that women and their woes are a pretext for male bonds, as evidenced by the end of the poem, when Collatine and all the men come together to wage war upon Tarquin. The poem thus works in a circular fashion: it began with Collatine's friendship with Tarquin, and ended with Collatine and all his friends vowing vengeance upon Tarquin: thus the codes of male friendship were central to the understanding of *RoL* as they were to the understanding of *Cymbeline*.

As the foregoing account evidences, Shakespeare remains, as in the title of Jan Kott's 1962 book, our contemporary. In an English Studies classroom of our times the study of his texts can bring together diverse and discrete cultural contexts: both temporal and geographical. To make the students aware of, and participatory in this project, the teacher needs to enable the making of discursive linkages, across eras and contexts, in doing which the English classroom can provide room to examine and study events, viewpoints and processes that otherwise would not enter the classroom. This is furthered by the cross-section of students we find in classes such as the one I teach. Drawn from many Indian states, with varied backgrounds in terms of class and caste they can, and do, find common ground when speaking of oppression and suffering, especially in the context of patriarchy. Issues relating to patriarchal oppression are particularly resonant as gendered power equations impact the lives of most women in India, even allowing for minor variations due to class, caste, religion, etc. The men in the class similarly are able to recognise the working of patriarchal structures within their own families and across society and are usually swift to see the very unequal power equations in texts and society, at large, even when it works to their advantage.

While making Shakespearean texts topical and contemporary can be a risk-filled undertaking as it elides, to a certain degree, the significance of the Shakespearean contexts, it also enables students to understand Shakespeare and gain access to his works. But this project of showing students how Shakespeare is relevant today also helps students in several ways: many who arrive in my classes convinced of the incomprehensible nature of the Shakespearean text discover that not only can they read a Shakespearean play but they can make meaning of it, for themselves and for others. For many of the students their mastery over a Shakespeare text becomes the key with which they can unlock careers in English Studies. But in a larger context, these classes also help the students to see that English Studies is not this discipline wherein they study texts that have no connection to their lives, texts written by long-dead white men. Instead, by learning to think about what they read, by making connections between texts and real life as they know it, they see not just the relevance of Shakespeare but also the relevance of English as a discipline and the importance of the Humanities.

Notes

1 The said student wrote up her notes on this in an assignment wherein she also compared Cymbeline's faith in the soothsayer to the faith many Indians have in astrologers and such.

2 Locker room talk is defined by the Merriam-Webster Dictionary as "of a coarse or sexual nature" while the Urban Dictionary defines it as "Any manner of conversation that polite society dictates be held privately – with small groups of like-minded, similarly gendered peers – due to its sexually charged language, situations or innuendos."

Works cited

Burns, Alexander et al. "Donald Trump Apology Caps Days of Outrage over Lewd Tape". *New York Times*. 7 October 2016. www.nytimes.com/2016/10/08/us/politics/donald-trump-women.html?action=click&module=RelatedCoverage&pgtype=Article&region=Footer Accessed 15 December 2018.

Cameron, Deborah. "Performing Gender Identity: Young Men's Talk and the Construction of Heterosexual Masculinity" in *Language and Masculinity*. Eds. Sally Johnson, Ulrike Hanna Meinhof, Wiley, 1997. 47–64. Print.

Chatterji, Shoma. "Rapist to Victim: Will You Marry Me?" *India Together*. 25 April 2007. www.indiatogether.org/rapevict-women Accessed 16 December 2018.

Forsyth, Jennifer. "General Introduction". *Cymbeline. Internet Shakespeare Editions*. University of Victoria, 28 Dec 2014. http://internetshakespeare.uvic.ca/doc/Cym_GenIntro/complete/#about Accessed 15 December 2018.

"Hyderabad: NRI Woman Ends Life Over Husband's Harassment". *Telangana Today*. 13 October 2018. https://telanganatoday.com/hyderabad-nri-woman-ends-life-over-husbands-harassment Accessed 15 December 2018.

Karat, Brinda. "When a Judge Suggests a Woman Marry Her Rapist". *NDTV*. 1 July 2015. www.ndtv.com/opinion/jayalalithaa-this-rape-victim-needs-your-attention-777041 Accessed 16 December 2018.

Kokra, Sonali. "14 Year old Rape Victim …". *Huffington Post*, 31 July 2017. www.huffingtonpost.in/2017/07/31/14-year-old-rape-victim-forced-to-marry-alleged-rapist-to-suppor_a_23057348/ Accessed 16 December 2018.

"Locker Room Talk". *Urban Dictionary*. (2017) www.urbandictionary.com/define.php?term=Locker%20Room%20Talk Accessed 15 December 2018.

"Locker-Room Talk". *Merriam Webster*. (n.d.) www.merriam-webster.com/dictionary/locker-room Accessed 15 December 2018.

Mallick, Aditi. "In Heart of Hyderabad, Father Chops off Girl's Arm for Marrying a Dalit". *The Times of India*. 20th September 2018. https://timesofindia.indiatimes.com/india/in-heart-of-hyderabad-father-chops-off-girls-arm-for-marrying-a-dalit/articleshow/65879179.cms Accessed 25 November 2018.

Menon, Nivedita. *Seeing Like a Feminist*. Delhi: Penguin India and Zubaan Books, 2012. Print.

"Pranay's Fears Came True". *Telangana Today*. (n.d.) 17 September 2018. https://telanganatoday.com/pranays-fears-came-true Accessed 25 November 2018.

Scroll. "'Personal Relationships Are Core of India's Plurality': Supreme Court Restores Hadiya's Marriage". *Scroll.in*. 8 March 2018. https://scroll.in/latest/871253/personal-relationships-are-core-of-indias-plurality-supreme-court-restores-hadiyas-marriage Accessed 16 March 2019.

Shakespeare, William. *Cymbeline, King of Britain. The Norton Shakespeare*. Stephen Greenblatt et al., ed. New York: W.W. Norton & Company, 2008. *Print*.

———. *The Norton Shakespeare*. 2nd ed., Stephen Greenblatt et al., ed. W.W. Norton & Company, 2008. Print.

———. *The Rape of Lucrece. The Norton Shakespeare*. Stephen Greenblatt et al., ed. New York: W.W. Norton & Company, 2008. *Print*.

———. *The Tragedy of King Lear: A conflated text. The Norton Shakespeare*. Stephen Greenblatt et al., ed. New York: W.W. Norton & Company, 2008. Print.

———. *The Tragedy of Othello the Moor of Venice. The Norton Shakespeare*. Stephen Greenblatt et al., ed. New York: W.W. Norton & Company, 2008. Print.

3

ENGLISH, HUMAN RIGHTS AND LITERATURE IN THE POSTCOLONIAL CLASSROOM

Pramod K. Nayar

This essay narrates, and meditates upon, the teaching of a new interdiscipline, Human Rights and Literature, in an M.A. English class in the University of Hyderabad, a metropolitan, public university.

"Reading Right(s): The Culture of Human Rights" was offered as an Elective course in semester IV. However, over a dozen students from MA II also opted to audit the course. There were about six students pursuing their PhDs also in the course. The students in the course came from diverse socio-economic, regional, linguistic and ethnic/caste backgrounds.

The course mixed genres: poetry, fiction, life writing, speculative fiction, websites, photographic evidence (Abu Ghraib) and the graphic novel. A considerable amount of critical theory was also prescribed, from Judith Butler on precarity to Elizabeth Anker (2012) and Joseph Slaughter (2007) on the Human Rights (hereafter HR) novel.

This essay forwards the idea that two *lingua francas* emerged in the postcolonial classroom in the course of the term. One, the *lingua franca* of HR, whose history was traced, and its legal narrative (the Universal Declaration of Human Rights or UDHR, 1948) and its scope today discussed. Two, the English language and English literary studies itself as a kind of *lingua franca*. This latter means that for theoretico-political frames such as HR to be studied and employed universally as befits the *Universal* Declaration of HR, English language and a training in literary studies serves the purpose well. English (I use the term, unless otherwise specified, to indicate 'English Language and Literary Studies', as embodied in the BA [English] and MA [English] programs) enabled the class to sample texts from vastly different contexts such as Jean Amery's essay "On Torture" that detailed his experiences under Nazi Germany, Dalit poet Vijila's "Bitch" (about caste-based discrimination in India), Constantin Cavafy's "Waiting for the Barbarians" which highlighted the 'necessity' of having a cultural/racial Other to draw attention to and to build a national identity, East European poetry about war, displacement and genocide (by Czeslaw Milosz and Horst Bienek), Indian graphic texts about child abuse (*Hush*) and

DOI: 10.4324/9781003146209-4

47

speculative dystopian fiction about cloning (*Never Let Me Go*). It enabled them to discover ways of linking HR with literary studies. It builds on an earlier argument where I proposed:

> human rights demands a cultural apparatus in which the discourse of rights, cast in the language of international/transnational standards and norms circulates within a register of claims and in the narrative form of autobiography, personal stories and memoirs. As should be obvious, I am calling for the translation of global norms of human rights into a local context, even as local stories of violations must be translated to fit into a global narrative of campaigns, protests and legalistic measures.
>
> (2011: 23)

The essay reflects upon the critical and pedagogic practice enabled by English in a course and class when the genres studied were not strictly literary. It links this practice to both a postcolonial condition and a planetarity around HR, made possible precisely because all of us could read these texts in English. The essay *is* conscious, like the classroom itself was, of the risks of English-as-hegemony. Adapting James Dawes, the essay asks: "what is gained and what is lost when we import the terms and methods of universal HR" to postcolonial literary studies of texts of global provenance and "to the specific historical and contemporary justice movements"? (Dawes 2018: 11). In partial response to this line of questioning, the essay wonders whether, in cases where certain moral and other universals such as HR were at stake, English does serve the purpose of invoking the category of the 'human' rather than the idea of the 'citizen' which is tied to national identity.

I

English Literature courses can be variously designed, with greater or lesser emphasis on 'English' Literature or 'new' and postcolonial literatures, literatures in translation, among others. This course on HR sought to read texts avowedly postcolonial in content (post-Apartheid fiction, Dalit writing) but whose frames of reference were not explicitly either 'Eng-Lit' or 'postcolonial'. The main aim, at least in the instructor's mind, was to see if 'Eng-Lit' elective courses could co-evolve with a mélange of the postcolonial, canonical Eng-Lit, European Literature of war and posthuman texts, all framed within a universal concern with HR. To phrase it differently, could an elective course in MA English be made to speak, through diverse literary texts of multiple origins, to a concern such as HR?

The course was designed with the assumption that there is the possibility of 'translating' the language of Universal HR into a postcolonial pedagogic setting. We began, therefore, with a reading of the UDHR document itself, and some attention was paid to its language and conceptual framework.

To begin with, we discovered that concepts such as 'dignity', 'inalienable rights', 'person', 'sovereignty', among others, are heavily weighted concepts, which may also possess different valences in different cultures and contexts. However, the fact that the UDHR and its concepts has found resonance across geocultural borders implies a translatability of concepts (Merry 2006), but more importantly, a translatability of contexts in which the human finds her/himself reduced to the abhuman – broken, injured and suffering. It was possible to see, in other words, the broken human in Nazi camps, the tortured Iraqi in Abu Ghraib, and injured soldiers in war zones from around the world, without necessarily requiring footnotes.

That said, we examined briefly the history of the UDHR document, the various debates in its making that foregrounded the differences in points of view of 'person', for example. The fact that these cultural and philosophical differences in how cultures perceived the 'person' or the individual – the heart of the UDHR document and HR principles – were discussed within an Eng-Lit classroom in a course devoted to HR and literature in a postcolonial setting (university, country) was also noted. In a postcolonial context, conscious of a colonial past and linguistic diversity, and the ongoing contexts of caste-based oppression, patriarchy-driven honour killings, minority-hunting, among others, we translate UDHR's concerns of human dignity, the sovereign individual and such into local contexts, via English. How then does English help us understand the tensions in the making of the UDHR document? We know from historical accounts that Eleanor Roosevelt chaired the UDHR drafting committee, and the members included René Cassin of France, Charles Malik of Lebanon, Peng-chun Chang of China and John Humphrey of Canada (who prepared the Declaration's blueprint). Others associated with the drafting included Hernán Santa-Cruz from Chile, Alexander Bogomolov from the USSR, Charles Dukes from the UK and William Hodgson from Australia. We noted this multicultural, multinational and plural composition. We also noted Upendra Baxi's argument that many ideas and concepts of HR in history emerged from contexts such as slavery and anti-colonial movements from Africa, Asia and South America, thus implying non-European foundations for a universal document (see Dhawan and Randeria 2013, disputed by Moyn 2010, Chapter 3).

The process of drafting the UDHR, then, could also be read as a project of translation, first from various cultural and national origins – and contexts, ranging from a world war to genocide to the formation of new state borders – embodied in the constitution of the various drafting committees, then into English at the United Nations and then into numerous languages worldwide. Circulating widely via organizations such as Amnesty International or Doctors Without Borders, and processes and structures like international law, the UDHR comes to stand in for the globalizing of certain concerns drawn from diverse historical experiences of war, human suffering, and violations. As mentioned above, translating the UDHR's concerns to local contexts through the course exemplifies a two-way translation made possible via English: from diverse and diffuse geocultural contexts *into* the UDHR in 1948 and the UDHR itself from a global document *into* a specific postcolonial context. The fact that local-level organizations and campaigns, such as Dalit rights initiatives, draw upon the UDHR is an instantiation of this two-way translation.

Needless to say, the course requires fine-tuning to address serious issues of postcolonial nations, such as minority and indigenous rights, to be read via literary texts from Adivasis, religious and linguistic minorities, in contexts ranging from "narratives of neglect" from specific regions of the country (Dutta 2009) to women's memoirs.

II

Keeping the informing question of the course – 'could an elective course in MA English be made to speak, through diverse literary texts of multiple origins, to a concern such as HR?' – in mind, the opening sessions in the course were devoted to examining the narrative tradition of HR. HR becomes a concern globally with the UDHR of 1948. In postcolonial nations like India, HR is enmeshed in the political situations arising from the presence of armed forces in places like Kashmir and the northeastern states, the custodial deaths that are frequently reported in newspapers, vigilantism that has targeted minority lives, and related rights of tribals and the displaced.

Adapting the theoretical work of Anthony Langlois, Winfried Brugger, Lynn Hunt, Joseph Slaughter and others, we read the following literary texts: Maria Edgeworth's "The Grateful Negro", extracts from Samuel Richardson's *Pamela* and Alice Walker's "The Flowers". Two eighteenth century texts, including one canonical novel from a traditional Eng-Lit course, and a twentieth-century African American short story helped us trace a history of ideas of the human. The sentimental short story (Edgeworth), the sentimental novel (Richardson) and the *bildungsroman* (Walker) all constructed the human in certain ways.

Following Hunt, we noted how the sentimental slave in Edgeworth was constructed as a 'human', *just like the white slave owner*. The heroine in Richardson, pursued by the wicked master, not only documents her affective responses to her condition, she elicits a similar empathy from the reader. The girl child who discovers the body of a lynching victim in Walker's story has effectively concluded her summer and her innocence. Passages like these from *Pamela* came in for class discussion:

> I was proceeding, and he said, a little hastily—
> Because you are a little fool, and know not what's good for yourself. I tell you I will make a gentlewoman of you, if you be obliging, and don't stand in your own light;

And so saying, he put his arm about me, and kissed me!

Now, you will say, all his wickedness appeared plainly. I strug-gled and trembled, and was so benumbed with terror, that I sunk down, not in a fit, and yet not myself; and I found myself in his arms, quite void of strength; and he kissed me two or three times, with frightful eagerness.—At last I burst from him, and was getting out of the summer-house; but he held me back, and shut the door … I would have given my Life for a Farthing. And he said, I'll do you no Harm, *Pamela*; don't be afraid of me. I said, I won't stay. You won't, Hussy! Said he: Do you know whom you speak to? I lost all Fear, and all Respect, and said, Yes, I do, sir, too well!—Well may I forget that I am your Servant, when you forget what belongs to a Master. I SOBB'D and cry'd most sadly. What a foolish Hussy you are! said he: Have I done you any Harm?—Yes, Sir, said I, the greatest Harm in the World: You have taught me to forget myself, and what belongs to me; and have lessen'd the Distance that Fortune has made between us, by demeaning yourself, to be so free to a poor Servant.

(Richardson 1811:12)

This account was treated as an expression of the character's interiority, thereby communicating to us a sense of her *self*. The point was made, via Hunt among others, that the epistolary novel linked selfhood to qualities of 'interiority', which manifest when the characters expressed their inner feelings in their letters. We discussed, again via Hunt, how the epistolary novel depicted *all* characters/selves as possessing interiority, implying that all selves were equal.

Affect here communicates itself via stories of suffering. In the Eng-Lit classroom, using texts from contexts as diverse as late eighteenth century/early nineteenth century slavery or the lynching of African Americans enabled the class to approach the 'problem' of the human by *reducing* it to a foundational question: how does one define the human? The answer provided by these diverse authors was: as a sentimental being. On reflection, it appears more than likely that the attention to sentiment as a key mode of understanding the human comes, in part, from the training in Eng-Lit studies when, say, English Romantic poets are part of the syllabi. In the course devoted to the Romantics, attention is often drawn to these poets' sentimentalization of Nature, the self-portraiture of figures like Wordsworth as sentimental beings responding to Nature, the emphasis on the sentiments of certain classes of people in texts like the Preface to the Wordsworth-Coleridge *Lyrical Ballads* (where Wordsworth claimed that it is in the rural areas one finds true passion and uncontaminated sentiment), among others. That is to say, the students were already familiar with the emphasis on sen-timent as a marker of class, professions and even geocultural locations (urban/rural) *and* the individual self through their readings of texts like the

English Romantics. From this to discovering the definition of the human as grounded in sentiment and affect rather than in Reason and Rationality (as defined by the Enlightenment) was a logical progression. What is important here is to note that the reading of *English* texts for a particular thematic concern – the human as sentimental being – enables and prepares the students to read texts from different contexts and yet see overlapping patterns: the slave, the African American, the postcolonial, all defined in terms of affect. Whether this emphasis on English texts in classroom work, affect as a *lingua franca* for the work in both literary studies and HR is a moot point, but its role in the *recognition* of the human *qua* human is undeniable.

III

Instances of dehumanization that reduced the human to the abhuman or even the nonhuman were then studied. Once again, the texts came from varied contexts: Vijila, "The Autobiography of a Bitch" (Dalit poem), Jean Amery "On Torture" (autobiography, German-occupied France during World War II), Abu Ghraib (photographic images, from the 'war on terror'); Horst Bienek, "Exodus" (poem, post-war Germany). These were approached via a theoretical paradigm articulated by Elizabeth Anker in her work on HR fiction (2012), but also via media theorists who have written on the depiction of graphic violence (Tait 2008). Anker's argument that HR stories invariably focus on the corporeal even as they depict violated corporeality served the purpose here. This segment covered a range of ideas revolving around embodiment, infra- and dehumanization, trauma-memory citizenship to communities of mourning.

The key argument for this section, building on my work elsewhere (Nayar 2011), was that the HR texts map the collapse of the sense of self *and* the collapse of the body's boundaries and coherence. The frames of reference—bodily functions, bodily borders with the world, agency to perform an action—for locating a sense of the self are destroyed and the subject begins to see her/himself only in terms of pain and disintegration. It is the incremental destruction of the body rather than death that marks the HR torture novel, dying rather than death itself. Abject embodiment is the effect of the slow deterioration of the body's coherence due to protracted tortures. Since the body is the first site of subjectivity, it also becomes the site of subjectivity's repression and erasure, the site of power and discourses that make or *unmake* this subjectivity. We therefore discussed abject embodiment in Amery, Vijila and other authors, where the human is reduced to just 'flesh' (as Amery argued about his own case), to animal form (Vijila), to photographed and degraded victims (Abu Ghraib). In the case of Abu Ghraib, the role of the camera at the scene of dehumanization was discussed. We argued that the camera was integral to the process of dehumanizing the racial-cultural Other, that the camera is part of the structure of helplessness because one is reduced to the passive *object* of the lens (and of the torturer), and of the future archive in which these images could be stored for recirculation.

The principal advantage of the English language, in retrospect, when teaching such diverse texts was the availability of critical and theoretical material on almost all aspects one wished to cover: from philosophical reflections on corporeality to media theory. Then, the translated texts such as Jean Amery's and Vijila's being available in English enabled us to modify the theoretical frames adequately enough to speak of the corporeal disintegration in Amery contrasted with the disintegration of the social in Vijila, both then converging upon an argument of the collapsing self:

> The first blow brings home to the prisoner that he is *helpless*, and thus it already contains in the bud everything that is to come. One may have known about torture and death in the cell, without such knowledge having possessed the hue of life; but upon the first blow they are anticipated as real possibilities, yes, as certainties. They are permitted to punch me in the face, the victim feels in numb surprise and concludes in just as numb certainty:

> they will do with me what they want
>
> (1980: 27, emphasis in original)

The passage above is Amery describing the first moments of his torture. The translation into English captures the agony and humiliation, not to mention the sense of vulnerability, of the first blow delivered upon the body. While Amery would go on to reflect on the consequences of the blows and the tortures (most notably his comments on "trust" and "never at home in the world" after torture), these kinds of passages have a visceral quality that, even in translation, gives us an affective punch. Discussing such passages in class, the conversation turned around the body, oddly deracinated, denationalized, and dealt with solely as an injurable, and injured, *body*. Dehumanization, it would appear, has only one language – bodily harm. When Vijila's poem discusses animalization as a consequence of caste (which is her immediate context) – and the outcast *as* animal – again, it speaks a language of its own, that of exclusion. If Amery is singled out as a *singular* body for torture, the Dalit or the outcast is singled out for persistent *social* humiliation. References were made to clear parallels in India, notably custodial deaths of arrested victims.

What one sees emerging here is the possibility of cross-cultural empathizing, contexts not withstanding of a vulnerability all victims (both potential and actual) share across the world. While the class may not exactly understand the Ku Klux Klan's history of lynching or the outcome of genocidal displacements in Germany, the social ostracization of Jews, blacks and minorities across the world made perfect empathic sense in a context where Dalits are 'outcast' people. Unfamiliar cultural contexts, in other words, are rendered familiar through the study of collapsing social ontologies and the failure of cultural apparatuses like the law or democratic processes. HR discourse with its emphasis on vulnerability, social ontology, embodiment and dehumanization works across racial and geographical categories, as we discovered.

In both cases (the individual and the social), in different contexts and origins (war, social inequality respectively), the self collapses. Did the original language of the two texts matter, then? Reading these different examples together, we obtained an insight into the different forms of dehumanization in history: corporeal torture, insults and humiliation, social exclusion, in texts from the Nazi era to contemporary India, and convergent upon the idea and image of the collapsing self.

Whether such a convergence, which runs the risk of flattening out the contexts of HR violations, is desirable or detrimental to a discourse of rights, when studying these discourses in English, is of course a point to be kept in mind. However, that said, it appears impossible not to see the emergence not only of a global discourse, in *English*, on rights but also a global literature made available in English on the subject. Literary texts about the Armenian, Rwandan, Bosnian genocides, Argentinian 'dirty war', Korean comfort women, Sri Lankan civil war, Dalit oppression – and I am only referencing the twentieth century – now jostle for narrative and critical space with works on the Holocaust, and all in English translations or originals. While it is true, as commentators have noted, that the Holocaust becomes the paradigm for trauma studies, recent work by Michael Rothberg (2011), for instance, alerts us to the possibilities of multidirectional memory, and points to what Marianne Hirsch termed "connective histories" (2014). In my own work (2011), if I may be forgiven the autobiographical turn, I have examined texts from several of the above contexts, to see parallels in, say, dehumanization of the racial other.

When global intellectual histories are being made possible (notably in the work of Samuel Moyn and others) through English, it seems completely understandable that literatures in English, sharing concerns such as dehumanization-discourses in varied contexts, cumulatively contribute to a global debate – and *lingua franca* – on the right to one's body, ontological security and social ontological security for the first two.

A discussion of the global HR movement when read to the backdrop of globalizing processes, including the global 'war on terror', terrorism, climate change, poverty and inequality, and others necessitates the evolution of global parameters, in discourse, of measuring violations. While the *langue* of such discourses remains the broken human form and collapsing social ontologies, the *parole* of a discourse of rights takes recourse to images, words and representational strategies that derive considerable *global* visibility and critical purchase when available in English. *Langue* here is the signifying system of broken bodies which are enunciated (*parole*) in various, and diverse contexts: the victim of social exclusion, the refugee in wartime, the dissident and the suspected 'terrorist'. While one hesitates to forward the proposition that there exists a universal grammar or signifying system to represent abused victims, it does appear that victims around the world make sense to us because of their community: as people who have lost this humanity.

In works that do not have any verbal text, such as the graphic novel *Hush*, we found we could still use a common language – images – to understand the horror of child sexual abuse. Again, theoretical paradigms for reading silences and rhetorical listening came from English language sources, but the interpretations were based entirely on the images.

IV

Notions of social justice and inequality, often informed by Marxism, marked another instance of a globalized *parole* through which the subject of HR may be studied. When studying texts that explicitly foreground social inequality – such as Dalit texts – and state-determined socially exploitative processes – such as cloning in the service of humans in *Never Let Me Go* – the Marxist paradigm, central to much postcolonial studies and integral to Literary Theory classes in Eng-Lit programs, was dominant. Part of the process, and consequence, of such readings, it appears to me on reflection, is to show the fungibility of victims. If one can see the categories of injured – the suspected terrorist, the displaced and the tortured – as interchangeable (despite their different contexts) but unified in terms of a fundamental condition – corporeal vulnerability – then it is possible to see the Dalit as a similar but *not* identical victim as the slave or the abused. We may seek verisimilitude but not exact correspondence. To word it differently, one can *see* the Dalit in the process of excavating the victimhood of the Jew, the refugee and the injured (Rothberg's work [2011]), already cited, makes these connections between African Americans and the Holocaust via W.E.B. Du Bois's writings).

While the framework for studying HR was, in the main, indebted to the work of critics already mentioned (Slaughter, Anker, Hunt, etc.), there were discussions that appeared to shift the focus slightly towards the political economy of HR. The discussion veered between the moral discourse in global HR regimes and the political economy undergirding contexts in which dehumanization occurs. While left unstated, this line of thought foregrounding the political economy of rights was reminiscent of Samuel Moyn's recent work where he notes:

> the spirit of human rights and the political enterprise with which people associate them has shifted from nationally framed egalitar-ian citizenship to a globally scaled subsistence minimum. Human rights have become our language for indicating that our cosmo-politan aspirations are strong, not stopping at the borders of our particular nation. They have been a banner for campaigns against discriminatory treatment on the basis of gender, race, and sexual

orientation. But they have also become our language for indicating that it is enough, at least to start, for our solidarity with our fellow human beings to remain weak and cheap. To a startling extent, human rights have become prisoners of the contemporary age of inequality.

(2018: 6)

Moyn's point that HR discourse is content to provide *sufficiency* rather than *equality* and that the cosmopolitanization of HR has been made compatible with market fundamentalism resonated with discussions of neoliberal economies, globalization and the neocolonial states such as India in which social inequality remains unalleviated. What the students concurred with was this: the moral discourse of equality and political citizenship had very little of useable intersections with the material conditions of equality and civic citizenship. From affirmative action to land rights of tribals – instances were cited of the tribal dwellers' campaign for land rights, and their victimization by the state in Kerala – the neoliberal state with grandiose moral discourses of emancipation and equality does very little in actual material terms to generate equality.

A specific instance where discourses of equality, sufficiency and economy intersected in our discussion was Ishiguro's novel. In *Never Let Me Go*, Ishiguro ponders over state-sponsored science that, with impunity, creates clones as living cadavers, whose purpose is solely to provide vital organs so that diseased humans may lead full lives. The clones lack all rights, including reproductive ones, and may well represent, as commentators note, a new slavery. During discussions, questions of social inequality made possible by state-sponsored science and its links to global 'tissue economies' – from organ trade to surrogacy – were employed. Emphasizing global biocapitalism and its pernicious effects on specific classes of people – in the novel, represented by the clones – the discussion returned to the points of departure and the contexts of slavery. Are the clones slaves? Is their childhood, as mapped by Ishiguro, a version of the Western *bildungsroman*, a genre associated by Joseph Slaughter with the rise of HR ideals?

Genres such as the *bildungsroman*, associated with canonical Eng-Lit (via Henry Fielding, Oliver Goldsmith, etc.), have been repurposed, we discovered, to speak of contemporary science and worse, contemporary slavery. The genre makes perfect sense even when speaking of cloning and biocapitalism, even though its origins were in contexts radically different from today's. The Eng-Lit genre *enabled* us to read Ishiguro's novel and connect it to questions of HR. Biocapitalism, genetic citizenship, animal rights and posthumanism are now of global concern mainly because of the globally linked tissue economy that (as the work of Kalindi Vora 2008, 2009 and Waldby and Mitchell 2006, shows) traverses First and Third Worlds via the bodies of the poor, the Fanonian 'wretched of the earth'.

Informed by postcolonialism which has, as Robert Young points out (2012), continued relevance in the world of neocolonial domination and continuing racialized oppression in the new 'Empire' (Hardt and Negri 2000), discussions of the world's oppressed in biocapital regimes position such texts as Ishiguro's within a global tradition. Where texts from the European Enlightenment and Abolitionist era produced affects and protests around biocapital regimes such as slavery, plantation, and indentured labour, works like Ishiguro's offer us, as students of English studies, a *history* of resistance and new ways of thinking about race. If the eighteenth century focused on race, contemporary cyberpunk dystopias such as Ishiguro's or Margaret Atwood's *MaddAddam* trilogy – an eco-dystopian work that examines life after the apocalypse, but which also chronicles the science and the biocapitalist culture that led up to the collapse – focus on species.

Conclusion

English as language but also as a field of literary studies offered generic, thematic, formal and discursive antecedents to the contemporary field of HR studies in this course. Two *lingua francas*, English and HR, intersected in this interdiscipline. Discourses of the body, vulnerability and social ontology required texts arriving from different cultural locations, informed by the broadest foundational document possible – the UDHR itself originated in a post-war multicultural crucible – and interpreted within theoretical fields opened up by Eng-Lit studies.

If, as Geoffrey Galt Harpham has argued (1999), literature has always been concerned with 'outsiderhood', it suggests that literary texts are interested in the included and the dominant as much as with the marginalized and the ignored: the white man and the slave, the monarch and the soldier, the queen and the prostitute, the brahmin and the Dalit. It is also, then, interested in *processes* (which I have referenced here as cultural apparatuses of social ontologies) of exclusion and inclusion. This means, a course that forges links between traditional Eng-Lit studies read via the paradigm of HR (Slaughter, Hunt, Anker, Goldberg, Moore) and HR documents and discourses would generate challenges to reading practices and interpretive frames to help us foreground new forms of outsiderhood. We see such challenges and frames evolve when dealing with emergent genres and media like the graphic novel or dystopian texts like Ishiguro's.

For postcolonial classrooms English as language and as the dominant field of Literary Studies provides the necessary tools, as I see it now, to deal with the uneven cosmopolitanism of HR represented in literary *and* non-literary texts. If literary studies is infused with the HR discourse's aspirations and frames of reading the human, as we sought to do throughout the course, we bring together these two crucial fields to address texts as diverse as the postcolonial *bildungsroman*, the postcolonial dystopian novel and the postcolonial global novel. The literature being produced from formerly colonized nations, then, enables us to understand the "universal" component of UDHR, to give the document an additional charge when we read novels about, say, caste-based discrimination for readers across the world to see parallels with racial and patriarchal discrimination. Conversely, reading UDHR and the global HR texts, some of which appeared in the classroom discussed here, feeds into postcolonial concerns. The postcolonial global novel becomes central to envisioning and revisioning the field of Human Rights even as the global discourse of Rights forms a subtext to the literary productions of Dalit or Aboriginal authors.

Works cited

Améry, Jean. *At the Mind's Limits: Contemplations by a Survivor on Auschwitz and its Realities*. Trans. Sidney Rosenfeld and Stella P. Rosenfeld. Bloomington: Indiana University Press, 1980. Print.

Anker, Elizabeth S. *Fictions of Dignity: Embodying Human Rights in World Literature*. Ithaca and London: Cornell University Press, 2012. Print.

Bienek, Horst. "Exodus". *Against Forgetting: The Poetry of Witnessing*. Ed. Carolyn Forché. New York: WW Norton, 1993. 468–469. Print.

Brugger, Winfried. "The Image of the Person in the Human Rights Concept", *Human Rights Quarterly* 18.3 (1996): 594–611.

Butler, Judith. *Precarious Life: The Powers of Mourning and Violence*. London: Verso, 2004. Print.

———. *Frames of War: When is Life Grievable?* London: Verso, 2009. Print.

Cavafy, Constantin. "Waiting for the Barbarians". *Against Forgetting: The Poetry of Witnessing*. Ed. Carolyn Forché. New York: WW Norton, 1993. 490–492. Print.

Cavarero, Adriana. *Horrorism: Naming Contemporary Violence*. Trans. W. McCuaig. New York: Columbia University Press, 2011. Print.

Dawes, James. *The Novel of Human Rights*. Cambridge, MA: Harvard University Press, 2018. Print.

Dhawan, Nikita and Shalini Randeria. "Perspectives on Globalization and Subalternity", *The Oxford Handbook of Postcolonial Studies*. Ed. Graham Huggan. Oxford, UK: Oxford University Press, 2013. 559–586. Print.

Dutta, Nandana. "Narrative Agency and Thinking about Conflicts." Beyond Counter-Insurgency: Breaking the Impasse in Northeast India. Ed. Sanjib Baruah. Delhi: Oxford University Press, 2009. 124–144.

Düwell, Marcus et al. Ed. *The Cambridge Handbook of Human Dignity: Interdisciplinary Perspectives*. Cambridge, UK: Cambridge Univeristy Press, 2014. Print.

Edgeworth, Maria. "The Grateful Negro". (n.d.). Online. https://repository.library.northeastern.edu/downloads/neu:m0415d75k?datastream_id=content Accessed 12 January 2021.

Hardt, Michael and Antonio Negri. *Empire*. Cambridge, MA: Harvard University Press, 2000.

Harpham, Geoffrey Galt. *Shadows of Ethics: Criticism and the Just Society*. Durham: Duke University Press, 1999. Print.

Hirsch, Marianne. "Connective Histories in Vulnerable Times", *PMLA* 129.3 (2014): 330–348. https://doi.org/10.1632/pmla.2014.129.3.330 Accessed 20 January 2021.

Hunt, Lynn. *Inventing Human Rights: A History*. New York: W.W. Norton, 2007. Print.

Ishiguro, Kazuo. *Never Let Me Go*. London: Faber and Faber, 2005. Print.

Merry, Sally E. *Human Rights and Gender Violence: Translating International Law into Local Justice*. Chicago, IN: Chicago University Press, 2006. Print.

Milosz, Czeslaw. "Child of Europe", *Against Forgetting: The Poetry of Witnessing*. Ed. Carolyn Forché. New York: WW Norton, 1993. 439–442. Print.

Moyn, Samuel. *The Last Utopia: Human Rights in History*. Cambridge, MA: Harvard University Press, 2010. Print.

———. *Not Enough: Human Rights in an Unequal World*. Cambridge, MA: Harvard University Press, 2018. Print.

Nayar, Pramod K. "Subalternity and Translation: The Cultural Apparatus of Human Rights", *Economic and Political Weekly* 46.9 (2011): 23–26. www.jstor.org/stable/41151832 Accessed 20 January 2021.

Richardson, Samuel. *Pamela or Virtue Rewarded*. Manchester: Richard and Allen, 1811. (Free EBook, Google).

Rothberg, Michael. "From Gaza to Warsaw: Mapping Multidirectional Memory", *Criticism* 53.4 (2011): 523–548. www.jstor.org/stable/23133895 Accessed 20 January 2021.

Scarry, Elaine. *The Body in Pain: The Making and Unmaking of the World*. New York: Oxford University Press, 1985. Print.

Sontag, Susan. "Regarding the Torture of Others", *New York Times* 23 May 2004.

Tait, Sue. "Pornographies of Violence? Internet Spectatorship on Body Horror", *Critical Studies in Media Communication* 25.1 (2008): 91–111. https://doi.org/10.1080/15295030701851148 Accessed 20 January 2021.

Thomas, Pratheek and Rajiv Eipe. *Hush*. Bangalore: Manta Ray Comics, 2010. Print.

Vijila. "The Autobiography of a Bitch", trans. Lekshmy Rajeev, *The Oxford Anthology of Malayalam Dalit Writing*. Eds. M.V. Dasan, V. Prathiba, Pradeepan Pampkirikunnu and C.S. Chandrika. New Delhi: Oxford University Press, 2012. 39–40. Print.

Vora, Kalindi. "Others' Organs: South Asian Domestic Labor and the Kidney Trade", *Postmodern Culture* 19.1 (2008). http://doi.org/10.1353/pmc.0.0036 Accessed 20 January 2021.

———. "Indian Transnational Surrogacy and the Disaggregation of Mothering Work", *Anthropology News* (2009): 9–12.

Waldby, Catherine and Robert Mitchell. *Tissue Economies: Blood, Tissues and Cell Lines in Late Capitalism*. Durham, North Carolina: Duke University Press, 2006. Print.

Walker, Alice. "The Flowers". *The Complete Stories*. London: Hatchette, 2011. Print.

Young, Robert J.C. "Postcolonial Remains", *New Literary History* 43.1 (2012): 19–42. www.jstor.org/stable/23259359 Accessed 20 January 2021.

4

CRITICAL PEDAGOGY

Theorizing the literatures of Northeast India

Sukalpa Bhattacharjee

Teaching is much more difficult than learning because teaching makes calls "to let learn" (Heidegger 1968: 15). The teacher, initiating the process of learning 'to let learn' must unlearn her own double-bind of remaining faithful to a hand-me-down tradition of close reading, leading to a sacrosanct meaning 'in' the text, and a poststructuralist resistance to textual closure. The challenge is to allow for a play of texts and contexts to show how multiple meanings become possible. But a class is not a stereotypical space with a unidirectional flow of knowledge from the teacher to the student. There has been an intellectual shift towards critical pedagogy in the classroom where the teacher is no longer the sole possessor of a "secret knowledge" that students aspire to (Knights 2017: 6). The classroom has been a contested space where the teacher always already held the epistemic centre pushing students to the periphery. However, contemporary critical pedagogy perceives the classroom as a shared liminal space of collaborative alter/native knowledge systems through a production of mutual affectation between the teacher and the students (as opposed to mere subjective emotions). This in turn opens the possibility of conceiving of classroom encounters as particularly intense sites for the making, unmaking, and remaking of selves in ways that surpass theories of 'learning' that rely on traditional, linear understandings of temporality. That is, learning is less about the accumulation of knowledge and more about embodied encounters that transform the embodied selves in concrete relations. Gayatri Spivak designates the classroom as "that changeful site" that generates a critique of racism, sexism and other forms of dehumanizing violence accompanying global capitalism (Snaza 2015: 50).

Therefore the strategies of evaluation/interpretation of a text in a classroom continue to evoke questions of agency –who speaks in the text? Who reads and interprets? Most teachers of our generation are trained both in close reading of texts as well as reading against the text. The question is to negotiate between an objective reading of the text (if there is any such reading) by remaining faithful to it and simultaneously opening up the text to multiple readings from myriad subject positions. As Gayatri Spivak puts it, "The formulation of... questions is itself a determined and determining

DOI: 10.4324/9781003146209-5

gesture" (Spivak 1988a: 95) and thereby a classroom often gets transformed into a political space.

Teachers in general and English teachers in particular often wonder 'can the student speak?' particularly in institutions where students come from a 'vernacular' medium of education. Voice retrieval of students has been an important project of critical pedagogy. Sometimes students have to be given short-term courses in listening comprehension of English lectures in the classroom. We have also argued about the temporality and materiality of teaching and the 'burden' of English in the Indian classroom. Before teaching genres of marginal literatures now emerging in India students have to be aware of the shift of paradigm from 'learning to curse' in English to the appropriation of the burden of English, which is greatly shaped by the patterns and politics of publishing and distribution of Indian writing in English in India and abroad. Students need to be made aware of the increase in publication of marginal literatures in English such as Dalit Literatures and Literatures of Northeast India, which have also found place in the syllabi of universities (Dutta 2018: 201). Indian Writing in English (IWE) in general has acquired institutional legitimacy through inclusion in college and university curricula, reflecting both original writings in English by Indian writers and English translations from Indian literatures. In the context of new literatures emerging in India, on the one hand, and diasporic literatures produced by Indians in the Anglophone world, the question is how 'Indian' is IWE or is there an acceptable category which can be called 'Indian'? The deconstruction of the presumably unified category called 'Indian' is inevitably linked to the politics of writing –*writing from* or *writing back* in English, which in turn generates a critique of the Indian nation-state. The nature of contemporary debates on nationalism in India and the consequent institutional reaction to them often disrupts free discussion on how the nation can be mapped in marginal literatures. Are there formal, structural, or aesthetic components distinguishing such marginal writings in English within the broad category of IWE? This leads to other questions: are there overt or covert ideological pressures in canonizing IWE particularly in the context of alter/native literatures (like the Tribal, Dalit or NE) emerging at the peripheries of mainstream India? What are the parameters of contestation between these marginalized categories and gendered subaltern writing? Recent studies on Tribal and Dalit Literatures have shown that gendered subaltern writings have produced critique of patriarchal structures inbuilt within these categories. Can these conflicts explain the shift within postcolonial IWE to a space that generates a critique of the postcolonial? What implication does this critique have for postcolonial literary/cultural studies in their pedagogical politics? Therefore in teaching literary theory and criticism in the classroom one is not sailing with students to a distant world of Byzantium where a golden bird made by a Grecian goldsmith sings to the emperor from a golden tree. One is engaging with contemporary everyday realities. What a theory teacher performs in the classroom, despite her best intentions to remain objective is something like Balzac's castrato referred to by Barthes:

> In his story 'Sarrasine', Balzac, speaking of a castrato disguised as a woman, writes this sentence: "It was Woman, with her sudden fears, her irrational whims, her instinctive fears, her unprovoked bravado, her daring and her delicious delicacy of feeling" Who is speaking in this way? Is it the story's hero, concerned to ignore the castrato concealed beneath the woman? Is it the man Balzac, endowed by his personal experience with a philosophy of Woman? Is it the author Balzac, professing certain "literary" ideas of femininity? Is it universal wisdom? or romantic psychology? It will always be impossible to know.
>
> (Barthes 1997: 142)

In the classroom the teacher's subjective voice remains unrecognizable like that of the castrato. Ben Knights' observation that teaching of English Literature has to acknowledge the 'unstable' and 'permeable' nature of this discipline is based on the fact that English Literature today is positioned between literary genres and a host of proximate subjects such as Cultural Studies, Film Studies, Gender Studies, etc. It is on the borderland of such a literary space that the teacher of literature has to negotiate between 'centrifugal' and 'centripetal' forces of the discipline (Knights 2017: 3). While there is need for stability in terms of the genres and the course prescribed, critical pedagogy always draws the teacher towards the beyond of the genre and the course. The irony of such a position is that one is always inspired to read/teach against the grain, turning the genre against itself. As one is engaged with the text or the genre, a counter-discourse of the text/genre emerges in the classroom here and now. The question that looms large here is whether there is an objective reading/teaching of texts/contexts. How does the subject position of the teacher/student affect the interpretation/reception of texts in a classroom?

Interesting accounts by English teachers regarding their subject positions as insider or outsider in a certain cultural context, express both their predicament as outsider and their frustration at being considered an outsider in the class. Leslie Sanders, who taught at York University in Toronto, has written about the need to recognize that students bring to the classroom very different experiences that the instructor must acknowledge and even learn from. Sanders states that, although she raised a number of significant questions, the students were interested in addressing only one dimension of interpretation. Her inability to affect a dispassionate and discriminating reading of the text made her feel frustrated that the class had made her an outsider because she was a white instructor teaching an African text to a group of black students (in Kanaganayakam 2005: np). Again, Arun Mukherjee, teaching a Canadian text in a classroom in Canada, laments the fact that regardless of how much she tried, her class insisted on reading the text along very traditional, universalist lines. She expresses her disappointment at the resistance she encountered in trying to introduce a political dimension to her discussion. She says, "My classroom, I believe, is one of the arenas where this process is enacted and participated in by way of struggle against the status quo as well as resistance to change" (Mukherjee 2004: 192). Sanders is conscious of a strong identification between students and the text while Mukherjee laments the resistance among students to unfamiliar areas of experience. Similarly, Gayatri Chakravorty Spivak, admits that her different positions as feminist, deconstructionist and member of the Subaltern Studies group are all constitutive of her approach to the study of a text in the class. She expresses her frustration that in some cases neither the student nor the teacher is willing to read texts historically and/or politically (Spivak 1994: 127). My own engagement in the context discussed above is that of a cautious move not to reduce my students in the classroom to respondents of my own scholarly project of producing a counter-discourse of ethnicity, caste, or gender. Through a systematic dismantling and interrogation of readily accepted categories such as tribe and Tribal Literatures, I have tried to make the class address them as critics. I have drawn parallels between textual descriptions and empirical evidence so as to enable responsible readings, similar to what Spivak describes as 'ethical singularity' which is not only the act of producing response from the listener, but also the "ethical stance of making discursive room for the other to exist" (Spivak 1995: xxv). This is meant to create an intimate relationship between the teacher and the students in non-essentialized and non-crisis terms producing responses from both sides.

In engaging with issues of ethnicity, identity and tribe while theorizing the Literature of Northeast India in a classroom located in the space of its production, one has to begin with awareness of the ethnic composition of the classroom even though one presupposes that a literature classroom is a liberal space for addressing critical thoughts objectively. There is an inbuilt struggle for a teacher to project herself as an objective critic of a text which is always already complicated with political discourses of inclusion/exclusion, us/them divides. Initially, the teacher is not too certain whether her own ethnic/religious/caste identity as reflected in visible markers such as appearance or name has not been a hindrance for the class to accept her as a fellow scholar in generating an academic critique of sensitive terms such as tribe or in generating an internal critique of a community. What would it mean to teach or 'let learn' the Literatures of Northeast India in a metropolitan university in contrast to teaching it in institutions where the everyday lived life of the region forms the backdrop or the context of these texts and for pedagogy? One needs to keep in mind that the contemporary political climate of the region is hugely charged with notions and claims of ethnicities, tribe, representations, identities, and citizenship. Students and teachers in their day-to-day life are often polarized or affiliated to opposing schools of thought and action and located at different representational domains of the political theatre. It may be mentioned that these are class-rooms with English postgraduate and PhD students at NEHU (North Eastern Hill University), located in Meghalaya, one of the hill states of Northeast India. It is not necessarily a multicultural classroom and so there is already a pre-existing shared experience of an ordered life-world and institutionalized religious practice among the majority in the class. The teacher who does not come from a similar ethnic or religious background has the anxieties of being an Other to the dominant ethos of the class. The challenge is to attract the students to critical academic discourses by inspir-ing them to unlearn their deep-rooted ethnic or religious biases, by learning to rise above them. Therefore the discussions on critical and sensitive issues are usually in a dialogic mode through conversation and intertextuality.

I have been teaching modern and poststructuralist literary theory for some decades now and have traversed generic and disciplinary boundaries in contextualizing what I teach. Needless to say, in teaching theory one often encounters resistance, since most students have not been exposed to contemporary theory at the graduate level. Therefore the teacher needs to continuously and constantly contextualize the theories using different forms of literary, social, and political texts. It is through such a methodological practice of explaining theory/text/context simultaneously, that I got round to theorizing the Literature of Northeast India since it is the most immediate socio-political context to which the class and in this case also the teacher could relate to. My subjective experiences and scholarly interest and empathy with ideas like Elaine Showalter's 'gynocriticism' or Hélène Cixous 'ecriture feminine' influence my approach. Doing theory also reflects a habit of mind that relates the literary to the immediate social or political around us. Robert Eaglestone in "What Do We Teach When We Teach Literature?" says that, particularly in teaching theory, we are committed to the question of students' experience and so we teach them to be literary critics. Citing Ben Knights, Eaglestone says

> that disciplines in general, and English in particular, are not simply made up by knowing texts (we might call this 'knowing about', perhaps) but by 'communities of practice' ('knowing how to'), and that these communities embody knowledges and behaviours that cannot simply be written down or listed…
>
> (Knights in Eaglestone 2019: 4–5)

Knights seems to emphasize that studying disciplines such as English involves identifying with the behaviours associated with the subject. It is in this pursuit of the literary practice as a habit of mind that one is persuaded to make a critique of the postcolonial itself particularly with reference to the emergence of texts from the margins and the space they occupy in the syllabi of undergraduate and postgraduate English departments.

One of the most important re-visionings of English Studies has been reflected in the inclusion of canonical and non-canonical texts from the margins of India like the Northeast. For a teacher of English Studies, who is experientially and culturally sensitive to the issues of exclusionary politics, claims of citizenship, reverse racism and ethnic cleansing in such regions, the major challenges in a classroom situation are: (a) how to deconstruct the stereotypical binary of the centre and periphery represented in most English texts from the region? In other words, how to morally justify the emergence of a counter-canon that itself creates new centres at the peripheries, by privileging the written over the oral and by privileging writings in English over the vernacular? (b) How to make a distinction between 'tribe' as a derogatory category constructed by the colonizers and 'tribe' as a term of self-description by creative writers? As one looks for a space of intervention, ethics of self-representation interfere with the realm of 'top-down' working of the English language in producing a gentry of English language writers in the indigenous communities. Such a use of the English language marks a sense of localization of the global English, delivered in the milieu of decoloniality of the local literatures. This decolonized English functions as a prosthetic bridge between the local and the global accommodating the native imageries of place and identity while also consciously distancing the local from the global for producing a discourse of otherness. This distance is intersubjective as it works like a norm of othering the English while appropriating it in a variety of indigenous and local contexts of life, or rather in lived experiences. How does one theorize this as a phenomenal event that dominates the very scene for language, literature and music and enters into learning in an interdisciplinary mode? One could term it as a novel experience of the global in the local and hence an experience of the metropolitan West in the local tribal and indigenous contexts of teaching and learning.

Given this, the English classroom inevitably becomes more of a radical and political space for creating a scholarly sensibility among students, for examining whether a creative writer writing in English from India's Northeast is capable of appropriating the dominant canons of language and literature to *write back* or is *writing in*. It has been said that the classroom becomes the site for the everyday struggle of a teacher. Among many other contexts of my everyday struggle in the classroom in dealing with Tagore's ideas of Nationalism, Ambedkar's discourses of caste and Eve Kosofsky Sedgwick's discussions on human sexuality, the most glaring has been the contextualization of Edward Said's *Orientalism*. The struggle is because of the imperative to unpack both semic and semiotic codes in the text, which invariably becomes an ideologically loaded exercise and yet the teacher is expected to distance herself from the immediate political. As mentioned earlier, my postgraduate and PhD classroom comprises students from the hill states of Northeast India who are ethnically mostly tribals and some of them also write poetry and present them in poetry reading circles in

Northeast India. My experiences of teaching Contemporary Theory and critical approaches to literature in both classes involved discussing various constructions of the native orient by theorists and finding parallels of such constructions by colonizers in the ethnic worlds of the region. As I begin reading aloud Arthur Balfour's speech in the House of Commons from "Knowing the Oriental" in Edward Said's *Orientalism*, the parallels of various categories of 'them' and 'us' that emerge in the mind of both the students and the teacher in the context of contemporary movements in Northeast India are obvious. Balfour says:

> We know the civilization of Egypt better than we know the civilization of any other country. We know it further back; we know it more intimately; we know more about it. It goes far beyond the petty span of the history of our race, which is lost in the prehistoric period at a time when the Egyptian civilisation had already passed its prime. Look at all the Oriental countries.
>
> (in Said 1979: 32)

Although I was supposed to be discussing only orientalism, imperialism and postcolonialism in relation to the prescribed course in Contemporary Theory, my class urged that I contextualize my theory classes with texts and narratives of/about the region. So I bring in my analysis accounts of white ethnographers, British officers, and missionaries where similar images of the natives have been used. What the first chief commissioner of Assam, Colonel Richard Harte Keatinge, stated while narrating his responsibilities in Northeast India is very significant:

> There is no part of our vast Indian frontier about which we have so little military or geographical information as the north-east…there is no like extent of it bordering upon savage tribes, so sparsely garrisoned; yet in this remote corner of our empire there is more English capital invested in land than in any like extent of our dominion.
>
> (Mitchell 1883: 9)

One can read such descriptions against Robert Lindsay's narrative on his experiences in the Khasi Hills in 1789 where he compares the beauty of the land to the Garden of Eden but is shocked to find 'wild looking' people dancing on the land (Lindsay 1849: 177). Postcolonial critique generated by such an imperialist representational mode invites a critical stance on the issue of representation. It is also a political imperative to look into the history of nomenclature of indigenous communities in Northeast India, which is being interrogated by contemporary scholars on Northeast India. The politics of naming has been central to the idea of representation. In such a representational context Aime Cesaire remarked: "The colonizer, who in order to ease his conscience gets into the habit of seeing the other as an animal, accustomed himself to treating him like animal, and tends objectively to transform himself into an animal" (Nandy 1983: 30).

It is impossible to explain oriental constructions of natives without generating a critique of knowledge and power –the two 'Baconian' themes which dominate Said's *Orientalism*. As we discuss the possibilities of a postcolonial recovery from colonial constructions through literary writings, it is with the term tribe that we are faced with a dilemma. The obvious question from the class now is: – has the subject of orientalism in Northeast India been able to write/strike back through literary genres categorized now as Tribal Literatures or Literatures of Northeast India? A student from Nagaland, familiar with Temsula Ao's poetry, says: Yes Ao has been able to critique oriental construction in "Prayer of a Monolith" (Ao 2013: 293–295). I then asked the student to substantiate her point. She started reading out from her mobile:

> I stand at the village gate
> In mockery of my former state. ...
>
> They dislodged me from my moorings
> They tore me from her side
> They chipped and chiseled
> They gave me altered proportions
> ...
> And planted the 'made-over' me
> As their new-found trophy.

I asked the student whether we should call it tribal poetry. The student replied in the affirmative saying that in tribal myths the self is a continuum between past and present and tribal identities are described through association to sacred and profane spaces. A student from Arunachal Pradesh agreed and said: "Mamang Dai in *The Legends of Pensam* says that we have come from solitudes and miracles." Another student joined in to state that many Naga tribes believe themselves to have originated from the rock called Khezakhenoma. I strengthened her point citing from Mamang Dai's "An Obscure Place":

> The history of our race
> begins with the place of stories.
> We do not know if the language we speak
> belongs to a written past.
> Nothing is certain.
> (Dai 2011: 5–6)

But now the class becomes alert to the fact that the term 'tribe' is an oriental construct, even though it is also a term of self-description of many indigenous communities. I complicated the matter further by mentioning that in the context of representation of indigenous people of Northeast

India by themselves and by the other, another dimension of dispossession needs to be addressed –the loss of the indigenous script and the importance of the 'spoken word' in transmitting a cultural and a written tradition. A deconstruction of the colonial usage 'tribe', used as a signifier by white ethnographers and missionaries in their 'civilizing' mission becomes inevitable. Charlotte Seymour Smith writes:

> the concept of tribe was largely a colonial creation...tribal division and tribal consciousness were largely a creation of the efforts of colonial rulers to impose order and supralocal unity among the previously largely autonomous local communities, and where there was previously a loose and contextually relative sense of ethnic identity, colonial rule often imposed a tribal division which then acquired increasing concreteness due to the need to adapt to the administrative and political demand of colonial rule.
>
> (Smith 1986: 281)

At this point the class is eager to establish the point that the recognition of 'Northeast Literature' as part of marginal literatures has been a positive step towards appropriation of the colonial discourse of orientalism. However, ethnic cultures of Northeast India call for a recognition of their distinct self-identity which is based on a certain world-view and an affirmation of difference with the ethnic other. Has the language of literary expression been able to articulate a differentiated self-identity? The class now realizes that 'Northeast Literature', as it is called in the syllabi of academic institutions and in the catalogue of publishing houses, includes only writings in English from the region, including translations into English from other languages. Therefore, apart from religion and culture, language becomes another contested field for imperial imposition. A student suddenly interrupts and asks: "does it mean that there was never a moment of postcolonial recovery in the hills of Northeast India since our writers mostly write only in English and not in their native languages?" Without addressing her question directly at that point I move into other similar contexts. We then discuss how in response to the systematic violence done to their own languages, some postcolonial writers and activists either advocated a complete return to the use of indigenous languages or used the imposed English language to appropriate the dominant European tongue, re-forming it in new literary forms. In the former category one finds the Kenyan writer Ngugi wa Thiong'o who said that African writers should write in African languages while in the latter category one has writers like Chinua Achebe and those of the so-called Third World who like Shakespeare's Caliban adopted the strategy of *writing back* to the empire. Such an appropriation is particularly visible in novels from postcolonial countries like Africa and India where authors struggled to represent indigenous themes and conflicts within the parameters of a western genre. As the student repeats her question, I now try to answer more in terms of *what ought to be* rather than *what is*. Postcolonial Literatures in English therefore have to contest the imperial 'worlding' of the indigenous life-world and reproduce a counter-narrative of their own societies as distant cultures, exploited but with rich intact literary heritages waiting to be recovered, interpreted. Here the issue of the agency of representation becomes important –the indigenous life-world as represented by the indigenous *self* and that represented by the *other*.

The student further probes:

> But what about the Literature of Northeast India? Has it not made self recovery possible for the indigenous communities of both the hills and the plains? So many of our writers are being translated and read. A few of them have got prestigious awards and recognition…

But I insisted that self-recovery of the indigenous people through their representational agencies also involved a recovery of their cultural specificities not only in relation to the colonizers but also with reference to other indigenous cultures with which they were clubbed. But can the postcolonial Indian imagination in a collective sense address ethnographic and historical misrepresentation of indigenous people and cultures of Northeast India? For that matter, can the Literature of the Northeast as a counter-canon represent also its ethnic other who is otherized on the basis of ethnic claims and identities and yet who also lays claim to Northeast as her homeland? The representational possibilities of Northeast Literature seems to shrink in the context of our classroom discussion at that point. Some other students intervene at that moment and cite the incidents of racism in the national capital where students are attacked in a colony for eating beef or girls eve-teased as 'chinky',etc. So now the question was to examine the relationship between a mainstream politics of otherizing the region, culture, and people in the metropolis vis-à-vis the reaction to it by way of reverse racism in the region. It is therefore impossible to theorize the Literature of Northeast India without engaging with contemporary political discourse of/in the region. I decided now to read to the class a few lines from Robin Ngangom's poem "The Invented Land":

> My homeland has no boundaries.
> At cockcrow one day it found itself
> inside a country to its west…
>
> My people have disinterred their alphabet,
> burnt down decrepit libraries
> in a last puff of nationalism…
> My native place has not been christened yet
> my homeland, a travelogue without end…
>   (Ngangom 2012: 13)

So it is not as though there is a stereotypical representational mode that writers use to describe their roots, their homelands, and their destinies. It is therefore quite inadequate to characterize the Literature of Northeast India as a homogenous body of writing engaged with common themes.

But I still have not been able to answer the student on the Literature of Northeast India as a counter-canon to mainstream IWE in terms of language and an inclusive representation of different shades of identities in the region. I haven't yet been able to tell her how indigenous communities in Northeast India would have to appropriate both western and mainstream Indian representational categories and the stereotyping of the indigenous as 'native' or 'tribal'. The Literature of Northeast India as a postcolonial marginal genre and as prescribed in the syllabi of different universities has not been representative of the diversity of people who inhabit this region. Gayatri Spivak's query, "Can the Subaltern Speak?" (Spivak 1988b) evokes two senses of representation: the scholarly representation of knowable objects and the democratic representation of political subjects. The question exposes the slippage between a scholarly project of portraying 'others' and a political project of speaking for 'others', both of which deny these voices of 'others' and the complex subject position that would be irreducible to static images or statistical averages. Such representational modes one could argue, create a category of internal orients like 'internal minorities' (Lloyd 1987) who are often termed as *the other of the other*. A student from the Bangladesh border in the Garo Hills now asks: "Who is *the other of the other*? Are they represented in the Literature of Northeast India?" I answer him by saying that the *other of the other* mostly writes in her native language and therefore she does not enjoy the privilege of publication as those who write in English or both in English and their own mother tongue. Stuart Hall arguing that representation, culture, and language are tightly connected in the process of producing meaning writes:

> In part, we give things meaning by how we represent them – the words we use about them, the stories we tell about them, the images of them we produce, the emotions we associate with them, the way we classify and conceptualize them, the values we place on them.
>
> (Hall 2003: 3)

Politics of representation leaves room for misinterpretation and unfair assessment of culture and values associated with a community. Therefore one has to evolve a hermeneutic strategy of recovery:

> from the lost terrains of historical and temporal sense of being that finds its closure within contemporary language games. Such lost terrains consist of (a) an originary sense of place and the subsequent loss of the place and (b) the construction of an other as an

antithesis to the self in the form of racism, xenophobia and other such forms of violence.

(Biswas 2011: 122)

So we move to the defence of the rubric "Northeast Literature", which sometimes is used interchangeably with "Tribal Literature", and look for the possibilities of a postcolonial recovery. I begin with the premise that literary intervention has been a dominant mode of postcolonial recovery in Northeast India. Creative authors of indigenous communities of the region, particularly those writing in English, have appropriated the dominant colonial weapon –the English language –to represent themselves and their communities. But a critical question that one has to encounter is: can their writings be called "Tribal Literatures"? In the context of postcolonial literature, the word 'tribal literature' used in the Scandinavian Writers' Conference in 1967 sought to denote by this term the distinctive feature of representing people, things, and ideas with their cultural authenticities (Ghose 2006: 34). But will the rubric "Tribal Literature" fit into the postcolonial descriptive categories like "Third World Literature or "Indian Literature" or will this term make up for the in-between in "post" and "colonial"? Or will it be the "blank space" of Postcolonial Literature in the sense of unidentified and unexplored peoples and regions? (McClintock 1995: 24). Aijaz Ahmad has vehemently argued against the theoretical category of "Third World Literature" because of

its equally homogenizing impulse to slot very diverse kinds of public aspirations under the unitary insignia of 'nationalism' and then to designate this nationalism as the determinate and epochal ideology for cultural production in non-Western societies.

He continues:

I find it all the more difficult to speak of a 'Third World literature' when I know that I cannot confidently speak as a theoretical coherent category of an 'Indian' Literature... The difficulty lies, rather, in the very premises that have governed the narrativisation of that history, which has (1) privileged High Textuality of a Brahminical kind to posit the unification of this literary history; or (2) assembled the history of the main texts of particular languages (in a very uneven way) to obtain this unity through the aggregative principle; or (3) attempted to reconstruct the ... themes in several languages but with ... the canonizing procedures of the 'great books' variety, with scant attempt to locate literary history within other sorts of histories in any consistent fashion.

(Ahmad 1994: 243)

The methodological problem is that we neither succeed in situating the Literature of Northeast India or "Tribal Literatures" within the established pedagogical categories of Indian Literature or Postcolonial Literatures nor are we able to justify its claims to self-representation. Postcolonial narratives are considered to be contested terrains where the discourses of imperialism and its subjected others struggle for control over the field of representation. In such a contestation the category of "Third World Literature" or "Indian Literature" definitely does not provide for a conceptual or normative framework for the inclusion of 'difference' characterized by "Tribal Literature" or a tribal world-view. In her essay, "Where Have All the Natives Gone?" Rey Chow examines the construction of images of the 'native' which, despite their ubiquity, remain elusive. 'Native' works, bifurcated as either timeless (the art museum sentiment) or historical (the ethnographic museum), are determined in post-imperialist discourse by the search for 'authenticity.' Chow argues that questions about the native are questions about the irreversibility of modernity (Chow 1993: 48). The concept of time in a tribal life-world cannot be represented within the western notion of a linear or chronological time internalized by dominant postcolonial societies. Therefore, in a theoretical sense it is a postcolonial imperative confronting indigenous writers of Northeast India to transcend the qualitative space given by the connotation attached to the term 'tribe' from a colonizer's point of view as discussed above. The complex and dynamic nature of postcolonial identity formation is undoubtedly manifesting itself in the manner in which writers from indigenous communities of the region are positioning themselves against dominant cultures which they attempt to counter through their literary texts. From a literary perspective, it is important to examine the author's conception of the symbiotic relationship that exists between fiction, the society, and the author. Representative authors from indigenous communities of the region writing in English and published by mainstream publishing houses have projected the specificities of their cultural life-world. But the question is: Can these literary works be placed under the rubric "Tribal Literature"? In other words, are the writings of these authors at least over the past decade necessarily 'tribal' in their content? Again, how do writers writing in their own indigenous languages encounter the postcolonial? What is the postcolonial discursive space represented by "Tribal Literature" in the emerging genre of "Literature of Northeast India"–a canon that is gradually getting attention in the institutional space of metropolitan universities in India and abroad?

To the question of whether those who write in unrecognized tribal languages are a part of the postcolonial canon or not has been widely debated the world over. The literary works from below or the margins written in a lesser known language, without the privilege of being expressed in an alien cosmopolitan tongue, is the predicament of a majority of writers in the post-colonial tribal world of the Northeast. Unfortunately, most of these writers do not gain primacy over the English language writers. In the very popular mode of theorizing the post-colonial in English or in French, writers writing in their native tongues often get excluded from the post-colonial canon unless they also write in English. This throws up a double problematic: (1) indigenous writers writing in English on indigenous themes get reduced to only a special genre within the post-colonial rubric, and (2) writing in English takes away much of the refinement available in tribal and indigenous languages. This problematic can neither be resolved within the rubric of the uncontaminated tribal or indigenous nor can it be reduced to the mere post-colonial. One might say that this displaces the tribal into the post-colonial, while it cannot also recover the 'tribal' in the form of the 'Tribal Literature'. When and how does one exactly dismantle the binary between the 'tribal' and the 'post-colonial'?

As one looks for a space of literary intervention, an ethics of self-representation interferes with the realm of 'top-down' working of the English language in producing a gentry of English language writers in the indigenous communities. This is also a moment of transforming the agency of the indigenous writer into the dominant canons of language and literature to *write in* or to *write back*. The contemporary phase for post-colonial theory considers this aspect of 'transformation' by describing

> how cultural and political schemata imprint themselves upon bodily experience and thus motivate agents in powerful ways... What does seem clear is that there is little payoff in separating the world of emotion and affect from the world of language and self-representation.
>
> (Appadurai 1997: 148)

What is then the possibility of an ethical intervention in what is unavailable for reflection and representation? Can we hear the pre-ontic murmur of the tribal self and the tribal world beyond the devices of representation? One has to take an epistemological stance here moving beyond both the anthropological as well as the ethical. The epistemological stance here is not concerned with an object or subject of knowledge; it is rather concerned with a choice of what is beyond the alterity of the tribal. By 'beyond the alterity', one would mean a non-nativist non-symptomatic reading of ways of world-making as it happens in Tribal Literatures of India's Northeast. For example, how do tribal spiritual experiences constitute the multifarious lived experiences of the tribes? Can this be defined in a language of representation? Or, does it produce an alternative to existing 'modern' ways of writing about oneself? Mrinal Miri articulates this epistemological stance when he argues:

> One thing that can certainly be said in favour of the tribal vision is that the disjunction between the disengaged original self and the samsaric world of the received view of spirituality (...) does

not exist in this vision. The world of the tribesman is seamlessly continuous between the inanimate, the animate and the human; she/he is concerned with the contingencies of time and space as anything else in the world. Self-knowledge for the tribesman, therefore, must be bound by these contingencies. The episteme of the tribal vision is similarly continuous between the natural, the moral and the spiritual.

(Miri 2010: 116)

This epistemic continuity acts as the mediating factor amongst incommensurable worlds of alternatives and assists in recovering the tribal world from its representational gaps. But it is also to be noted that such a recovery would serve as a decoy that would also substitute the ethnology and anthropology of the tribes by a visionary understanding of the 'signifying spaces' of the tribal universe. The question that my class now asks is:

does such a signifying space that establishes continuity between apparently disjointed spaces of self-representation and spaces of signification within the tribal world act as a condition for recovery of the tribal world?

The question can be answered with a methodological departure into Critical Pedagogy.

Critical pedagogical practices demand such a deconstructive reading of genres and terms because every literary rubric or epistemological category carries within itself the seeds of its own deconstruction. Such is the case with the term tribe and the Literatures of Northeast India. In engaging with the theoretical possibilities of mapping a genre like Literatures of Northeast India in the classroom, one is constantly challenged by its limits and (im)possibilities of representing an identity-in-difference. Postcolonial narratives need to thrive on a celebration of identity-in-difference and it is in articulating this identity-in-difference that the Literatures of Northeast India or "Tribal Literatures" can occupy a very prominent place within the genre of Postcolonial Literature beyond the hierarchy and individuation which categorizes canonical/institutional Postcolonial Studies.

Thus in our theoretical journey in attempting to examine the rubric "Northeast Literature" in the classroom, we now discover the ambivalent position of postcolonial critics within their own critical predicament of having to say 'no' to a structure which they critique and yet they inhabit intimately, because of the hegemonic mode of self-vigilance of a theory that paralyzes thought into binaries and yet cannot represent the unrepresentable of native culture and history. Tribal narratives have the potential to claim cultural or linguistic autonomy as never fixed and isolated but always on, an ongoing articulation of differences. In doing postcolonial studies in the mixed space *between* centre and periphery, between First and Third

Worlds, postcolonial intellectuals have always experienced the unstable combination of power and powerlessness, identity, and difference. Tribal Literature could be the in-between of the literature of the First and Third Worlds without seeking narrative closure. The vast space of the tribal cultural world with its multitude of rituals and practices is the field of symbolic decoding that constitutes what can be called "Tribal Literature". In this vast field, the post-colonial is a moment of recovery not confined to devices of self-representation, but moving beyond it in an epistemological and methodological sense. The body of work that passes as "Tribal Literature" from India's Northeast reverses the top-down effect of post-coloniality and instead firmly places itself back into the symbolic multiverse of the tribal world, whose multiple and productive prosthesis go into production of a tribal subjectivity that is a constituent of what is called 'post-colonial'.

Work cited

Ahmad, Aijaz. "'Indian Literature': Notes towards the Definition of a Category" in Aijaz Ahmad ed. *In Theory: Classes, Nations Literatures*, Delhi: OUP, 1994. Print.

Appadurai, Arjun "Life after Primordialism" in Arjun Appadurai ed. *Modernity at Large: Cultural Dimensions of Globalization*, New Delhi: Oxford University Press, 1997. Print.

Ao, Temsula, *Book of Songs: Collected Poems (1988–2007)*, Dimapur: Heritage Publishing House, 2013. Print.

Barthes, R. "Death of the Author" in Roland Barthes ed. *Image, Music, Text*. Trans. S. Heath. London: Fontana, 1997. 142–148. Print.

Biswas, Prasenjit. "Ethnophilosophy: Conceptual Artefacts, Wisdom and Critique of Anthropocentrism in India's Northeast" in S. Dasgupta et al. eds. *Literatures and Oratures as Knowledge Systems: Texts From the North-East*, Centre of Advanced Study, Department Of Comparative Literature, Kolkata: Jadavpur University, 2011. Print.

Chow, Rey. *Writing Diaspora: Tactics of Intervention in Contemporary Cultural Studies*. Bloomington: Indiana University Press, 1993. Print.

Clark, Lauren B. "Critical Pedagogy in the University: Can a Lecture Be Critical Pedagogy?" 16.8: (2018). 985–999. https://doi.org/10.1177/1478210318787053. Accessed 12 January 2019.

Kanaganayakam, Chelva. "How to Teach *The Guide* as a Culturally Different Text." *Postcolonial Text* 1.2: (2005). Np. Web.

Dutta, Nandana. "View from Here: English in India: The Rise of Dalit and NE Literature." *English* 67.258: (2018). 201–208. https://doi.org/10.1093/english/efy025 Accessed 15 January 2021

Dai, Mamang. "An Obscure Place" in Tilottama Misra ed. *An Oxford Anthology of Writings from North-East India: Poetry and Essays* New Delhi: OUP, 2011. Print.

Eaglestone, Robert. "What Do We Teach When We Teach Literature?". *The Use of English*. (2018). https://www2.le.ac.uk/offices/english-association/schools/UE67.3Eaglestone.pdf. Accessed 18 Oct 2018

Eaglestone, Robert. *Literature: Why It Matters*, Cambridge: Polity Press, 2019. Print.

Ghose, Anuradha. "The Notion of Identity Formation and the Paradigm of Cultural Resistance in the Novels of Chinua Achebe," in Mala Pandurang ed. *Chinua Achebe: An Anthology of Recent Criticism*, Delhi: Pencraft International, 2006. Print.

Hall, Stuart. "The Work of Representation" in Stuart Hall ed. *Representation: Cultural Representations and Signifying Practices*. London: SAGE, 2003.

Heidegger, M. *What is Called Thinking?* Trans. J. G. Gray. New York: Harper & Row, 1968. Print.

Knights, Ben, Ed. *Teaching Literature: Text and Dialogue in the English Classroom*, Basingstoke: Palgrave Macmillan, 2017. Print.

Lindsay, Robert. "Anecdotes of an Indian Life," in Lindsay, Lord ed. *Lives of the Lindsays* Vol. 3, London: John Murray, 1849. Print.

Lloyd, David. "Genet's Genealogy: European Minorities and the Ends of the Canon", in *Cultural Critique*, Spring, 1987. 161–185.

Mitchell, John F. *Report (Topographical, Political and Military) on the North-East Frontier of India*, Calcutta: Superintendent of Government Printing, 1883. Print.

McClintock, Anne. *Imperial Leather: Race, Gender and Sexuality in the Colonial Contest*, New York: Routledge, 1995. Print.

Miri, Mrinal. "The Spiritual and the Moral" in Tilottoma Misra ed. *The Oxford Anthology of Writings from North-East India: Poetry and Essays*, New Delhi: Oxford University Press, 2010. Print.

Mukherjee, Arun P. "'You Don't Even Want to Go There': Race, Text, and Identities in the Classroom" in Cynthia Sugars ed. *Home-Work: Postcolonialism, Pedagogy, and Canadian Literature*, Ottawa: University of Ottawa Press, 2004. 189–212. Print.

Nandy, Ashis. *The Intimate Enemy: Loss and Recovery of Self under Colonialism*, New Delhi: Oxford University Press, 1983. Print.

Ngangom, Robin. "My Invented Land (after Mario Meléndez)" in *Classic Poetry Series:Poemhunter.com – The World's Poetry Archive*, (2012) www.poemhunter.com/i/ebooks/pdf/robin_s_ngangom_2012_6.pdf Accessed 28 April 2019.

Said, Edward. *Orientalism*, New York: Vintage, 1979. Print.

Smith, Charlotte Seymour. *Macmillan Dictionary of Anthropology*, London and Basingstoke: Macmillan Press Ltd., 1986. Print.

Snaza, Nathan. "Class Time: Spivak's 'Teacherly Turn'." *Critical Literacy: Theories and Practices*. 9.1: (2015). 49–61.

Spivak, Gayatri Chakravorty. *In Other Worlds: Essays in Cultural Politics*, New York: Routledge, 1988a. Print.

———. "Can the Subaltern Speak?" in Cary Nelson and Lawrence Grossberg eds. *Marxism and the Interpretation of Culture*, Urbana, IL: University of Illinois Press, 1988b. Print.

———. "How to Read a Culturally Different Text", in Francis Barker, Peter Hulme, and Margaret Iversen eds. *Colonial Discourse/ Postcolonial Theory*, Manchester: Manchester University Press, 1994. 126–150. Print.

———. "Translator's Preface" *Imaginary Maps: Three Stories by Mahasweta Devi*, New York and London: Routledge, 1995. Print.

5

THE FISSURED SURFACE OF THE TEXT

Reading the gaps and silences in
A Passage to India

Binayak Roy

An Indian classroom in a semi-urban area is a specific kind of cultural melting pot where students and faculty members from diverse race and class backgrounds, ethnicity, culture, traditions, ideologies, religious and disciplinary affiliations, values, thoughts and life-experiences huddle together. This might be equally true of the metropolis but the region in which the institution is situated lends its own cultural and linguistic character to the mix. It is, therefore, imperative on the part of the teachers to interweave these diverse worlds to create an inclusive and compassionate learning space in the classroom. Moje et al., basing their ideas on Moll et al.'s concept of "funds of knowledge", argue that every individual possesses funds of knowledge from the multiple social worlds that she/he inhabits. They selectively draw from these as per the demands of the situation, time and place. Bakhtin argues that in the absence of any common shared meaning, interlocutors must dialogically negotiate meanings of acts as unique acting agents from particular subject positions within the context of the particular act itself. Bender expatiates that meaning is constructed "in the relationship of understanding [between the speaker and the addressee – real or imagined] from a particular perspective and the obligation of acting from that position;" and as such the truth or the meaning of any utterance is essentially partial, ever unfinalized and subjective (1998: 189).

Any meaning making process, according to Bakhtin (1981), is essentially dialogic and must attempt to include both sides of the conversation. However, when Bakhtin speaks of dialogue, he means more than the actual act of conversation between interlocutors. Every utterance is dialogic in that it anticipates an addressee and can never be free from the influence of the anticipated response to the utterance. An utterance emerges from the desire to be answered; it is "not designated to dissipate in a vacuum" (Braxley 2005: 13). The response could be "either in words or in action", spoken or written and directed to the speaker or not, but there's always a

DOI: 10.4324/9781003146209-6

listener and "the listener will respond eventually" (Braxley 2005:13). Therefore, meaning is always negotiated and, as Volosinov/Bakhtin (1973) writes, "can only arise in interindividual territory" (Volosinov/Bakhtin cited in Dyson 1993: 4). Bakhtin argues that precisely because meaning cannot be shared with others, "the 'ethical act' is grounded in an awareness of difference" and is unique "within the act itself"; its truth cannot be accessible outside "the act itself", in which "the unique self plays a crucial part" (Bender 1998: 188). Bakhtin's notion of participative thinking "emphasizes that I can only understand theoretical ideas and other people within specific actions that exist in relation to myself" (Bender 1998: 188).

The active integration of multiple funds of knowledge and discourse is important in teaching students how to navigate the texts and literary practices necessary for serious research and prepare for the "complex, diverse, and sometimes dangerous world" they will be part of beyond the educational institution (Moore, Bean, Birdyshaw, and Rycik 1999). Herein lies the significance of *adda* (intellectual debates in an informal manner, often in the form of talk-sessions) in classroom discussions. *Adda*, in the Indian and Bangladeshi cultural context, is freewheeling conversation, a pastime pursued for its own sake by a group of intimates. Ideally, each participant is at once a speaker and a listener. Its informing spirit is one of entertainment rather than edification. It is more serious than small talk but less formal than debate. In fact, it is a cross between the two. It reflects a sceptical, argumentative, humorous Indian temper. *Adda* acknowledges multiple accentuality, varying points-of-view, different 'funds of knowledge,' and functions within the ethics of answerability. *Adda* helps in the consolidation of group identity/community. *Adda* is essentially dialogic.

Discourses generated in *adda* often have an immediate use-value for students' social worlds, no matter how worthless such discourses might seem to adults observing from the sidelines. "Consciousness-raising", believes Dutta, "should be the purpose and goal of critical humanities education – a goal larger than what is generally ascribed to the discipline (2015: 45). "Consciousness-raising" implies not only being aware of the inequalities that exist in our society but "it also entails being aware of and sensitive to our ethical responsibilities in the world" (2015: 45). A humanities scholar therefore conceptualizes the social world as interconnected and assumes an active role for each component in that world. Sheila Schwartz argues that the first essential characteristic of a humanities educator is "a *tolerance for ambiguity*" (1968: 9, emphasis original). The humanities teacher "cannot function with an emotional need for closure, for neat packages, for the completion of subjects or ideas, or for dependence on examinations" (1968: 9). Therefore, a critical humanities educator needs to actively seek out connections between the multiple social worlds of the youth and between the multiple funds of knowledge that they bring to school in order to make the dialogism inherent in our society, and in each of us, more visible to the students.

E.M. Forster's *A Passage to India* (1924[1965]) has been an enigmatic text for readers. It is a challenge for any teacher to unravel its complexities in the classroom, especially to undergraduate students. This chapter is based on my experience of teaching this text in a college in rural north Bengal over a few years, using the form of the *adda* that is a popular mode of conversation, in order to open up the classroom and the text for exchanges with and among the students.

My first challenge was to impress upon these young, impressionable minds that this novel is much more than a tourist guide to India, as they might have conjectured from the title. Fresh from the historical romance of *A Tale of Two Cities* (a text on their syllabus), they are all on a sudden confronted with the bitter reality of colonial India with its miasma of racism, and the perceived hostility of nature. It allowed them to vicariously explore the limits and ultimate futility of racism, the deep emotional currents unleashed by a decision to marry, the difficulties of friendship among colonial administrators and their subjects, and the need to prevent imperialist injustice.

In a narrative as multi-layered as *A Passage to India*, it is always a challenge to decide what issues to bring to the foreground in the class, what episodes and characters in the text to isolate and analyse. The novel's endorsement of syncretism and humanism that downplay cultural differences and divisiveness assume immense significance even a hundred years later when the world is torn apart by a resurgence of right wing extremist politics. Despite his celebration of cultural pluralism, an acute sense of the sameness of man across "looking glass borders" and temporal divides underlies Forster's work. The desire of Fielding to meet Aziz as free citizens transcending the divisions of colonizer/colonized, white/non-white, self/other does not lose its appeal in spite of its failure. The novel celebrates the depths of human experience and the achievement of the self's reciprocal relationship with the other. Forster distrusts the nationalist political and official discourse of faceless and dehumanizing statist machinery which is detached from the actual lives of the people. He rather imagines their discursive-epistemic spaces as forms of openness for a genuine transcultural open-ended dialogue. In meeting the other, he remains open and responsive to them, rather than defining them from his own perspective. Alterity, i.e. the unknowable and unreachable nature of the other, cannot be attained, but can be imagined and hence activated.

The theoretical manifesto for reading

In his influential book *The Implied Reader: Patterns of Communication in Prose Fiction from Bunyan to Beckett*, Wolfgang Iser asserts that the

> phenomenological theory of art lays full stress on the idea that, in
> considering a literary work, one must take into account not only

the actual text but also, and in equal measure, the actions involved in responding to that text.

(1974: 274)

Alluding to the work of the Polish phenomenologist Roman Ingarden, Iser argues that the text offers various schematised views or perspectives that the reader 'concretizes' in the process of reading; the reader "sets the work in motion" (1974: 275). For this reason, the literary work has two poles, the artistic and the aesthetic. The former refers to the "text created by the author" (274), the latter to the "realization accomplished by the reader" (1974: 274). The work cannot be completely identical with the text, or with the realization of the text, but, in fact, must lie halfway between the two. The "text only takes on life when it is realized" (1974: 274). This realization is by no means independent of the individual disposition of the reader. The convergence of text and reader brings the literary work into existence, a convergence that "can never be pinpointed, but must always remain virtual" (1974: 275) and impossible to identify either with the "reality of the text or with the individual disposition of the reader" (1974: 275). It is the "virtuality"(1974: 275) of the literary work (he calls the work later a "gestalt"[280]) that renders it "dynamic" (1974: 275). The literary text "activates our own faculties, enabling us to recreate the world it presents. The product of this creative activity is what we might call the virtual dimension of the text, which endows it with its reality" (1974: 279). This virtual dimension is not the text itself, nor is it the imagination of the reader: it is the coming together of text and imagination.

The "activity of reading" is a sort of "kaleidoscope of perspectives, preintentions, recollections" (1974: 279). The reader is given the opportunity to bring into play his own faculty for establishing connections – "for filling in the gaps left by the text itself" (1974: 280). Since they may be filled in different ways, any text is

> potentially capable of several different realizations, and no reading can ever exhaust the full potential, for each individual reader will fill in the gaps in his own way, thereby excluding the various other possibilities; as he reads, he will make his own decision as to how the gap is to be filled.

(1974: 280)

In this very act, the "dynamics of reading" (1974: 280) are revealed. Iser contends that the "'picturing' [...] done by our imagination is only one of the activities through which we form the 'gestalt' of a literary text" (1974: 282). In addition to the "process of anticipation and retrospection" (1974: 283), the reader will engage in a "process of grouping together all the different aspects of a text to form the consistency that the reader will always

be in search of" (1974: 283): the reader will always "strive, even if uncon-
sciously, to fit everything together in a consistent pattern" (1974: 283). By
"grouping together the written parts of the text, we enable them to interact, we observe the direction in which they are leading us, and we project
onto them the consistency which we, as readers, require" (1974: 285). The
'gestalt' produced thereby is "coloured by our own characteristic selection
process" (1974: 284) and not given by the text: it arises, rather, from the
meeting between the written text and the individual mind of the reader with
its own particular history of experience, its own consciousness, its own
outlook. The 'gestalt' is not the true meaning of the text; at best it is a con-
figurative meaning. Roland Barthes also celebrated the birth of the reader
and claimed the reader as "the space on which all the quotations that make
up writing are inscribed. (Barthes 1967: 118) But unlike Iser, Barthes's reader
is without history, biography, psychology.

Tabish Khair, too, emphasizes the active and creative role of the reader in
Reading Literature Today: "Some gaps and silences ask to be excavated,
and hence demand the participation of the reader" (2011:11). The reader as
the critic is not "a blank receptor of the intentions of the author or the text"
but is someone who "actually reads" (2011:15). To read, for Khair, is to
"think, suppose, guess; discern the meaning of; inspect and interpret"
(2011:15). Borrowing Seamus Heaney's metaphor of "digging" in his poem
"Digging", Khair calls reading "an act of digging" and the reader "an active
thinker and interpreter" (2011:15). Khair sides with Iser and distances
himself from Barthes when he dismisses the birth of the Reader-without-
History. He asserts that the Reader-without-History is "a non-reader, [...] a
passive receptor, [...] a simple celebrator of the text, not [...] someone who
interprets, guesses and digs" (2011: 19). Conceding that fiction differs from
fact and a novel differs from either sociology or history or autobiography,
yet there is, asserts Khair, "an intricate relationship between facts and
fiction, between sociology/history/autobiography and creative writing"
(2011: 23). A reader's blindness to these narrative gaps is an "insult"
(2011: 23) to both the writer's art and the reader's skills.

Reading *A Passage to India* in the classroom

My endeavour in the early part of our discussion of *A Passage to India* was
to make my students better readers of the text and to explore the connection
between the linguistic world of the narrative and the extra-linguistic
material world. I tried to develop an *adda*-epistemology in class discussions
via a permeable curriculum through which students were encouraged to
come up with their own interpretations of this text. This meant creating a
dialogic learning space within the classroom that would be engaging for
students, encouraging them to select a concept from the textual discussions

and try to present their arguments. The continuous interaction with each other transformed the classroom into a space in which the text was constructed and reconstructed constantly with Indian realities in view; in the process, more inclusive and less Eurocentric perspectives started coming to the surface. The infusion of *adda*-epistemology develops "a *metaliteracy* in students for the purpose of raising their social consciousness" by connecting critical discourses on "contentious histories and uses of literacy" to the students' everyday lived-experiences (Alim 2011: 140; emphasis original). It thereby creates an engaging, meaningful and dialogic learning space for students where their multiple funds of knowledge, thoughts and ideas are acknowledged rather than dismissed, the "peer sphere" and "home sphere" of the students interweave with the "official sphere".

After a series of class lectures and a screening of David Lean's adaptation of the novel, I observed that they were quite keen to discuss its core issues. My continuous focus was to read the text closely and not to straitjacket it within the bounds of a particular literary theory. This had the advantage of creating an engaging, meaningful and dialogic learning space where students' thoughts and ideas are given proper respect and used for informing praxis. The core issues that were taken up for discussion were the colonial divide, the colonizers' stereotypical concept about the Indians, "Mosque" and the possibility of communication between the English and the Indians, the "Caves", the "shadow" of Mrs Moore, Adela's "Trial" and the "Temple".

Close reading, students' interpretation and filling in gaps

The close textual analysis that I attempted in the class evoked students' keen interest in the text and they were able to come up with some interesting observations. The first was, of course, the observation that two European travellers (namely Mrs Moore and Adela Quested) who do not know India are replaced by a new pair (Ralph and Stella) at the end of the novel. A student, taking part in the discussion, pointed out that the only happy marriages presented in the novel are the ones in which one spouse is already dead (Mrs Moore's and Aziz's), and the living one takes solace in memory. Furthermore, Aziz's wife is not the only figure to exercise influence after death; so do Mrs Moore and the Rajah in the last section, "Temple". The spirit of Mrs Moore mystically compels Adela to withdraw her accusation against Aziz in court. I was very much impressed by an interesting parallelism that I had overlooked in my reading of the text (nor found in the available discussions on the novel) between the description of the body of the punkawallah in the court in Chandrapore and a servitor in Mau who carries the idol of Krishna into the waters: "He was naked, broad-shouldered, thin-waisted — the Indian body *again* triumphant" (*APTI* 1924:1965: 309–310, emphasis mine). The very word "again" reverts the readers' mind to the unseen physical presence of the punkawallah in the court. By excavating a labyrinthine network of traces and joining the unconnected segments, the reader is able to open up possible areas of interpretation, becoming a co-creator of meaning.

Students' misconception about the "assault" on Adela Quested

Any reader who reads *A Passage to India* feels compelled to ask what exactly happened to Adela in the Marabar caves and my students were no exception. Some of them even nurtured the idea that the 'mystery' of the unidentified seducer of Adela would be resolved by Fielding and the novel was a piece of detective fiction set in colonial India. The question now veered to: What happened to Adela in the Marabar caves and who was the assaulter? The answers to this ranged from the physical to the psychological, from sexual hallucination to the metaphysical and in order to restore some order into these speculations I attempted to interpret the event textually from the gradual build-up to Adela's entry into the caves.

I initiated my discussion with the concepts of nation and nationalism. As Partha Chatterjee explains in his influential book *Nationalist Thought and the Colonial World*, the origins of the nation in the West have much to do with the pursuit of a set of human ideals often identified as the European "Enlightenment". European nationalism is "part of the same historical process which saw the rise of industrialism and democracy" and "nationalism represents the attempt to actualize in political terms the universal urge for liberty and progress" (1999: 2). There is, however, a conflict right at the heart of nationalism, which Chatterjee terms the "liberal dilemma": nationalism may promise liberty and universal suffrage to the colonizers but only brings undemocratic forms of government and domination to the colonized. Representing the Western nation as the best product of human civilization becomes a way of legitimating colonial expansion.

It has been a cliché of literary criticism that in *A Passage to India* Forster severely criticizes British colonial power structures and sympathizes with Indian political aspirations. What has largely been overlooked in the discussions of the novel are the seemingly discordant images of India that the narrative projects: whether "the hundred Indias which fuss and squabble so tirelessly are one" (*APTI* 256) or whether there are gaps and silences between these concepts of India. My examination of these multiple Indias in the narrative began with British India, i.e. the colonial encounter. The colonial masters split the Indian space into two compartments, encouraging "the colonizers to impute to themselves magical feelings of omnipotence and permanence" (Nandy, 1983: 35). The "two zones" are opposed, "they both follow the principle of reciprocal exclusivity" (Fanon 2001: 30). The settler's town, for Fanon, is invariably "a strongly-built town", "a well-fed" and "an easy-going town; its belly is always full of good things" (Fanon 2001: 30). On the contrary, the space inhabited by the colonized people is "a place of ill fame, peopled by men of evil repute", "a world without spaciousness; men live there on top of each other, and their huts are built one on top of the other" (Fanon 2001: 30). Students were quick to point out the division of space in Chandrapore and came up with their textual illustrations. The civil station of Chandrapore "is sensibly planned, with a red-brick club on its brow [...], and the bungalows are disposed along roads that intersect at right angles. [...] it shares nothing with the city except the overarching sky" (*A Passage to India*, 10; hereafter *APTI*). The Chandrapore of the natives presents streets that are "mean, the temples ineffective, [...] down alleys whose filth deters all but the invited guest" (*APTI* 9). Everything is "so abased, so monotonous": "Houses do fall, people are drowned and left rotting, but the general outline of the town persists, swelling here, shrinking there, like some low but indestructible form of life" (*APTI* 9). The roads, named after victorious generals, signified "the net Great Britain has thrown over India" (*APTI* 18). I thus tried to begin my discussion with the dialectical character of the two spaces.

Students' participation in the discussion

The egalitarian spirit fostered by the democratic *adda* space encouraged students to initiate discussions on certain key issues in the novel. This was based on their reading of the text as well as the critical literature surrounding it. One of the students came up with her argument about the colonial Club, which boasted an atmosphere of exclusiveness and superiority by keeping Indians out of its anglomorphic zone. Another raised an interesting point about the significance of the baithak-khana in nineteenth- and early twentieth-century Bengali Literature as a space of conversation and its difference from the English club.

Welcoming these ideas and throwing open further issues, I explored the antithesis of the bustling bazaars of India, with its walls serving "as a metaphor for its bounded and limited culture" (DeLoughrey 2004: 302), and the European Club, which for Orwell, was "the spiritual citadel, the real seat of the British power, the Nirvana for which native officials and millionaires pine in vain" (14). Smarting from his humiliation at the hands of the Callendars, Aziz explained to Mrs Moore in their first meeting at the mosque that Indians "are not allowed into the Chandrapore Club even as guests" (*APTI* 24). The Club's alienation from India is emphasized further at the end of the evening's dramatic production when the British National Anthem is played by the orchestra, which "reminded every member of the Club that he or she was British and in exile" (*APTI* 27). While the Bridge Party in the Club gardens, the tea party at Government College and the excursion to the Marabar Caves are the liminal spaces to establish "contact zones" between the British and the Indians, the closed doors and windows of the Club emphasize their cultural difference. The group of Indian ladies scornfully referred to by Mrs Turton as "'Oh, those purdah women!'" (*APTI* 41) emerges as one micro space amongst the many micro spaces in the narrative. When the Anglo-Indian community gathers in the Club following the alleged assault on Adela Quested, the space has "the air of the Residency at Lucknow" (*APTI* 178), where the British have gathered behind "the palisade of cactuses" (*APTI* 177)).The trope of the siege is invoked throughout the chapter with references to the "Mutiny" of 1857 and the counter-insurgencies. When the Club is described as "an outpost of Empire" (*APTI* 179) and suggestions are made for absolute military control of the colonized land to re-affirm their battered identity, the irreversible split between the British and the Indians receives the final stamp.

The central question raised at the very beginning in Mahmoud Ali and Hamidullah's discussion – "whether or not it is possible to be friends with an Englishman" (*APTI* 12), receives its answer in its last sentence –"'No, not yet ...No, not there'" (317). The anarchic Other, conceived as the negation of the progressive, rational Western Self, is consigned to the periphery, invisible to the Western gaze. The colonial world creates a Manichaean dialectic between the rulers and the subjugated and conceives the native to be "a sort of quintessence of evil", "insensible to ethics", who "represents not only the absence of values, but also the negation of values" (Fanon 2001: 32). This stereotyping of the other underpins colonialism in as much as it presumes "the colonized as a population of degenerate types on the basis of racial origin, in order to justify conquest and to establish systems of administration and instrument" (Bhabha 1994: 70).

Students' presentation and a close reading of the text

After initiating this discussion, I assigned students the task of finding from the text suitable illustrations to carry the ideas forward. They did so enthusiastically and the next day came up with their reading in a PowerPoint presentation, the gist of which is given here:

> The all-pervasive presence of the British Raj thwarts any attempt of the Indians and the English to come closer to each other. The English cherish a set of stereotypical received notions about the Indians and overlook the variety which surreptitiously upholds their supremacism. The unfriendly attitude and pure malice of the English is evident in Mrs Callendar's remark that the "kindest thing one can do to a native is to let him die" (*APTI* 28). At the "Bridge Party", Mrs Turton haughtily instructs Mrs Moore and Adela, "'You're superior to everyone in India except one or two of the Ranis, and they're on an equality'" (*APTI* 42). The presumed racial superiority of the Britishers and the racial inferiority of the Indians and hence their incorrigibility justify the conquerors' perpetual rule over the conquered for the sake of civilizing them. The central allegation that Aziz has sexually assaulted Adela in the

Marabar Caves simply corroborates the racial prejudices of the English like McBryde. The Englishmen's fear of Indian sensuality, lasciviousness, and polygamy is revealed in his prejudicial statement at the trial that "'the darker races are physically attracted by the fairer, but not vice versa — not a matter for bitterness this, not a matter for abuse, but just a fact which any scientific observer will confirm'" (*APTI* 213). Premised on white supremacism, McBryde's remark projects the white body as the norm, and anything else counts as a deviation and enforces the sweeping generalization that "'[A]ll unfortunate natives are criminals at birth; for the simple reason that they live south of latitude 30'" (*APTI* 164). By foisting upon the Orient the West's image of it, the former denies the non-European other any identity of its own.

This, for my young students, was a commendable achievement. The spirit of *adda*, culturally ingrained in them, enabled them to create a space for fruitful interaction on an equal footing with their teacher, quite unlike the racist nature of the colonial club itself.

Moving ahead with the text, and inspired by the students' response, I tried to explore the Englishmen's stereotypical concept of India and Indians and India's internal schisms which are inextricably linked in the narrative. While the English conjure their safe haven in the frigid Anglo-Indian Club, the Hindus and the Muslims create their own little worlds in their entanglements with each other. The Muslim festival of Muharram invariably generates riots. Aziz, in his turn feels like an "outsider", "excluded" (*APTI* 300) from the Hindu rites at Mau. Hamidullah and company relish their derogatory remarks about Professor Godbole and Dr Pannalal who, they mockingly comment, "hang together like flies and keep everything dark" (*APTI* 101). Going a step better they condemn the Hindu Professor as a source of infection and scornfully generalize that "'All illness spread from Hindus'" (*APTI* 102). Dr Pannalal, a Hindu, feels morbid and "nervous of the den of fanatics into which his curiosity had called him" (*APTI* 104). At Mau, the split is not between the Hindus and the Muslims; the cleavage was between the Brahman and the non-Brahmans. The narrative thus manifests the 'nature' of India which leads to the assertion that "[T]he fissures in the Indian soil are infinite" (*APTI* 288).

In his essay "Notes on the English Character" Forster asserts that middle-class Englishmen brought up in the public-school system have no conception of the "richness and subtlety" (*Abinger Harvest* 1967: 15; henceforth *AH*) of the world outside. This clan of men "go forth into it with well-developed bodies, fairly developed minds, and undeveloped hearts" which is "largely responsible for the difficulties of the Englishmen abroad" (*AH* 15). When I presented these observations by Forster and asked the class to identify the character who fits this image, the immediate response was Ronny Heaslop.

Students' identification of the sections that best illustrate Ronny's traits

Ronny Heaslop's religion was of this "sterilized" Public School brand, which never goes bad, even in the tropics" (*APTI* 250): "Wherever he entered, mosque, cave, or temple, he retained the spiritual outlook of the Fifth Form, and condemned as 'weakening' any attempt to understand them" (*APTI* 250). There is a streak of Puritanism in Ronny which makes him interpret the world according to clear-cut straitjackets –the binaries of right and wrong. For him India "isn't a drawing room" (*APTI* 49), "'Nothing's private in India' [...] India isn't home'" (*APTI* 33, 34) and he is just a tool of the colonial administrative machinery that crossed the oceans "to do justice and keep peace".

(*APTI* 49)

I pointed out that Ronny's initial friendly gestures towards the Indians, as for example when he invited the lawyer Mahmoud Ali to have a smoke with him, gradually disappear when he becomes conscious of his bureaucratic position. This invites the narrator's scathing observation that "every human act in the East is tainted with officialism" (*APTI* 184) and that "where there is officialism every human relationship suffers" (*APTI* 207). A staunch champion of the Empire, Ronny bluntly declares that he is "out here to work, mind, to hold this wretched country by force" (*APTI* 50). The duty-conscious colonial official obsessed with clear-cut inflexible generalizations cannot absorb the complexities of either the colonized country or personal relationships. thereby exhibiting an emotional failure.

Sudhir Kakar, in *The Colours of Violence: Cultural Identities, Religion and Conflict* (1996), distinguishes between pre-colonial "religious" conflicts and post-colonial "communal" violence in the Indian sub-continent. While religion is "a matter of personal faith and reverence for a particular set of icons, rituals, and dogmas", asserts Kakar, communalism entails one's "exclusive attachment to his or her community combined with an active hostility against other communities which share its geographical and political space" (1996: 13). The overarching identities as "Muslim" and "Hindu" were highly charged by the divisiveness of the Partition of 1947, "the most momentous event in the shaping of Hindu-Muslim relations in independent India"(1996: 37). A permeable academic curriculum fosters love and solidarity, the very basis of community formation. The dangerous potential for violence and aggression in the creation of exclusivist collective identities is succinctly explained by Regina Schwartz: "Imaginary identity as an act of distinguishing and separating from others, of boundary making and line drawing, is the most fundamental act of violence we commit" (2000: 187). Students in India, itself the cradle of many religions of the world, are enlightened about a secular approach to religion and life from their schooldays. The text provided me with an opportunity to explain the significance of inter-community solidarity and the limitations of the parochialism of nationalism and the religious divide. While a typical middle class Englishman like Ronny Heaslop is taught at his public school that "feeling is bad form" (*AH* 1967: 15) and that he "must bottle up his emotions, or let them out only on a very special occasion" (*AH* 1967: 15), an Oriental believes that "[E]motion has nothing to do with appropriateness. It matters only that it shall be sincere" (*AH* 1967: 16). The first section of the novel, "Mosque", not only develops the contrast between the English civil station and the native section, it also presents the fundamental difference between an Englishman and an Indian, between the stolid and "unfeeling" Ronny and the impulsive Aziz. Smarting from humiliation at the hands of the snobbish Callendars, Aziz's chance meeting with Mrs Moore throws open the possibility of an impersonal communication based upon warmth and sympathy transcending racial boundaries. This precisely is Fielding's humanistic credo. For him "[T]he world [...] is a globe of men who are trying to reach one another and can best do so by the help of good will plus culture and intelligence" (*APTI* 62). Aziz's peremptory attitude at Mrs Moore's minor inadvertent mistakes in the mosque melts because of her underlying sympathy, the "flame that not even beauty can nourish was springing up" (*APTI* 117) and Aziz intimately calls her "'an Oriental'" (*APTI* 24). While Ronny interprets his mother's affectionate meeting with Aziz as an instance of native insolence, his fiancée Adela believes that Mrs Moore has had a glimpse of "'the real India'" (*APTI* 31). Fielding rams home the point that the perfect mode to experience the "real India" is to "'Try seeing Indians'" (*APTI* 27). It was Adela's misfortune that she would always see India as a "frieze, never as a spirit", while Mrs Moore had a glimpse of the "spirit" of India itself (*APTI* 47), an oceanic feeling which interweaves the earth and the space above:

> In England the moon had seemed dead and alien; here she was caught in the shawl of night together with earth and all the other stars. A sudden sense of unity, of kinship with the heavenly bodies, passed into the old woman and out, like water through a tank, leaving a strange freshness behind.
>
> (*APTI* 30)

The institutional attempts to bridge the gap between the English and the Indians like the Bridge Party or Fielding's tea party end in failure. The English ladies appear too haughty and their Indian counterparts too reserved to share a wavelength and initiate an animated involvement. The Hindus and the Moslems too are irreconcilable with their mutual exclusions, suspicions and hatred as evidenced at the dinner at Hamidullah's house. However, as in the chance encounter between Aziz and Mrs Moore in the mosque, the narrative captures vital moments of tremendous potential. The seemingly incompatible Ronny and Adela are suddenly drawn together, "encircled" by the night's anonymity which seemed "absolute" (*APTI* 86). Always aware of their differences, conscious of the unbridgeable gulf that divided them, Fielding and Aziz are brought closer to each other when Fielding visits the sick Aziz at his home. Their "compact" is solemnized by the photograph of Aziz's dead wife: "[...] they were friends, brothers, they trusted one another, affection had triumphed for once in a way" (*APTI*119).

"Equality before God — so doubtfully proclaimed by Christianity", believes Forster, "lies at the very root of Islam" (*AH* 294). Reflecting on religion in *Alexandria*, he speculates that "Islam means peace. [...] and its buildings can give a sense of arrival, which is unattainable in any Christian church" (1967: 45). The mosque performs this function to perfection in the narrative, "it serves as a focus for the developed heart": "What the mosque celebrates is not so much communion with God as with men — in the communal enjoyment of the beautiful" (Moody 1968: 10, 9). For Aziz, Islam is "an attitude towards life both exquisite and durable, where his body and thoughts found their home" (*APTI* 20). Once Aziz has been assured that Mrs Moore is behaving as "tradition and propriety enjoin", he happily embraces her as a participant in the secret understanding of the heart. However, it is Aziz's religious dogmatism itself on which hangs the relationship between the self and the other, between the Indians and the Englishmen, keeping the possibility of interpersonal communication in a precarious balance. For him India is coterminous with the "Mogul Empire at its height and Alamgir reigning at Delhi upon the Peacock Throne" (*APTI* 65). He cherishes the splendour of the Mughal Empire but not the generous, syncretic efforts of Akbar to unite the variegated religious sects of India. He calls Akbar "'half a Hindu; he was not a true Moslem'" (*APTI* 143). Whenever Aziz is described in terms of the physical landscape of India, the land is inhospitable: "There is something hostile in that soil. It either yields and the foot sinks into a depression, or else it is unexpectedly rigid and sharp, pressing stones or crystals against the tread" (*APTI* 19). The narrator undercuts Aziz's professed liberal attitude with the observation that "his outlook was limited and his method inaccurate" (*APTI* 71).Therefore, the possibilities of transcultural friendship that are initiated in the opening section are also threatened with failure from within.

Proceeding along this line, I gradually started preparing my students for the next assignment on the second section of the novel "Caves", the shattering experiences of Mrs Moore and Adela Quested that propel the narrative and also take the classroom discussions forward. My discussion now started revolving around the complexities of a concept– "India". Far from containing a mere fragment of human experience, India represents the whole of human experience ranging from the sheer casual approach to hospitality of the Bhattacharyas to the ecstasy of human and divine love as expressed in Godbole's song. The Indian intricacies challenge the undeveloped head and confuse the undeveloped heart as John Beer contends: "India's muddle needs all the efficiency which British administrators brought to it: at the same time its mystery asks for the reverence of a fully developed heart" (1970: 214). The muddle is represented by the mutual suspicions of the Hindus and the Muslims, the Muslims with their proud isolationism and alienation and the Hindus relatively withdrawn from mainstream social and political involvement yet strong defenders of caste divisions. Thus contextualized, the Marabar Caves signify the robust, hostile nature of the Indian landscape, the nature of which the narrative cannot fathom intellectually, because it pushed language to the limits of its representational capacity. They challenge the west with its irreducible difference:

> 'Primal', 'dark', 'fists and fingers', 'unspeakable', fearsomely advancing to the lion with the sunset –these phrases signal the fear and insecurity the imperialists experienced, confronted with what they could not master; to reduce it to stasis was to contain that fear and hold that threat at bay.
>
> (Pathak et al. 1991: 200)

For Forster the caves were "a solid mass ahead, a mountain round or over or through which [...] the story must somehow go". An area in which "concentration" could take place, the caves were "something to focus everything up; they were to engender an event like an egg" (1953: 30–31). For Wilfred Stone, the caves are the archetypal form of the inner cell of the World Mountain, and the "architecture of the temple is a late and sophisticated shaping of a dim racial memory –of something primal, elemental, antecedent to consciousness":

> The caves hint at something existing before gods, before differentiation, before value. Though the temple remembers this form and shapes itself around it as a shell around an egg, it is at a far remove from the caves' 'unspeakable' nothingness.
>
> (1966: 304)

The caves are "like nothing else in the world", "they bear no relation to anything dreamt or seen", "no carving, not even a bees'-nest or a bat distinguishes one from another", "nothing, nothing attaches to them, and their reputation [...] does not depend upon human speech" (*APTI* 124). The caves are empty and do not excite curiousness: "Nothing is inside them, they were sealed up before the creation of pestilence or treasure; if mankind grew curious and excavated, nothing, nothing would be added to the sum of good or evil" (*APTI* 125). Any utterance or sound inside these dark chambers resonate a "terrifying echo" which is "entirely devoid of distinction":

> Whatever is said, the same monotonous noise replies, and quivers up and down the walls until it is absorbed into the roof. 'Boum'

is the sound as far as the human alphabet can express it, or 'bou-oum', or 'ou-boum', — utterly dull. Hope, politeness, the blow-ing of a nose, the squakaqueak of a boot, all produce 'boum'. [...] echoes generate echoes.

(APTI 145)

It is into this vacant space that the two English ladies embark on a jour-ney: the elder Mrs Moore in a mood of apathy, the younger Adela with an air of excitement. The experience they have forms the crux of the novel.

Students' presentation of Mrs Moore's experience in the caves

Students were now invited to make their own presentations. Two of them volunteered, choosing to speak on Mrs Moore's experience in the caves and connect it with the other segments in the text which had been discussed earlier, especially the intricate distinction between "a mystery" and "a muddle" about which many were quizzical. They highlighted this on a PowerPoint presentation as an epigraph to their presentation:

'I like mysteries but I rather dislike muddles', said Mrs Moore.
A mystery is a muddle.
Oh, do you think so, Mr Fielding?
A mystery is only a high-sounding term for a muddle. No advan-tage in stirring it up, in either case. Aziz and I know well that India's a muddle'.

(APTI 68)

Mrs Moore enters a mosque and is soothed by its serenity; she enters a cave that is disquieting and her world crumbles. Her faith in God and Love impelled her to treat a wasp on her peg with affection; her alarming experience in the caves makes her realize the insignificance of human val-ues as she encounters the "shadow" before time and space: "Something snub-nosed, incapable of generosity –the undying worm itself" (*APTI* 203). The metamorphosis initiated by her experience in the mosque, and fostered by her feeling of oneness with nature and Godbole's song, reaches its culmination inside the dark chamber with the echo, as caught com-pletely off-guard, unprepared / uninitiated by both her culture and her religion, she encounters a state that is beyond religion and even beyond language

[...] that state where the horror of the universe and its smallness are both visible at the same time –the twilight of the double vision in which so many elderly people are involved. [...] in the twilight of the double vision, a spiritual muddledom is set up for which no

91

high-sounding words can be found; we can neither act nor refrain from action, we can neither ignore nor respect Infinity.

(*APTI* 202–203)

The caves are in themselves nothing; they affect, they reflect, what enters them. Her faith in personal relationships which, in fact, had been her gospel, is shaken, as she enters a state of trance.

I was really impressed by a query from a particularly attentive reader who pointed out one of the major ironies in the novel. Why did Mrs Moore who felt "at one with the universe! So dignified and simple" (*APTI* 203) feel traumatized in that "scoured-out cavity of the granite" (*APTI* 203) inside the Cave?

At this point I turned the students' attention to Forster's essay "De *Senectute*" where he reflects upon the intuitive wisdom of the old, the ultimate insight preceding death which qualifies Mrs Moore's vision inside the Marabar caves. The wisdom of the old, writes Forster, far from "making decisions or […] the conveyance of information, […] is indirectly connected with the possession of knowledge". It does not specialize in sympathy. But it has the power, without proffering sympathy, of causing it to be perceived, and it is certainly not cynicism" (1957: 17). The withdrawn, indifferent Mrs Moore passes into the state of impassivity or calmness, which the Greeks called "*ataraxia*".

The echo produced in Mrs Moore a profound spiritual muddledom. Even when she was approaching the Marabar caves by train she felt quizzical about the significance of human relationships and pondered that much "fuss" has been made over marriage: "centuries of carnal embracement, yet man is no nearer to understanding man" (*APTI* 134). After her brush with the monotonous meaningless echo, she starts unravelling the layers of meaninglessness in human relations as she lost all urge to communicate her experience to even her children in England. Moral and religious values had lost all their appeal to her as "Religion appeared, poor little talkative Christianity, and she knew that all its divine words from 'Let there be Light' to 'It is finished' only amounted to 'boum'" (*APTI* 148). The echo silently undermines her hold on life:

Coming at a moment when she chanced to be fatigued, it had managed to murmur, 'Pathos, piety, courage –they exist, but are identical, and so is filth. Everything exists, nothing has value.' If one had spoken vileness in that place, or quoted lofty poetry, the comment would have been the same — 'ou-boum'.

(*APTI* 147)

Mrs Moore was very passionate about making plans all through her life as she was proud of her "well-equipped mind" (*APTI* 135). Coupled with her orderliness was her inclination towards resignation. India had torn her plans to shreds and claimed her as part of itself. K.W. Grandsen rightly claims that the "echo is her epitaph": "it is the Last Judgment: all distinctions, all the superstructures erected by man's wit and pride, are reduced to nothing" (1962: 97, 94).

A dialogical response from a student

A student (who is now herself a teacher) raised the issue of the physical perspective, i.e. the intensifying heat; the narrative warns the readers that "April, herald of horrors, is at hand"(*APTI* 111). Although Adela reiterates that she "'won't be bottled up'" in the hot weather, the fear that she can be bottled up exists.

It was a welcome observation and I had to "dig" into the text, going back a few chapters, to the section on how a foothold in the rocks in Marabar reminds Adela of the patterns made by the wheels of Nawab Bahadur's car, the collision with the unknown animal that throws up the realization that "[s]he and Ronny –no, they did not love each other": "The discovery had come so suddenly that she felt like a mountaineer whose rope had broken. Not to love the man one's going to marry! Not to find out till this moment! Not to find out till this moment!" (*APTI* 150). The realization of her loveless engagement coexists with her discerning of Aziz's handsomeness and regret at hers and Ronny's lack of physical charms. Her "appalling, hideous" question about the number of wives Aziz has repels Aziz and he lets go of her hand, as Adela lingers on in the cave, unbalanced, alone, split psychically, frigid:

> She followed at her leisure, quite unconscious that she had said the wrong thing, and not seeing him, she also went into a cave, thinking with half her mind 'sight-seeing bores me', and wondering with the other half about marriage.
>
> (*APTI* 151)

That she suffered from sexual hysteria, was hence a viable contention.

David Lean's screen adaptation and its deviation from Forster's text

One of my students asked about a scene in David Lean's screen adaptation in which Adela visits a Hindu temple whose erotic sculptures and the activities of monkeys cause Adela to have some kind of nervous attack. This was an instance of interpolation in the film itself because the Marabar caves as presented in Forster's narrative do not contain any sculptures. I mentioned that such negative stereotypical representations of the East as a place of sexual threat and liberation are quite common in Western culture and literature, as Edward Said ponders in *Orientalism*: "Why the Orient seems still to suggest not only fecundity but sexual promise (and threat), untiring sensuality, unlimited desire, deep generative energies, is something on which one could speculate"(1978: 188). Forster makes Adela's problem not primarily sexual, but conceptual and linguistic. She hasn't the words to describe the experience.

I had to explore the most complicated section of the text now –the inner world of Adela, which was, and always is, an intellectual challenge. I presented my arguments to the students with the help of Jung. Psychically, Adela had a glimpse into the everlasting no, "the pit of *nada*, the ultimate negation lying at the bottom of the unconscious. She had seen what can be explained mythologically as the archetypal emptiness preceding existence itself" (Stone 1966: 335). Louise Dauner suggests that Adela met what Jung describes as the Animus, the male archetype that woman carries within her (Dauner 1961: 268, cited in Stone 1966: 335). Stone has a stronger pre-scription when he equates Adela's experience with what Jung describes as the Shadow, "that deepest and darkest bottom of the unconscious which strikes unspeakable horror into those unequipped to encounter it" (Stone 1966: 335). Jung writes:

> The meeting with oneself is, at first, the meeting with one's own shadow. [...] where the realm of the sympathetic system, the soul of everything living, begins; where I am indivisibly this *and* that; where I experience the other in myself and the other-than-myself experiences me.
>
> (*Collected Works* 2014: 45)

This is akin to the "twilight of the double vision"; one evokes terror in Adela and compassion in Godbole. The Westerner, brought up in the public school system as conceptualized earlier, experiences the Shadow as an assault/rape upon her personality. In the realm of consciousness, argues Jung, individuals are masters of their own, but if "we step through the door of the shadow we discover with terror that we are the object of unseen factors" (2014: 23). Swinging between the poles of "hard common sense and hysteria", Adela has no grasp about the nature of her experience as she tries to recollect it frame by frame:

> 'I went into this detestable cave', she would say dryly, 'and I remember scratching the wall with my finger-nail, to start the usual echo, and then, as I was saying, there was this shadow, or sort of shadow, down the entrance tunnel, bottling me up'.
>
> (*APTI* 189)

The experience not only shattered her psychologically, it was an assault upon her body as well. Although her senses were "abnormally inert" and "the only contact she anticipated was that of mind", "[E]verything now was transferred to the surface of her body, which began to avenge itself, and feel unhealthily" (*APTI* 189). When Miss Derek and Mrs McBryde examine her with magnifying glasses picking the spines out of her flesh, "[S]he lay passive beneath their fingers, which developed the shock that had begun in the cave" (*APTI* 189). Their fingers substitute for the Marabar rocks, sustaining the image of the violated body and the cave as the assailant.

Her mind is assailed by the echo, "the noise in the cave" which "prolonged over the surface of her life" (*APTI* 190). She realizes the meaninglessness of personal relationships and the fact that she is not fit for any. This couples with the desire to get back at the roots: "'I feel we all ought to go back into the desert for centuries and try and get good. I want to begin at the beginning'" (*APTI* 193). She knows full well that the only person who can dissipate the nature of evil/echo in her ears is Mrs Moore. Her despairing cry that she cannot get rid of the echo receives a cold response from Mrs Moore: "'I don't suppose you ever will'" (*APTI* 195). When she begins to confront the possibility that she is wrong and Dr Aziz is innocent, the echo vanishes. It resounds when she considers her accusation, diminishes when she thinks of retracting the false charges, and disappears only when she tears apart the veil of illusion and releases Aziz. After the trial when she no longer has any secrets, the evil echo leaves her, discharging itself into the Indian atmosphere of hatred, hostility, nation and animosity. Words, Mrs Moore asserts, are meaningless:

'Say, say, say, [...] As if anything can be said! I have spent my life in saying or in listening to sayings; [...] I'll retire then into a cave of my own [...] Somewhere, where no young people will come asking questions and expecting answers. Some shelf.'

(*APTI* 195–196)

She knows that the British preoccupation with the trial is mechanistic and soulless; and that Adela will come to terms with the insight that she herself has achieved: "'She has started the machinery; it will work to its end'" (*APTI* 201). Adela's experience of the inhuman and the absolute in the Marabar Caves is transmuted into a moral process which reaches its apotheosis in the court. Harvey contends that Adela "shares Mrs Moore's vision in the caves, but unlike Mrs Moore she cannot realize it for what it is" (66). The trial is Adela's baptism by fire as she holds on to her own by cowering away from her English community by refusing to utter the rehearsed words. She also makes a dive into the darkness of her mind and attempts to converge her language with the remembered images from the caves. The two figures who act as catalysts in her tribulation in the court are the detached punkahwallah and the participation mystique embodied by the ritualistic incantation "EsmissEsmoor" as Mrs Moore is revived as an Indianized goddess. The narrative extols the punkahwallah's physical beauty despite his low caste and his apparent blankness of mind and detachment from the scheme of things: "Almost naked, and splendidly formed […] he stood out as divine […] sending swirls of air over others, receiving none himself, he seemed apart from human destinies, a male fate, a winnower of souls" (*APTI* 212). He performs a commonplace task, but, viewed symbolically, he presides over the destinies of others, unnoticed, unheralded. The aloofness of this figure impressed Adela and she interrogated her own self in a tone of rebuke:

> In virtue of what had she collected this roomful of people together? Her particular brand of opinions, and the suburban Jehovah who sanctified them — by what right did they claim so much importance in the world, and assume the title of civilization.
>
> (*APTI* 212)

Coupled with this the invocation of Mrs Moore's name as "Esmiss Esmoor", the court that Adela had feared as "the place of question" (*APTI* 222), was transformed into a place of vision:

> Something that she did not understand took hold of the girl and pulled her through. Though the vision was over, and she had returned to the insipidity of the world, she remembered what she had learnt. Atonement and confession –they could wait. It was in hard prosaic tones that she said, 'I withdraw everything.'
>
> (*APTI* 223–224)

Aziz feels betrayed when Fielding stands by Adela in the aftermath of the trial when she is deserted by everybody. There is a greater poignancy in the scenes between Fielding and Adela than between those of Fielding and Aziz. They realized the similarity of their outlooks and perhaps, their position. Mrs Moore is a spiritual presence in these scenes: "people are not really dead until they are felt to be dead" (*APTI* 247). They also realized that both have reached the end of their spiritual tether, life is not a "scientific manual" (*APTI* 273) and perhaps "life is a mystery, not a muddle [....] Perhaps the hundred Indias which fuss and squabble so tirelessly are one, and the universe they mirror is one. They had not the apparatus for judging" (*APTI* 256). The muddles/confusions of India can be discerned, but the mystery of India is unknowable. Forster's concept of India is crystallized in the character of Professor Godbole with whom Mrs Moore shares a spiritual affinity. An embodiment of the seamless but interweaving nature of Hindu thought, Godbole holds the key to the understanding of the book to which I now turned.

Students' reaction to Professor Godbole

There were peals of laughter from the students when the Deccani Brahmin Professor Godbole who "only ate — ate and ate, smiling" (*APTI* 71) was introduced to them in the first section. The very physical appearance of Godbole who wore a "turban that looked like pale purple macaroni, coat, waistcoat, dhoti, socks with clocks" (*APTI* 71) suggested to them a figure from the history books. I urged them to take note of the richly suggestive lines which followed: "[…] his whole appearance suggested harmony –as if he had reconciled the products of East and West, mental as well as physical" (*APTI* 71). The presentation of the thoughts of this enigmatic figure is always preceded by "as if" and "perhaps". One of my students even suggested that he is a word-spinner reminiscent of a Shakespearean fool. His deference for rituals delays him for the train to the Marabar expedition. When Fielding visits him after Aziz's arrest, the unaffected Godbole narrates to him a legend of a Hindu Raja who went to the Marabar hills, which Fielding received in "gloomy silence" (*APTI* 176). My students were immensely sceptical when I mentioned that Godbole's Hindu view of life is the philosophy which the narrative upholds. I had to re-present my arguments once again to convince them about this issue.

Godbole brings in the inextricable web of Hindu Vedantic philosophy to explain his take on the event:

> When evil occurs, it expresses the whole of the universe. Similarly when good occurs. […] Good and evil are different as their names imply. But, […] they are both of them aspects of my Lord. He is present in the one, absent in the other, and the difference between presence and absence is great, as great as my feeble mind can grasp. Yet absence implies presence, absence is not non-existence […].
>
> (*APTI* 175)

It is this Hindu view of life in which chaos turns into order to which Forster finally turns in the significant last section of the novel called "Temple": the reconciliation of all opposites as well as the intricate co-existence of the creator and the destroyer in the same being. Godbole, the mouthpiece of the contemplative life, reveres Tukaram, the greatest mystic of Maharashtra, the pre-eminent exponent of the *bhakti* cult which preached man's communion with God through love. In a moment of ecstasy, he has a vision of Mrs Moore: "he did not select her, she happened to occur among the throng of soliciting images, a tiny splinter, and he impelled her by this spiritual force to that place where completeness can be found. Completeness, not reconstruction" (*APTI* 282).

I was really impressed by a query from a student who pointed out one of the major ironies in the novel. Why did Mrs Moore who felt "at one with the universe! So dignified and simple" (*APTI* 203) feel traumatized in that "scoured-out cavity of the granite" (*APTI* 282). Just as Mrs Moore had blessed the wasp earlier, Godbole "loved the wasp equally" (*APTI* 282), thereby establishing the spiritual affinity between the duo. Mrs Moore's gospel was infinite love; "'God...is...love [...] God has put us on earth to love our neighbours and to show it'" (*APTI* 51). Those words are repeated in inverted form in Mau by the Indian Professor "God is love!"(*APTI* 284), removing differences, annihilating distinctions. Aziz wipes out the wrong done to him at Marabar and in a fresh act of love spontaneously utters the same words to Ralph Moore which he had done to his mother: "'Then you are an Oriental'" (*APTI* 306). It is in this context that the boating scene assumes immense significance; the riotous atmosphere after the Moharram processions in Chandrapore have been replaced by the harmonious celebrations of the birth of God. Stella believed that Marabar is wiped out. The "peace of Mau" improves the estranged relationship between Fielding and his wife; in the "language of theology, their union had been blessed" (*APTI* 314). The memory of Mrs Moore restores the broken unities to those who can communicate with her "Esmiss Esmoore", i.e. as a reincarnation of a Hindu goddess. "[T]he syllables of salvation that had sounded" (*APTI* 308), during Aziz's trial at Chandrapore liberates Aziz from the self-imposed cells of isolation and he writes a friendly and amiable letter to Adela. Stella's body as she shrank into Fielding's arms on one side and flung herself against Aziz on the other in the waters brought about a symbolic reconciliation between them: "They plunged into the warm, shallow water, and rose struggling into a tornado of noise" (*APTI* 310). The fragments of oars and the letters of Ronny and Adela float in the waters; the rain washes over the world, refreshing and also recreating and reuniting all the ruins, suggesting reconciliation: "Artillery was fired, drums beaten, the elephants trumpeted and drowning all an immense peal of thunder, unaccompanied by lightning, cracked like a mallet on the dome. That was the climax, as far as India admits of one" (*APTI* 310). The final answer to the question of friendship, though, is emphatically negative: English and Indians cannot be friends until Indians are politically independent. Aziz's vow to Fielding, "'India shall be a nation! [...] We may hate one another, but we hate you most [...] we shall drive every blasted Englishman into the sea, and then [...] you and I shall be friends" (*APTI* 317), echoes the belief of the Hindu nationalist Bankim Chatterjee: "So long as the conqueror-conquered relationship will last between English and Indians, and so long as even in our present degraded condition we shall remember our former national glory, there cannot be any hope of lessening the racial hatred"(cited in Meyers 1971: 335). *A Passage to India* suggests that Orientals hate their European oppressor. After the celebrations of Gokul Ashtami are over and the benedictions of religion have ebbed away, the political differences resurface again under a hostile sky. The spirit of India embraces and reconciles all opposites, not the physical landscape as explored in the discussion above. The land itself is unpredictable, inhospitable. The ending of the novel thus presents a contradiction: the well-intentioned Aziz and Fielding trying to come closer to each other, but the land (here the concept embodied through the horses) forces them apart. Literature thus invites the reader to excavate the gaps in the narrative and uses those gaps to push language to the limit.

The students, after the many interactions in the class, developed a completely different perception about the significance of religious institutions in human life as also the need for human solidarity by transcending all political, national and sectarian divisions. In the world of cut-throat competition, social media and cyberspace, where individuals are continuously cocooned within their own selves and pinned to their cellular screens, *A Passage to India* still provides a powerful warning about the human predicament. It urges the reader not to sever ties with his instincts, to link reason with intuitions, to integrate our selves because

> Separation from his instinctual nature inevitable plunges civilized man into the conflict between conscious and unconscious, spirit and nature, knowledge and faith, a split that becomes pathological the moment his consciousness is no longer able to neglect or suppress his instinctual side.
>
> (Jung: 2014: 289)

The students, and also their teacher, thus began their passage to India.

Works cited

Alim, H.S. "Global Ill-Literacies: Hip Hop Cultures, Youth Identities, and the Politics of Literacy." *Review of Research in Education,*35, 2011,120–146. www.jstor.org/stable/41349014 Accessed 16 August 2018.

Bakhtin, Mikhail M. "Discourse in the Novel". *The Dialogic Imagination: Four Essays*. Ed. M. Holquist. Austin, TX: University of Texas Press, 1981. Print.

Barthes, Roland. *Writing Degree Zero*. 1953. Rpt. 1972. Trans. Annette Lavers and Colin Smith. London: Jonathan Cape, 1967. Print.

Beer, John. "The Undying Worm". *E.M. Forster: A Passage to India. A Casebook*. Ed. Malcolm Bradbury. London: Macmillan, 1970, pp. 186–215. Print.

Bender, C. "Bakhtinian Perspectives on 'Everyday Life' Sociology." *Bakhtin and the Human Sciences: No Last Words*. Ed. M.M. Bell and M. Gardiner. London: SAGE Publications: 1998, pp. 181–195. Print.

Bhabha, Homi K. *The Location of Culture*. London and New York: Routledge, 1994. Print.

Braxley, K. "Mastering Academic English: International Graduate Students' Use of Dialogue and Speech Genres to Meet the Writing Demands of Graduate School." *Dialogue with Bakhtin on Second and Foreign Language Learning: New Perspectives*. Ed. W.J.K. Hall, G. Vitanova, L. Marchenkova. New Jersey: Lawrence Erlbaum Associates, 2005, pp. 11–32. Print.

Chatterjee, Partha. *Nationalist Thought and the Colonial World: A Derivative Discourse? The Partha Chatterjee Omnibus*. New Delhi: Oxford University Press, 1999. Print.

DeLoughrey, Elizabeth. "Island Ecologies and Caribbean Literatures." *TijdschriftvoorEconomischeenSocialeGeografie*, 95, 3, 2004, 298–310. https://doi.org/10.1111/j.1467-9663.2004.00309.x Accessed 18 August 2018

Dutta, Ritam. ""Let's Talk": Promoting Dialogue and Answerability in Critical Humanities Education with Permeable Curriculum and an Adda-Based Pedagogy."*Kultura – Społeczeńs Two – Edukacjanr*, 1,7,2015, POZNAŃ, 35–59. https://doi.org/10.14746/kse.2015.1.3 Accessed 27 July 2018

Dyson, A.H. "Negotiating a Permeable Curriculum: On Literacy, Diversity, and the Interplay of Children's and Teachers' Worlds." *NCTE Concept Papers* No. 9: 1993, pp. 1–40. Urbana, IL: National Council of Teachers of English. https://archive.org/stream/ERIC_ED359548/ERIC_ED359548_djvu.txt Accessed 12 May 2018

Fanon, F. *The Wretched of the Earth*. 1963. Rpt. London: Penguin, 2001. Print.

Forster, E.M. *Abinger Harvest*. 1936. Rpt. Harmondsworth: Penguin Books, 1967. Print.

———. "The Art of Fiction", *The Paris Review*, 1953. Print.

———. "De Senectute". *The London Magazine*, IV, 1957. Print.

———. *Aspects of the Novel. 1927. Rpt.* Harmondsworth: Penguin Books, 1962. Print.

———. *A Passage to India. 1924. Rpt.* Harmondsworth: Penguin Books, 1965. Print.

———. *Alexandria: A History and a Guide. 1922. Rpt.* With an Introduction by Lawrence Durrell. London: Michael Haag, 1982. Print.

Grandsen, K.W. *E.M. Forster*. Edinburgh & London: Oliver and Boyd, 1962. Print.

Harvey, W.J. *Character and the Novel*. London: Chatto & Windus, 1965. Print.

Iser, Wolfgang. *The Implied Reader: Patterns of Communication in Prose Fiction from Bunyan to Beckett*. Baltimore: Johns Hopkins Press, 1974. Print.

Jung, Carl Gustav. *The Collected Works*. Ed. Herbert Read. New York: Routledge, 2014. Print.

Kakar, Sudhir. *The Colours of Violence: Cultural Identities, Religion and Conflict*. Chicago: University of Chicago Press, 1996. Print.

Khair, Tabish. *Reading Literature Today*. Co-ed. Sébastien Doubinsky. New Delhi: Sage Publications, 2011. Print.

Meyers, Jeffrey. "Cited in Jeffrey Meyers The Politics of A Passage to India." *Journal of Modern Literature*, 1, 3 (Mar., 1971), 329–338. www.jstor.org/stable/3831057Accessed 18 August 2018.

Moje, E.B., Ciechanowski, K.M., Kramer, K., Ellis, L., Carrillo, R., Collazo, T. "Looking for Third Space: An Examination of Everyday and Secondary School Literacy, Knowledge, and Discourse." *Reading Research Quarterly*, 39, (1), 2004, 38–70. https://doi.org/10.1598/RRQ.39.1.4 Accessed 24 June 2018

Moll, L.C., Amanti, C., Neff, D., Gonzalez, N. "Funds of Knowledge for Teaching: Using a Qualitative Approach to Connect Homes and Classrooms." *Theory into Practice*, 31, (2), 1992,132–141. www.jstor.org/stable/1476399 Accessed 12 July 2018.

Moody, P.*A Critical Commentary on E.M. Forster's A Passage to India*. London: Macmillan, 1968. Print.

Moore, D.W., Bean, T.W., Birdyshaw, D., Rycik, J.A. "Adolescent Literacy: A Position Statement". *Journal of Adolescent &Adult Literacy*, 43, 1999, 97–111. www.jstor.org/stable/40017055Accessed 24 April 2018.

Nandy, Ashis. *The Intimate Enemy: Loss and Recovery of Self under Colonialism*. New Delhi: Oxford University Press, 1983. Print.

Orwell, George. *Burmese Days*. 1934. Rpt. London: Penguin, 2001. Print.

Pathak, Z., Sengupta, S., Purkayastha, S. "The Prisonhouse of Orientalism". *Textual Practice*, 5, 2, (1991), 195–218. https://doi.org/10.1080/09502369108582112 Accessed 24 May 2018.

Said, Edward W. *Orientalism. New York*: Vintage, 1978. Print.

Schwartz, R. Cited in Manfred Stege. "Epilogue" *Gandhi's Dilemma: Nonviolent Principles and Nationalist Power*. New York: St. Martin's Press, 2000. Print.

Schwartz, S. *Teacher Training for the Humanities. Selected Addresses Delivered at the Conference on English Education*. No 6, Part 2, National Council of Teachers of English, 1968, pp. 9–14. www.jstor.org/stable/i40004803 Accessed 3 March 2018.

Stone, Wilfred. *The Cave and the Mountain: A Study of E.M. Forster*. California: Stanford University Press, 1966. Print.

6

CULTURAL INTERSECTIONS AND NATURE WRITING

Teaching nature poetry

Dolikajyoti Sharma

This chapter attempts to look at some important questions in the teaching of nature and English Literature within an Indian classroom, in a region considered one of the most significant biodiversity hotspots in the world – Northeast India. I draw on my own experiences of teaching Emily Dickinson and Ted Hughes, using one particular point of entry, ecocriticism, in its implications in the particular milieu of Northeast India in general and Assam in particular.

Concepts of nature and its experience vary across cultures and geographical regions around the world. The primary reason for this is the diversity of environments and habitats requiring specific kinds of responses from local communities that have, over time, integrated into the cultural lives of those communities. The classroom is not a neutral place where academic discussions take place without any reference to the lived realities of the people occupying that space. Rather, it becomes a powerful space where cultural, political, ethical, ontological and epistemological questions can be raised in an open and receptive platform that links directly with the location and experiences of the students and the teachers. Moreover, the students often bring with them startling ways of looking at images and metaphors that owe much to cultural beliefs and experiences peculiar to their communities.[1] This was a realization that became especially apparent to me in my classes on Dickinson and Hughes since the particular thrust was on nature, environment and the relationships between the human and the non-human. Two different threads seemed to run through these classes and this chapter is organized around them: one, trying to familiarize the students with the environment and cultural attitudes to nature in Britain and America; and the second, attempting to read these poets from the location of the class in this part of the world, thereby making for more relevant readings of these poets.

A few days back when I started teaching Ted Hughes's poetry in this year's (2019) MA English Second Semester class at Gauhati University, I began by asking them to read his "Pike" (one of the texts prescribed) very closely for a few minutes and then give their immediate responses to it.

DOI: 10.4324/9781003146209-7

There ensued a pin-drop silence as most, if not all, pored over their texts and took stock of their responses. Across that silence, one could hear an oriole calling close to the classroom. The call of the bird coincided with the sounds of construction within the building the department is housed in, as new windows and grilles were being installed. As the students finished reading, I asked them if they heard any sounds. Most of them replied that they could hear the noisy construction work. Except for one or two, none had heard the oriole. Ironically, though, they *were* actually busy reading the poem on the pike; but in reading it as a text, they missed the point that the poem describes an actual fish, very much like the actual oriole outside. They were not observant enough or inquisitive enough about the world they live in; this was not merely true of their lives within the classroom but of their general awareness of their surroundings and contexts as well.

In teaching the nature poetry of Emily Dickinson and Ted Hughes, both of whom use a wide range of animal imagery, I found it useful to engage the students in visualizing those images. The primary reason was that the students would automatically shift into the terrain of metaphor and allegory before actually trying to read the poems closely.

In a typical class, I came across very few students who could actually visualize the movements or the behavioural traits of these animals and from there, could go on to connect these with why the poets chose these particular animals as subjects of their poems. The students who could do so usually had pets themselves and hence, could connect to the animal subjects. The rest were more or less oblivious (at least in their responses) to the plant and animal lives around them except when these had direct and immediate relevance to their lives. Most students were familiar with beliefs, customs, folk tales, and myths associated with animals and plants in India, particularly in the Northeastern cultures but also with such narratives in cultures around the world. But there was a noticeable disconnect between such knowledge and the reading situation in the classroom. The challenge was to encourage conscious engagement with their environments, which in turn would enable more nuanced reading of their texts.

The situation in the classroom could be identified as (1) inattention of students to their environment evident in their interaction (or lack of it) with the plant and animal life around them; (2) the unfamiliar animals, plants, and cultures described in the poems; and (3) a general lack of awareness and inquisitiveness regarding the ethical issues emerging out of discussions on human violation of the environment. In the case of the third challenge, while the students on the whole showed a theoretical familiarity with such issues (mainly because of course requirements), many found it difficult to connect these to their own milieus. My attempt in the classes, therefore, was to familiarize them with the notion of empathy and make them reflect on why it is significant at all and perhaps help them discover empathy as an emotion in themselves.

I

Northeast India is home to several indigenous communities, all of which share an intimate and complex relationship with nature.[2] These are grounded, first and foremost, on a relational notion of the self in nature, which implies 'respect' for nature and the environment. The United Nations Environment Programme states that

> Their [indigenous communities'] traditions and belief systems often mean that they regard nature with deep respect, and they have a strong sense of place and belonging. This sustains knowledge and ways of life that match up well with modern notions of nature conservation and the sustainable use of natural resources.
>
> (UNEP, "Indigenous people and nature: a tradition of conservation", 2017)

Such ways of life arise from an insider's engagement with the environment, establishing an "invisible and inaudible" but nevertheless an "intimate personal relationship with the bioresources" of a particular region (Jain 1998: 52). This manifests itself in cultural and everyday practices, for example, in taboos regarding food in all cultures in the region. In fact, extensive studies have been made by contemporary ethnobotanists, starting with Sudhanshu Kumar Jain, on the cultural dimensions of bioresources in India.[3] Much of the literature from this region, whether in the Indian languages or in English, represents such connections from diverse perspectives. The students bring with them local knowledge on plant and animal life in their respective communities. Most of them are also familiar with literatures in their own languages, which feature images and metaphors drawn from a sense of place. They have lived with the ideas of the sacred associated with certain aspects of nature. Folk tales and myths as well as children's rhymes revolving around the landscape and its human and non-human inhabitants are again quite familiar to them, all of it embedded seamlessly in their psyches. But when they enter into the world of nature poetry in the Anglo-American literary tradition they are faced with dualisms between nature and culture, human and nature and related ideas, and terms underpinning the history of ideas in Western culture, even if these are questioned and contradicted. There was also the practical fact of the relative unfamiliarity of the students with particular, everyday aspects of these cultures, though they were more or less familiar with them in a vague general way. For example, even though a few had heard of fox-hunting, they could hardly be expected to know the particulars of that customary English sport, or of contemporary debates on it in Britain. Even fewer had any kind of familiarity with the pike, though they could speak at length on the English landscape described by Wordsworth. Thus, my first task was to help the students bridge the two worlds of the English and American nature poetry they read in the classroom and the Indian/Northeast/Assamese and other cultures that defined their own beings.

As a way of preparing the ground for myself and for them I went back to the basics and acquainted my students with the plants, insects, birds and animals of the poems – the pike, the robin, the daffodil – through audios and videos. At the end of the semester some students had developed a greater awareness of their surroundings as well as of other cultures, and this would be reflected in the way they approached these poets. They could make sense of the choice of words to describe the appearances and behavioural patterns of the animal represented in the poems and to appreciate the effect of these words on the poems' contexts and structures. An interesting sidelight was the insistence on referring to the pike as "pike fish", an influence of the way different species of fish are referred to in the Assamese language (e.g. rou maas etc., 'maas' being the Assamese word for fish).

When they were able to connect these poems with their own milieu, and find similar experiences within their own immediate surroundings, the students could actually add newer and more interesting perspectives on the relationality of human selves in nature or in the environment.

II

The fox in Ted Hughes's poem, "The Thought-Fox", straddles the real and imaginary worlds: while the fox is a metaphor for the creative impulse and the poetic idea within the poet himself, the description of the animal as well as its behaviour recreates the actual living animal. The poet uses metonymy to describe the actions of the fox, as it "delicately" explores its surroundings and forages in the vegetation amidst the snow with its cold nose (lines 9 and 10). The fox's movement (tentative, alternating with bursts of speed) is shown as the defining feature of the animal. This is done through a frequency of phrasal pauses and the repetition of "now" in lines 11–13 (Hughes 2003: 21).

By way of starting a discussion on the poem, I asked the students of any encounter(s) with foxes or jackals (both called *xiyal* in Assamese though they are distinguished in other languages such as Hindi, which uses *lomri* for fox and *siyaar* for jackal) that they themselves may have had or that they had heard of. One student said that he had come across the practice of keeping foxes as pets, and that he had come to know of it through online acquaintances and friends who actually kept these animals as pets. All of these friends were from other countries; in India, it is illegal to keep foxes and jackals as pets as they are protected by the Wildlife Protection Act, 1972.

This raised the fundamental question of the ethics of keeping a wild animal in captivity as well as the more immediate question of whether it is a wild or a domesticated fox that Hughes is referring to. Since Hughes refers very obviously to a fox in the wild, the class discussed the linkages between animals, the wild, notions of wildness and animality, and the human/nature binary in order to make sense of the self-reflexive manner in which the idea in the poet's mind bypasses the poet's consciousness to arrive at a concrete manifestation in the form of the printed poem on the page.

Many of these students come from rural backgrounds and are, therefore, familiar with foxes and jackals. Moreover, the university campus itself contains a rich wildlife including these animals, which can be sighted at times. Many in the class, therefore, were familiar with the animal, though the milieu of the poem was obviously an unfamiliar one. This familiarity made them more inclined to observe the image of the fox in the poem closely; but in the process they reached a point that nonplussed them and me. The students who had seen foxes knew that they are shy creatures and generally retreat from humans. However, they were not really familiar with the behavioural patterns of the fox that are so central to the structure and movement of ideas in the poem. This was due to the fact that foxes, by virtue of their being so commonly seen, had become so much a part of their everyday lives that they never felt the need to look at them as distinctly 'other' presences.

What added to the confusion regarding why of all animals it is the fox that is foregrounded in the poem was the fact that while the fox is an apex predator (along with the otter, the owl and the eagle) in England ("Top of the chain" in RSPB website, n.d.), in India, it is completely outshone by the presence of bigger predators like the lion, the tiger and the leopard. Even the elephant and the Indian one-horned rhinoceros (found primarily in Assam and in some parts of Eastern India as well as some parts of Nepal) overshadow the fox by their sheer size. So, while fox hunting is linked to traditions in English culture and society, it was unfamiliar to students in my class who were rather more familiar with the history of big game hunting in India.

Moreover, as predators of livestock, it is wolves rather than foxes that have been hunted in this country, particularly in parts of Central and North India. Foxes are not often seen as a serious threat to livestock or to people (unlike the wolf), even though at one point of time, they used to be very common in India. It was, therefore, difficult for the students to imagine the fox along the lines of the poet's vision in "Thought-Fox", despite the fact that several of them had heard or were aware of folk stories revolving round the animal that portrayed it either as wily and/or wise on one hand, and as a fool/overreacher on the other. Rhymes like *"Xiyali e nahibi rati, tore kaan kati logame bati"* (*Don't come at night, O Foxie, Otherwise we will cut your ears and make earthen lamps with them* – a cautionary rhyme used as a lullaby for children) or *"Rodo dise boroxuno dise, Khora xiyalor biya, Ghansirikaye tamol kate, Aamako ekhon diya"* (*It's sun and rain at the same time; It's the wedding of the lame Fox; The sparrow is dicing the betel; O Sparrow give us one too*), were discussed in class much to the amusement of the students; at the same time, this allowed them to come forth with their own memories and made them more open to thinking of similar cultural engagements with the fox in English (and other) cultures.

It was only in the context of actually reading this poem that they consciously scoured their memories of fox-sightings to find anything that they could recognize as part of fox behaviour. These were mostly childhood memories, since the students themselves admitted that foxes (and jackals) were becoming rarer even in the rural areas. Reading the representation of the fox by Hughes and noting the manner in which the poetic self enters into a recognition of the fox as an autonomous being compelled the students to revisit their memories and reassess their own experiences from a perspective that was now more conscious of the embeddedness of human selves within nature.

III

There were similar responses to Emily Dickinson's poem on the oriole "One of the Ones that Midas touched" since the students were familiar with this bird especially in the university campus. Yet, as with Hughes's poem, the fact that the bird was the subject of a literary text was what facilitated a closer observation of the real bird in its natural habitat. This, of course, did not result in a simple one-to-one matching of the image of the bird with the real living bird, but went much deeper. Through the literary exercise of reading the poem closely, students were able to engage with themes and issues that were closer to their own location. In effect, we were no longer discussing an alien (or foreign) text with an alien (or foreign) milieu, but were finding it in our own context. In this sense, the binary between the local and the global, and more pertinently, boundaries between the local and the foreign were beginning to be questioned.[4]

Both Dickinson and Hughes demonstrate familiarity with animal behaviour, and use that knowledge to great effect in not merely fleshing out the subjects but in structuring the poems as well. For example, in Ted Hughes's "The Hawk in the Rain", the effortless gliding of the hawk in the air is a counterpoint to the painful trudging of the human across a muddy field (Hughes 2003: 19). As mentioned above, the typical behavioural patterns and the stealthy, tentative gait of the fox affect the formulation and progression of ideas in "The Thought-Fox". The short bursts of speed in the flight of the oriole becomes a guiding factor for the movement of Emily Dickinson's poem "One of the Ones that Midas Touched". These are only a few examples but they underline the need for a reader to be as conscious of her non-human environment as of the human.

I had an earlier experience of exploring this aspect when I taught modern Indian English poetry (also in the Second Semester) to several batches of students. Among the poems I taught was one by Keki N. Daruwalla titled "Wolf". Like Hughes's fox, Daruwalla's wolf also "[nudges] his way/into [the poet's consciousness]" as it circles around before lying down (Daruwalla, 2006: 196). This is an instinctive behavioural trait of the wolf that is aimed at self-preservation more than comfort, and a trait that it has handed down to its domesticated relative, the dog. All the students who had dogs as pets could immediately recognize this behaviour and this enhanced their interest in the poem. Although this seems too digressive to have any relevance while reading the poem, what such an entry into the poem enabled me to do was to open up my students to the idea of using animals and animal behaviour not merely as an abstract subject of a poem but as integral elements of its very structure. Daruwalla's poem progresses from the instinctive actions of the wolf in the first and second stanzas inter-weaving with the poet's subconscious and intuitive evocation of his child-hood memories of the animal and the cultural beliefs around it in the second and the third. The fourth (and last) stanza abruptly brings the poem to a moment of realization located in the poet's present, that wolves, so numerous and potent earlier, have now been hunted almost to extinction, and that it is the fear of human violence rather than animal that over-whelms the newer generations (embodied in the image of the poet's daugh-ter). The ethical position of the poet regarding human interference with and violence upon the environment is, thus, not expressed merely as an idea but seeps into the very fabric of the poem. Familiarizing the students with the immediate contexts and objects of study in this case, allowed them to immerse themselves deeply not merely into questions of ethics and empathy but into the literariness of the text as well.

With this experience in mind, I approached "The Thought-Fox" in a similar manner, and realized that here too, students were better able to link the instinct of the fox with the idea of poetic creativity as more of an intuitive expression than a conscious one strictly governed by reason (one recalls Hughes's hostility towards Movement poetry on this very ground).

The result of such readings was the emergence of a changed attitude to animal life and to the environment. This went beyond the relatively simple and at times mechanical act of reading literary texts and beyond using ecocriticism as a critical method to analyse and interpret literature; it entered into the very fabric of our social and emotional lives as humans.

IV

Val Plumwood, in her essay, "Nature, Self, and Gender: Feminism, Environmental Philosophy, and the Critique of Rationalism" (1991), offers a critique of environmental philosophy current during the last few decades of the twentieth century (including deep ecology and biocentrism) and argues that all these strands contradict the very positions they seek to establish regarding the human's relations with nature by "often mak[ing] use of or embed[ding] itself within rationalist philosophical frameworks that are not only biased from a gender perspective, but have claimed a negative role for nature as well" (Plumwood 1991: 3). This leads to these positions often vouching for the universal at the expense of the particular and drawing on

> the familiar view of reason and emotion as sharply separated and opposed, and of 'desire,' caring, and love as merely 'personal' and 'particular' as opposed to the universality and impartiality of understanding and of 'feminine' emotions as essentially unreliable, untrustworthy, and morally irrelevant, an inferior domain to be dominated by a superior, disinterested (and of course masculine) reason.
>
> (Plumwood 1991: 5)

In the light of hierarchies and dualisms emerging from this, Plumwood presents a relational rather than an oppositional account of the self – in relation to nature/environment that sees the human in terms of its continuities with the natural world. Doing this challenges traditional dualities and recuperates aspects like emotion, care, the personal, the body/corporeality, etc.:

> Part of a strategy for challenging this human/nature dualism, then, would involve recognition of these excluded qualities-split off, denied, or construed as alien, or comprehended as the sphere of supposedly inferior humans such as women and blacks-as equally and fully human. This would provide a basis for the recognition of continuities with the natural world. Thus reproductivity, sensuality, emotionality would be taken to be as fully and authentically human qualities as the capacity for abstract planning and calculation. This proceeds from the assumption that one basis for discontinuity and alienation from nature is alienation from those qualities which provide continuity with nature in ourselves.
>
> (Plumwood 1991: 17–18)

Such a relational approach to connections between human and nature is especially fruitful for a poet like Emily Dickinson. In another poem, "A Bird came down the Walk", the human perspective shares space with the bird's perspective that is rendered through a disruption of 'correct' grammatical language and the bird's responses to other worms and insects: the bird is individualised with a personal pronoun "he" as it drinks "a Dew" (not 'a drop of dew') from "a convenient grass" (not 'a blade of grass') and then gives way to a beetle to pass (Dickinson 1960: 156). The poet is aware of her own presence as an intrinsic part of the larger milieu that includes the walk, the bird, the earthworm and the beetle, yet is also conscious of the difference that her presence makes in that very world. At the same time, the poem calmly but graphically describes (in lines 3–4) the predatory nature of the bird when it eats the angleworm (Dickinson 1960: 156).

What takes the place of judgement is a sense of wonder at the bird eating the worm raw. This can be read as a self-conscious juxtaposition of the human and animal world and an irony on conventional human responses to animal behaviour that the poetic persona by implication, does not totally share. Dickinson's poetry defamiliarizes the natural world for the reader by presenting it through a juxtaposition of the perspectives of animals, insects and such orders of the non-human world with the human point of view. Dickinson's nature poetry presents an altogether new conception of self in relationship with a larger community that embraces the non-human alongside the human.

Christine Gerhardt argues in "'Often seen – but seldom felt': Emily Dickinson's Reluctant Ecology of Place" (2006) that with her training and interest in botany and geology as well as her consequent exposure to contemporary environmental concerns, Dickinson could not but acquire and articulate an ecological consciousness regarding place and the relationship between the human and the non-human worlds. This is reflected in her ambivalence to the human presence within nature:

> The oblique resonance with her time's environmental debates surfaces in the tension between her commitment to place and her simultaneous expression of doubt and reluctance vis-à-vis the natural world and our human capacity to relate to it.
>
> (Gerhardt 2006: 62)

A somewhat similar concern is present in Ted Hughes's "Pike". The poem presents three different images of the pike: the first is of the fish in captivity and the other two are of the fish in the wild. The perspective in the poem shifts between an anthropocentric one and one that seeks to look at the world with the eyes of the pike. The result is a poetic voice that registers a sense of precarious existence in a world dominated by the "eye" of the pike as the poet tries to fish for one in a deep, dark pond in the ancient ruins of a monastery. This destabilization of the anthropocentric gaze is crucial in establishing the human self's interconnectedness with the non-human, animal world. It does not, however, imply the total disappearance of the human gaze, but rather the coexistence of several different perspectives along with the human. This manner of looking at animals and insects, among others, seemed to be entirely new to most of my students, who could not get out of the habit of seeing them more as objects or beings who didn't matter, or, conversely (being from a culture that sees some animals as sacred), as creatures to be revered (like the cow) on certain festivals. The ones who could come to terms with the idea were those who had pets (mostly dogs) and therefore could see the latter as occupying an equal status as individual members of their family. But even here, the level of acceptance and recognition stopped with their own pets; the rest of the animals didn't really matter. In dealing with this limited view we went back to the poems, looking closely at the literary techniques used by the poet. We noted for instance Hughes' defamiliarization of the pike, known as a mere game fish, by representing it as an extraordinarily powerful and overwhelming presence in its own habitat, "[a] hundred feet long in their world" (Hughes 2003: 85). This literary exercise, I realized was also instrumental in making the interested students more observant not merely of texts but, subsequently, also of their own surroundings.

The students had no familiarity with the pike since it is not found in India. We therefore looked at images of the fish, their habitat and the regions they are found in, while also discussing their predatory behaviour. The fact that it is a game fish also surprised most, since in this part of the world, even though we do have fishing as a sport, the various species of fish are eaten as food. Since the poem highlights the predatory nature of the fish, the closest parallel I could bring in terms of the local context was the barali fish. The barali is a type of catfish common to South Asia and South East Asia.[5] It can grow to a huge size that has led to diverse legends around it. In Assam, it is believed that it is capable of devouring humans, and that it does devour carcasses, including those of humans. Many of the students were familiar with such beliefs, and could therefore appreciate the menacing images of the pike in the poem. What became quickly apparent, however, was the fact that, in a slight difference from "The Thought-Fox", here, the poet and the pike's subjectivities exist more in a relation of opposition, underlined by images of the submarine, hooks and clamps, and most importantly, by the image of the eye. The reference to England again underlines Hughes's preoccupation with what was for him an increasingly estranged relationship of Western culture with the natural world. This estrangement leads to the sense of alienation in the human observer who is both intrigued and overwhelmed by the eyes of the pike. However, while the anthropocentric gaze is definitely decentred, it does not entirely disappear, making way, rather (as reflected in his later poetry), for the coexistence of the human and the non-human in a symbiotic relationship with none losing their individual entities.

While the students took some time to go into the nuances of this rela-tionship, what they immediately appreciated was the sense of estrange-ment, given the rising cases of human– animal conflict in the State. As their habitat is steadily encroached by humans, elephants, leopards, and even rhinos (apart from other animals like snakes) enter into human ter-ritories in search of food, leading to frequent confrontations, sometimes fatal for either the animals or the humans and to large-scale destruction of property. This was also seen by the students as a shift in the cultural values of traditional societies in the region that was ultimately cast into a tradition versus modernity narrative. Accompanying it was the belief that traditional and indigenous ways of life in this region had historically advocated a relational connection between the human and the natural world but in the wake of modernisation and globalization was in danger of losing this tradition. Parallels were also drawn between these poets and contemporary writers of the Northeast whose writings reflect such tensions as well.

V

The question of place is central to ecocriticism and ecocritical pedagogy as it developed in the last three decades of the twentieth century, primarily as a repository of cultural beliefs embedded in an organic relationship between humans and nature (Buell 2005; Garrard 2010; Buell, Heise and Thornber 2011). This is motivated by a subscription to binaries or dualisms that are composed of essentialized categories such nature/culture, rural/urban, local/global, and so on. Greg Garrard in "Problems and Prospects in Ecocritical Pedagogy" (2010) argues that in such a rubric, "the distinctively destructive character of modernity is traceable ultimately to dualistic metaphysics and the privileging of instrumental reason, developments which were problematic at root" (Garrard, 2010: 235). This, however, fails to note that such divisions are extremely reductive since these refuse to take into account the frequent blurring of boundaries as far as such binaries are concerned: for example, the "possibility that environmental crisis might be a disastrous side-effect of developments that are in other respects welcome, such as reduced infant mortality" (Garrard 2010: 235). Thus, place as a static, essential idea is no longer feasible in the contemporary realities of the twenty-first century as questions arise on issues such as environmental justice, historical responsibility and the possibility of communities in countries of the Global South being as guilty of engaging in ecologically damaging activities as those in the Global North. Attitudes to nature are themselves no longer considered pristine but have come to be viewed as cultural constructions belonging to their respective communities that have become natural to these communities over time. Thus, the boundaries separating nature from culture have undergone a radical shift. Under such circumstances, the bringing back of a tradition/modernity thesis during discussions of Ted Hughes in the class seemed, at first, to be unduly reductive and one that did not seem to adequately acknowledge the nuances in the poems themselves. However, when one looked at the nature of the class, it began to make sense. Not everyone in the class came from a rural background and the familiarity with local beliefs or cultural practices also varied with the diverse backgrounds of the students. Whatever experiences they had in common, however, were connected with human - animal encounters that are usually widely covered in the local media. Given this, it seemed inevitable that modernity or modernization (especially in the context of the colonial history of India and the Northeast) would become a major issue. As the students grappled with the poets and their contexts, they began to look at ways in which certain issues or tropes regarding the human-nature relationship and human accountability came to have different manifestations depending on the local context. In the light of environmental movements in India like the Chipko movement, the Narmada Bachao Andolan (Save the Narmada Campaign), or (nearer home) the campaign against the Subansiri Hydel Project, human–environment relationships have come to be viewed under the lens of environmental justice as well. In the light of such circumstances, it is not possible to see the human–animal or human–nature relationship in isolation from the sociopolitical and economic contingencies in the Indian, and more specifically, in the Northeastern context.

The teaching trajectory reflected some of these complexities. We would usually begin with the sense of place that Dickinson and Hughes projected in their poems and with how this was influenced by the students' own experiences in and memories of those places. It would then move on to a discussion of what such a conception of place entailed in the questioning of the human-animal/nature binary in their poems; consider the implications of such questioning on the conceptualization of the self in a larger sense of community; and finally, discuss whether the self that seems to be constructed in these poems was an isolated self. The next stage would be to enquire if such a conception of the isolated self is possible in our context, whether it has been present in our cultures in the past or even in the present. If not, what was the reason? The discussion would then veer towards an exploration of human relationships with the non-human world as a rich site in which to look at the dynamic ways in which the ethical (and other) aspects of such relationships can be explored, which would bring us to the need for empathy and accountability. We would look at environmental movements around the world and link them with the movements taking place in our part of the world. This would be viewed again, in the context of the poets' own environmental consciousness that underlined their work. Finally, from such concerns of global relevance, we would come back to the local and see how these concerns inevitably shaped our conception of place even in the local context. Thus, the traditional notion of place itself came to be challenged in the classroom as the students took stock of their own contexts in reading place in the poems, since it emerged from these discussions that even Hughes's conception of place was underpinned by these larger global issues. From this perspective it was a discussion of Hughes more than of Dickinson that led the class in this direction, primarily because they could relate more closely to Hughes the later poet.

At the same time, it was also true that this happened only after the focus was turned to the text and to the structure and language used by the poets, during which, over time, a more nuanced view of nature and the environment began to emerge. Parallel to this was the opening up of the students to one another as they compared notes among themselves regarding their own encounters with animals and attempted to bring those experiences to bear on their responses to the two poets and their poems. One noticeable thing about the various batches of students was an unspoken divide or distance between students who had been brought up or had spent a considerable period of their lives in an urban setting and those coming from rural areas or small towns. A subtle sense of privilege seemed to run among the former and they were usually more confident of themselves and their experiences, while many from the latter group were relatively much quieter even when their experience of nature might have been deeper and much closer.

It is, in fact, usual in the higher educational institutions in Assam to see an unspoken divide between students belonging to an urban, privileged background and those coming from a rural (and in many cases, economically weaker) background. There is also sometimes a tenseness bordering on hostility between students from lower Assam who frequently speak in different dialects of Assamese and the students belonging to places in upper Assam where standardized Assamese is spoken; culturally this difference manifests itself in satires, parodies, and outright insults hurled by the two groups at one another (and this hostility is not limited to students but is present and often visible in the larger community). Besides this cultural divide *within* Assam, in any given year the class may have students from the other states of the Northeast whose modes of being in nature, culture and language might be vastly different. The question of language is inextricably tied with questions of class, identity and cultural belonging. Assam itself had seen a massive and violent language movement in the 1960s; in fact, autonomy movements launched by different communities in the state as well as in the entire Northeast, have often chosen language as the most evident marker of their identity. In addition, in Assam too, as in other parts of India, English as a medium of education has been a matter of some debate in the past, and the ripples of this are still visible in the English classroom with its students drawn from both English and other-language-medium educational backgrounds.

K. Narayana Chandran (2006) and K. C. Baral (2006) underline the pedagogical importance of English as a discipline of study in India in facilitating an openness to multiple perspectives and in developing a practice of close theoretical analysis and questioning of stereotypes in students. This is all the more relevant in a postcolonial, multicultural society like India which is fraught with power struggles and discrimination on the grounds of caste, class, gender, race, language, and religion. More recently, Suman Gupta, in his research on the teaching of English in Bulgarian universities (2010), is critical of the Anglocentrism that dominates contemporary English Studies and sees it as detrimental to the future of the discipline. Non-Anglophone classrooms, therefore, he argues, are more complex sites from which to question such a hegemony and thereby create a space for "continuous and interrogative disciplinary negotiations and productions, which tend to be neglected within mainstream accounts of the discipline" (Gupta 2010: 330). This is because the context of the non-Anglophone world by default necessitates teachers and students in such classrooms to constantly negotiate between the worlds and contexts of the Anglophone texts with the contexts and challenges in their own worlds:

> [D]isciplinary Anglocentrism produces a particular pressure on the pedagogic practice of English Studies in university classrooms of non-Anglophone contexts, which renders such a classroom a more critically salient space than its counterpart in habitually centred Anglophone contexts. The Anglocentric bent of the discipline's mainstream, and relative absence of systematic accounts of scholarship and pedagogy from non-Anglophone contexts, means that the English Studies classroom in the latter has to constantly negotiate and accommodate disciplinary boundaries in terms of where the classroom is located. The classroom has to draw upon and insert local exigencies and immediate viewpoints which are regarded as distant from the mainstream of English Studies. English Studies is, arguably, constantly reformulated and reoriented not just in the scholarship, but also in a transient yet continuous manner in the university classroom of non-Anglophone contexts.
>
> (Gupta 2010: 331)

Under these circumstances, the teaching of nature poetry in a classroom in Northeast India is a particularly challenging task, especially since it is a genre of poetry that is so heavily dominated by Anglo-American traditions of writing and interpretation. Even ecocriticism as a critical mode of reading has only recently (as late as the twenty-first century) begun to look at questions of postcoloniality, environmental justice, and similar aspects. However, this also creates a space to orient the class to cultivate a newer kind of empathy that is not restricted to certain humans or to the sole generation of an environmental consciousness in the students but is able to transcend the conventional boundaries set down in society. As mentioned earlier, Assam and the Northeast have experienced a long history of extreme violence rooted in questions of economic exploitation, identity, territoriality, race, language, and the use and exploitation of bioresources in the region. The ability to empathise is therefore crucial to survive in a world where it is so easy to become desensitized to all the violence one is exposed to in everyday life. Such empathy is also connected to sharper observation skills and an openness to the points of view of others.

As a larger goal for the kind of nature poetry I was teaching, I felt the need to make the students perceptive of and sensitive to the non-human environment around them. I would ask them questions like: if they were driving a car and saw a cat crossing the road, would they allow the cat to cross the road ahead of them to ward off the ill luck associated with it at the risk of running over it with their cars? Why is it that people here are so reluctant to let animals (dogs, cows) cross the roads safely but rather charge at them without a thought as to the usually fatal outcomes for the animals? It is significant that these are frequent occurrences on the streets and highways of Assam. Questions of animal rights and respect for the environment, thus, would inevitably come up in these classes, as well as myths and beliefs regarding the non-human world in different cultures (for instance, cats in ancient Egypt or in India, and in Assam).[6]

Teaching nature poetry in class, thus, creates a space for an alternative way of looking at our own existence in the universe by making us more empathetic to what are usually dismissed as the non-human aspects of our surroundings. This empathy, however, is not of an ideal or abstract kind but one that facilitates acknowledgement of the value of our natural surroundings and the plant and animal life inhabiting it. This empathy is also an articulation of a conscious sense of accountability to others, regardless of their being human or not. At least some of the students, over the many years I have been teaching nature poetry, seem to have become more conscious of and sensitive to their environment by the time they came to the end of the semester, going by the feedback I received from them after they completed the semester and/or the MA programme and often in their interest in going on to research in these areas.

Notes

1 One such example was an interpretation of the use of the metaphor of the rhino in Ionesco's *Rhinoceros* that went back to the derogatory association of the animal to a thick-skinned sensibility impervious to criticism or sarcasm (*goror sal*, meaning thick-skinned like the *gor*, or the rhinoceros).

2 Such relationships are present even in Hinduism, which is practised by a majority of Indians, including people from the Northeast.

3 The Indian ethnobotanist Dr Sudhanshu Kumar Jain's extensive work on this field is particularly relevant, given that it is among the first of its kind in India.

4 One of my students in another course on 'Migration and Literature', asked me about the point of reading Irish literature and Irish migration when there was a wealth of literature in India on the very same issues. I had been allotted two Irish short stories by Frank O'Connor and Liam O'Flaherty. This is a question that one often comes across in academic institutions in places such as India. Such questions, however, are vulnerable to certain reductive perspectives that are not able to or refuse to take into account the principles of relationality and intersectionality that are inevitably at work in English Studies in India. Being a student of English literature does entail a familiarity with literature emerging in Britain and the USA, but this familiarity need not be isolated from the perspectives and locations of the students and teachers belonging to other parts of the world. In fact, readings that embed 'mainstream' texts in local contexts often make way for newer and richer analyses of such texts, as academics like K. C. Baral, K. N. Chandran and S. Gupta have demonstrated.

5 There are two major species of this catfish found in South and South East Asia: Wallago attu (the barali) and Wallago leerii (found in South East Asia from Thailand to Indonesia). These catfish can grow to large sizes and are aggressive predators in their own habitat (Common Names List-Wallago attu (n.d.), Wallago attu).

6 There is a belief in Assam that if a cat is killed by a person, that person has to atone for this sin by giving a golden cat of the same size as the dead cat.

Works cited

Baral, K. C. "Postcoloniality, Critical Pedagogy, and English Studies in India," *Pedagogy*, 6, 3, Fall 2006, 475–491, DOI: 10.1215/15314200-2006-0061.

Buell, Lawrence. *The Future of Environmental Criticism: Environmental Crisis and Literary Imagination*. Malden, MA: Blackwell, 2005. Print.

Buell, L., Heise, U. K., and Thornber, K. "Literature and Environment." *Annual Review of Environment and Resources*, 36, (2011). 417–440. DOI:10.1146/annurev-environ-111109-144855.

Chandran, K. Narayana. "On English from India: Prepositions to Post-positions", *The Cambridge Quarterly*, 35, 2, (2006). 151–168. DOI: 10.1093/camqtly/bfl0.

Common Names List-Wallago attu. (n.d.). Retrieved from www.fishbase.se/ComNames/CommonNamesList.php?ID=10243&GenusName=Wallago&SpeciesName=attu&StockCode=10567.

Daruwalla, Keki N. "Wolf," *Collected Poems: 1970–2005*. New Delhi: Penguin Books, 2006. Print.

Dickinson, Emily. "One of the Ones that Midas Touched", "A Bird Came Down the Walk," *The Collected Poems of Emily Dickinson*. Ed. Thomas H. Johnson. Boston, MA: Little, Brown & Company, 1960. Print.

Garrard, Greg. "Problems and Prospects in Ecocritical Pedagogy," *Environmental Education Research*, 16, 2 (2010). 233–245, DOI: 10.1080/13504621003624704.

Gerhardt, Christine. "'Often seen – but seldom felt': Emily Dickinson's Reluctant Ecology of Place," *The Emily Dickinson Journal*, 15, 1, (2006). 56–78. doi: https://doi.org/10.1353/edj.2006.0020.

Gupta, Suman. "Critical Practice in the English Studies Classroom: Observations in Bulgaria," *English Studies*, 91, 3, (2010). 328–343, DOI: 10.1080/00138381003647566.

Hughes, Ted. "The Hawk in the Rain", "The Thought-Fox", "Pike", *Collected Poems*. Ed. Paul Keegan. New York: Farrar, Straus and Giroux, 2003. Print.

Jain, S. K. "Some Aspects of Biodiversity and Indian Traditions," *Indian Journal of History of Science*, 33, 1, (1998). 51–62. https://insa.nic.in/writereaddata/UpLoadedFiles/IJHS/Vol33_1_5_SKJain.pdf.

Plumwood, Val. "Nature, Self, and Gender: Feminism, Environmental Philosophy, and the Critique Of Rationalism," *Hypatia*, 6, 1, 'Ecological Feminism' (1991), 3–27. Retrieved from www.jstor.org/stable/3810030, 29-03-2014.

Top of the chain. (n.d.) www.rspb.org.uk/birds-and-wildlife/natures-home-magazine/birds-and-wildlife-articles/food-chains/top-of-the-chain/.

United Nations Environment Programme (UNEP). "Indigenous People and Nature: A Tradition of Conservation," (2017). www.unenvironment.org/news-and-stories/story/indigenous-people-and-noature-tradition-conservation.

Wallago attu. (n.d.). Retrieved from www.fishbase.se/Country/CountrySpeciesSummary.php?c_code=050&id=10243.

7

TRAVERSING DISTANCES AND DIFFERENCES

Teaching *Kanthapura*

Payal Jain

Introduction

Teaching an 'English' text in an Indian classroom is both an exciting and exhausting exercise. It not only requires underscoring of the so-called 'universality of literature' but also demands positioning the text in its scene of production. The foreignness of the text has to be negotiated delicately so as to keep a fine balance between its distance and proximity vis-a-vis the site of consumption. This commonplace experience of the socio-cultural and historical gaps between the locations of production and consumption has been addressed in several edited volumes dedicated to English studies in India (Joshi 1994; Marathe et al. 1993; Sunder Rajan 1992). However, not many recorded accounts are available on the experience of teaching Indian English texts in Indian classrooms. The reason may be because this seems to be a much easier job than teaching foreign literature. Nevertheless, many of these texts occupy an interesting position of both familiarity and strangeness due to the diversity that the geographical and cultural entity of India represents. At times, Indian English writing can prove as alien as any other English text and sometimes even more difficult for the students to appreciate than 'over-analysed' and critical literature supported texts like those of Shakespeare, Thomas Hardy or Jane Austen.

The present chapter is an account of my experience of teaching Raja Rao's *Kanthapura* (1936) in the fourth semester of the Postgraduate Course in English Literature (2018) in a premier institute of higher education in Guwahati. Guwahati is the capital city of Assam, a northeastern state of India. The seven states located in this northeastern region are marked by uniquely diverse cultural, ethnic, religious, and linguistic milieus because of their distinct histories and geographical setting. A classroom in Northeast India and especially in Guwahati, which is regarded as the educational hub of the region, generally consists of students coming from diverse socio-cultural, and ideological backgrounds in the different northeastern states of

DOI: 10.4324/9781003146209-8

India. With such a target group of learners, teaching a historical text like *Kanthapura* that is set in a little known, rigidly caste-ridden southern part of India, charts a particular phase of the Indian independence movement, and where the narrative is saturated with Hindu mythological references was surely not going to be an easy task. Traversing historical, cultural, and ideological distances between a very Indian text like *Kanthapura* and a set of present day Indian students located in the northeastern region of the country, in fact, proved to be much more difficult than teaching and facilitating the appreciation of an English modernist text like Virginia Woolf's *Mrs Dalloway* (1925), which I taught to the same batch of students in the same semester as part of one of their core papers.

A retrospection in this regard revealed multifaceted entanglements and dimensions which must have contributed to the tension between the text and its readers in this specific case. The present essay records some of these experiences and reflections. The first section of the essay situates the text of *Kanthapura* in the larger framework of the syllabus, describes the composition of the class and presents my teaching plan. The second section deals with the first-hand experiences of teaching a text steeped in Hindu mythology, caste structure and ideology to a multi-cultural and multi-religious Northeast Indian classroom. While the interaction on "Author's Note" witnessed animated discussions, the narrative of *Kanthapura* failed to excite and engage the majority of students, not only because of the gulf between their existing knowledge and the text in hand, but also because of its overtly Hindu ambience. In the third section of the chapter I refer to the apathy of a number of students towards this (dated) simplistic nationalist allegory, with which they could hardly relate. The troubled relationship of this region with the nation state of India is imprinted in the unconscious of most of the people of this region. Hence, the figure of Gandhi and India's independence movement are phenomena with which they have hardly any relation and my classroom deliberations attested to this fact. The next section deals with the prior orientation of the students and how and why *Kanthapura* was perceived as dull, monotonous, and monolithic. This *sthalapurana* with little psychological interest was often seen in contrast to the multi-layered *Mrs Dalloway* and declared boring. Besides, they felt it lacked the postcolonial concerns and postmodern modes they found interesting in contemporary Indian authors like Salman Rushdie and Amitav Ghosh. Raja Rao's narrative was very different from the already acquired taste of the class. In my final section I discuss the issue troubling most teachers of English in our times, i.e. how to make the present day Twitter-generation students read longish descriptive texts like *Kanthapura*. In conjunction comes the issue of the dearth of decent secondary material on Indian English Literature in general and on canonical texts in particular, and the challenge of competing with the readymade exam-oriented material available on Google and in the local market in the form of *kunjis* (generically also called *Ramji Lals* here). I conclude by reflecting on the need to keep the site and constitution of the real classroom in mind at the time of framing the syllabus, and of selecting the representative texts and adopting particular teaching methodologies with a clear understanding of disciplinary objectives/outcomes.

Situating the text in the larger context

Kanthapura features in the first part of a two-paper specialization in Indian English writing. This specialization is one among three options available to students in the last semester of their Master's program in English at Cotton University in Guwahati, the others being American Literature and Contemporary Critical Theory. In general, as per the University Grants Commission (UGC) model curriculum that is followed in most universities, students pursuing a Master's program in English Literature come with some familiarity with Indian writing in English gained during their undergraduate major program. However, such courses are introductory in nature, and at the Master's level they are expected to deepen their knowledge of the field. In the present case, my students not only had this kind of a background, but had also studied a compulsory paper on "Contemporary Indian English Literature" in the second semester of the Master's program. This paper mainly focuses on the postcolonial dimensions of Indian writing in English and the texts prescribed represent some of the dominant aspects of the post-independence contemporary Indian scenario. In addition to this, in the same semester, students are also expected to choose a paper on "The Brontes" or on "Salman Rushdie". The general tendency is that, those who opt for the Rushdie paper take "Indian English Literature" as their specialization in the final semester as they are by then familiar with some of the dominant trends in contemporary Indian English writings. The specialization in Indian English Writing is offered in two papers thar are taught simultaneously in the last semester of the program. The first paper titled "Indian English Literature I" features pre-independence writing and consists of three units: (a) "History and Ideas" containing writings from Aurobindo Ghosh, Rabindranath Tagore and M. K. Gandhi; (b) "Poetry" where they have texts from Henry Derozio, Toru Dutt and Sarojini Naidu, and (c) "Fiction" in which they would study the novels of Raja Rao, Mulk Raj Anand and R. K. Narayan. The unifying thematic concerns of this paper are nation and nationalism, independence movement, East–West encounters and social problems like untouchability, corruption, poverty etc. In the second paper titled "Indian English Literature II", the students are offered post-independence work and here they study the critical deliberations of Ashish Nandy, C. T. Mohanty and Dipesh Chakraborty, fictional works of Amitav Ghosh and Kavery Nambisan, plays of Girish Karnad and Vijay Tendulkar and the poetry of Nissim Ezekiel, Kamala Das, Eunice De Souza, Keki Daruwalla and Agha Shahid Ali. This paper provides a spectrum of postcolonial and postmodern concerns that challenges the essentialist concepts of nation, homogenous identity and binary oppositions between the self and the other at multiple levels. Thus, the specialization is intended to give the students an overview of Indian Writing in English across history and genres and the basic concerns and dominant styles in the field. As mentioned earlier, *Kanthapura* is a part of the first paper along with R. K. Narayan's *The Guide* and Mulk Raj Anand's *Untouchable*. In fact, it is one of the most popular texts in courses on Indian Writing in English in university syllabi across India (a course recognised as indispensable for MA programs in English by the UGC). Its position as one of the most significant milestones in the development of Indian English writing lies in its unique linguistic experiments, distinctive narrative style, and fictionalised representation of India's national awakening. The particular location of a text in a syllabus determines its modes of appreciation, interpretation and focalization and it was against this larger framework of the syllabus that I approached the text of *Kanthapura* in the classroom.

The group to which I taught this novel was a heterogeneous one, a characteristic of classrooms in all institution of higher education in Guwahati. All the 40 students who opted for Indian Writing in English were from the Northeastern region but except for this locational unity, there was hardly anything that could homogenize them. They belonged to different religions (Hinduism, Islam, Christianity), castes (Brahmins and non-Brahmins), linguistic groups (too many to even name), ethnic communities (broadly tribal and non-tribal but many constituent groups within the broad categories), and states (Assam, Nagaland, Mizoram, Arunachal Pradesh and Manipur), having unique political and historical experiences. While this definitely meant that they came with their own distinctive cultural baggage to the classroom, their prior knowledge also differed widely because of their earlier education at institutions of different kinds (missionary, public, or government). For example, there was a big disparity between the knowledge and perception of students coming from English missionary schools and those who came from the rural, vernacular medium schools. This was reflected especially in their understanding of Indian history and Indian culture (despite their religious affiliations). Though not very significant while teaching Western Literature, this gap became quite conspicuous at the time of teaching a 'Hindu' nationalist text like *Kanthapura*. Any classroom by default consists of unique individuals and obviously there can be no singular method of teaching, or a text that would suit all and as a teacher this idea is always at the back of one's mind. But this was a group that baffled me with its heterogeneous nature as I treaded the treacherous grounds of *Kanthapura* for the first time in my decade-long career of teaching English Literature.

Kanthapura is a chronicle of the gradual awakening of a small village in South India to the call of the national freedom movement. Set in the early decades of the twentieth century, the eponymous village represents a typical caste ridden society with rigidly gendered division of socio-cultural space.

This village undergoes transformation because of the efforts of a young Brahmin, Moorthy, who, influenced by the charisma of Gandhi returns to his village without finishing his university education and dedicates himself to the fulfilment of Gandhian dreams. Despite the tyranny of local land-owners, money lenders and the priest, the atrocities of the "redmen", and all the internal differences that divide them, the common people of Kanthapura get united and fight together to resist foreign rule. In the narrative, Moorthy works only as a facilitator and even during his absence and later disillusionment, the people of Kanthapura remain dedicated to the Gandhian cause. This story of nationalist arousal is, thus, more like the indigenous Indian *sthalapuranas*, the legendary history of a place, rather than the Western form of the novel. Despite its typical western features like first person limited point of view, historical narrative and linear plot with artistically balanced chapters, the impression that *Kanthapura* gives is not of being this tight, logical and formal work (Guzman 1980: 34–5). The narrative is chatty, digressive, and replete with allusions, myths, hymns, stories, legends, proverbs, memories and gossip. It is through these narrative elements and an English style that is enriched with "the cadences of Kannada as spoken by women in the Kara District of Karnataka" that Raja Rao captures "the texture of daily existence, the quarrels and alliances, the smell and sound of a village on the slopes of the Sahyadri mountains, where life is determined not by the clock or the Gregorian calendar but by seasonal rhythm" (Mukherjee 1993: 2607). Thus, *Kanthapura* is significant not only for its historical theme and as an example of early Indian English fiction, but also for its radical experimentation with English language in order to adequately represent the ways of living, being and perceiving in a small place in India. Placed in the specialization papers of the program, this novel had to be taught keeping in mind all these aspects and it was with this intention that I ventured to teach this text.

In a course that is dedicated mostly to the study of English Literature, the syllabus is generally framed in such a way that the literary texts are set against a comprehensive sense of the context of production. Thus, an account of the social-political background is essential to our teaching of any age of English Literature. However, what we think of as the context of textual production and how much this can be expanded laterally and temporally is likely to vary with different kinds of literary experiences. My background lectures were confined to the introduction of English in India, the emergence of Indian English Literature, the stages of its development, the debate between the *bhasha* literatures and Indian English Literature, the dominant themes of this literature, etc. While trying to give such a backdrop, the various aspects of Indian history and specific historical situation against which *Kanthapura* was written got sidelined (and, of course, there is never enough time to talk about everything in the class with the limited number of class hours available for teaching each text) and I naively assumed that the students would surely know of these as it was all about 'our own nation.' For background reading, I prescribed the histories of Indian English Literature by K. R. Srinivasa Iyengar (1962/2014) and M. K. Naik (2011), Meenakshi Mukherjee's *The Twice Born Fiction* (2017) and Priyamvada Gopal's *The Indian English Novel: Nation History, and Narration* (2009), but in hindsight I realize that none of these provided a comprehensive context for pre-independence Indian English Literature.

Teaching a novel in a classroom is always a difficult job as it is never possible to do it with as much detail as one would like, and yet it may not be fully appreciated if only major issues are discussed. In short, it requires a lot of involvement on the part of the students who are expected to go through the text on their own. My strategy for this genre is to do the first few chapters elaborately and introduce the main thematic and stylistic concerns and then use these to discuss the entire text. I planned accordingly. I was going to have only 12 class hours for this text. As I show in the following sections, many of these plans, aspirations, and efforts ran up against unforeseen challenges.

Challenges of bridging the cultural interspace

After a few classes on the general aspects of Indian English Literature, and just before starting discussion on the main text, Raja Rao's "Author's Foreword" was discussed in the classroom in detail. The significance of Raja Rao's "Foreword" is well established in the history of Indian English Literature (Mukherjee 1993; Trivedi 2006) and it has been aptly designated by Harish Trivedi, as the "manifesto of Indian writing in English" (2006: 9). Accordingly, it was highly appreciated in the classroom and led to animated discussions. The students could immediately understand the underlying significance as well as the dated nature of Raja Rao's position (in the 1930s) when they read: "We cannot write like the English ... We cannot write only as Indians ... Our method of expression therefore has to be a dialect which will someday prove to be as distinctive and colorful as the Irish and the American" (Rao 2014: xxxi). They could easily relate to Rao's point that "The telling has not been easy. One has to convey in a language that is not one's own the spirit that is one's own". (xxxi)

Such ideas were then connected to the concepts of 'the appropriation of the master's language' and 'the empire writing back'. All this was obviously facilitated by their familiarity with postcolonial theories and the literary practices of Rushdie and other postcolonial writers. Rao was identified as a predecessor of Rushdie and his achievement of chutnifying and Indianizing English. Reading the first chapter after the "Foreword" illustrated for students how beautifully Raja Rao was putting into practice what he had theorised. As we went through the first few pages of the first chapter of the novel, most of the students noticed how the language and the narratorial tone were so distinctive and different from the familiar conventional western historical novel, and so close to our own Indian roots. In these initial classes, the worth of *Kanthapura* as an early Indian English novel was well established insofar as its form and language were concerned. With this preliminary sense of achievement that students and teacher shared, I was hopeful that the text would be a success in the classroom and evoke enough interest, empathy and contextual appreciation of it as a nationalist historical novel for students to read the text as we proceeded.

However, the big challenge reared its head very soon when this 'Indian English text' emerged as an overtly Hindu one. Whereas the historical distance between students of present day Northeast India and a text about pre-independence rural south India could still be managed (though, for example, the students did have a difficult time in retaining the unfamiliar names of the characters in the first chapters of the novel initially), some other issues widened the rift between the text and readers. I soon realised that we, who are located in this part of the country, have only a vague knowledge of the distinctive cultures that form the category called south India. This umbrella term is a misnomer just like 'northeast'. Not only this, my students had little familiarity with the rigid caste system that is rooted so deep in the text, and hence, the territorial aspect of caste in the village was ludicrous to many of them. In fact, their knowledge of south India and untouchability was more or less derived from their often exaggerated and stereotyped depictions on Bollywood cinema and television. Thus, they were unable to comprehend Moorthy's predicament when for the first time he entered a pariah household (Chapter 8) and its aftermath and thought that he was behaving like a 'hypocrite'. On one of the occasions, a student suddenly asked me the difference between a shudra and a pariah and I found myself at a loss, unable to provide a proper explanation. In this region such divisions on the basis of caste or gender, while not entirely absent, are not too common and these again vary according to the place one is in or the community to which one belongs or even whether one is from an urban or a rural background. So the nuances of these distinctions may sometimes be lost. These experiences underscored how reading and teaching an Indian text to Indian students needs no less an understanding of cultural and historical background than a foreign text.

As mentioned earlier, my class was multi-religious and multi-ethnic and came with different levels of knowledge about Indian /Hindu mythology and religious texts. The historical narrative of *Kanthapura* is interspersed with references to Hari, Shiva, Rama, Krishna, Bharat and anecdotes from their lives. Out of the 40 students, only one could talk about these figures and their associations with some confidence. On such occasions, I felt the need for a handy annotated edition of *Kanthapura*, which would help bridge the basic gaps between the awareness of the readers and the text. Repeatedly, I was troubled by the question of how much background information can/should be supplied at this level of higher education within the limited time available to teach each text.

Yet, the biggest resistance to the text that came was sentimental and ideological. *Kanthapura* not only makes overt references to Hindu mythology and religious figures, but even the storyline of the novel, which is otherwise celebrated as nationalist and Gandhian, has been recognized as "fundamentalist" (Abraham 2003: 165). T. J. Abraham points out that the novel "addresses an exclusively Hindu community and is dysfunctional in multi-religious" and multicultural classrooms (163). The fact that "Rao's conception of India drew heavily on the resources of a High Sanskritic and Brahminical Hinduism", made him treat "the terms 'Indian' and 'Hindu' interchangeable[-y]" (Gopal 2009: 48). In the narrative, the nationalist fervour starts with the discovery of a half sunk *shivalinga* in Kanthapura, Gandhi is projected as an avatar of Shiva and frequently is associated with Ram, Krishna and Sankara. Not only this, non-Hindus have no place in the world of *Kanthapura* and are blatantly projected as evil, be it Bade Khan, 'maistri' or the 'redmen', a term used frequently in the novel to refer to the Britisher. In fact, the temple is the centre of *Kanthapura* and even political messages are conveyed through the bhajans (Abraham 2003:163). These instances were enough to establish the Hindu nature of this canonical nationalist text and thus, led to either silent resistance to the text or open criticism. A few students, in fact, were even critical of *Kanthapura* being given such a place of reverence in the canon. This essentialist Hindu nature of nationalism espoused by *Kanthapura* was quite disturbing not only because of the non-Hindu affiliations of many of us, but also because of the fundamentalist Hindutva ideology prevalent in the present times and the intolerance of differences – the effects of which are often expressed in violent attacks on students from Northeast India. The students' quite unguided recognition of these elements of the novel also alerted us to the strongly Hindu basis of the Indian national movement and its elision of different voices. The *ramrajya* envisaged by the narrator towards the end of the novel only drew disbelieving smiles from students who had become sceptical about such terms by the political realities of their time and they thought Raja Rao was much too idealistic in presenting this. It is common knowledge that religion was used as a tool to unite the people of India during the pre-independence period. But how do we interpret this kind of narrative in the turbulent and intolerant times we live in? I felt ill-prepared to face the overt and covert resistance the students showed towards the novel. Though the success or failure of a text in the class cannot be attributed to only one factor, I feel that this overtly Hindu component of the narrative clouded the students' perception so that most of them failed to grasp the fact that the canonical stature of *Kanthapura* in the history of Indian English Literature is surely not a result of its Hindu connotations.

The troubled reception of a nationalist text in an NE classroom

A literature class is not simply a matter of consumption of information or gathering knowledge. Rather, the people involved here are expected to practice empathy, identify relations, and understand relevance. All these require an attentive reading of the text in its larger context and understanding of its ideological underpinnings. As I was teaching *Kanthapura* to this class, one thing that came to the fore was that though a part of the Indian writing in English canon, *Kanthapura* was certainly not one of the most appealing texts in the syllabus. The simplistic nationalist stance of the text and dominance of the Gandhian ideas were two interrelated aspects with which my students from this region could hardly relate.

Nandana Dutta in her essay "Nationalism and Otherness: Reading Nation in the Literature Classroom" (2008) writes, "The northeastern part of India has historically been invisible to the rest of the country for reasons of topography and cultural difference, and the fact that it was seldom integrated into any centrist formation in the past" (73). The marginal role of the northeastern states in the Indian independence movement and their troubled relationship with the post-independence Indian government is something that is registered in the un/conscious of most of the people of this region. Dutta notes how this region is constructed in the imagination of mainstream India. She quotes Edward Gait's *A History of Assam*, which illustrates the fact "'the whole country [Assam] is famed in Hindu tradition as a land of magic and witchcraft'" (Gait quoted in Dutta 2008: 73). In fact, this exoticization and misrepresentation/misinterpretation of the region continues to date and most of us have our own personal narratives to share when we not only had to answer 'not so funny' questions about our looks, regional 'militancy', and our everyday cultural practices, but also how we are regularly targeted as 'Other' for our differences. Adding to this external perception is a constant grudge about the 'step-motherly treatment' this region gets from the Centre in its developmental policies.

While there is no doubt that a majority of these young adult students whom I was teaching did feel Indian, they were equally conscious of the complicated nature of the nation state India and how nation is more a matter of narration and imagination and any intrinsic unity between its peoples, their cultures and histories also needed the imaginative connection. This understanding could easily be attributed to their specific location and knowledge of postcolonial issues and the presence of novels like *The Shadow Lines* and *Midnight's Children* in the syllabus. In contrast to these texts, which undermine and question the fallacies of nationalist discourses and the integrity of the nation, ideas with which they could more or less comfortably relate, they found *Kanthapura* shallow. The story of the quick transformation of a sleepy, self-absorbed' village into a 'microcosm of India' high on nationalist spirit was too simplistic and propagandist a position to

126

appeal to many of them. Their vague familiarity with the course of the nationalist movement and its milestones, especially around the Civil Disobedience movement as these are charted in *Kanthapura* came as a surprise to me. In fact, quite a few of them mixed up the Civil Disobedience movement with the Quit India movement and despite my repeated requests, not many tried to brush up their knowledge of the Indian freedom struggle. For an otherwise well-informed and pro-active class, this lacuna in knowledge and interest was telling and it demonstrated their apathy towards a homogenous and monolithic conception of the nation, which they felt was belied by their own experience and the available discourse about the region's relations with the nation-state.

In addition to being a nationalist text, *Kanthapura* is frequently hailed as a Gandhian classic, a "Gandhi Purana" (Iyengar 2014: 391). According to Harish Trivedi, it is "one of the most evocative and nuanced novels about Gandhian nationalism not only in English but in any Indian language" (2006: 10). Though Gandhi does not appear physically in the text, his presence is constantly felt. He is seen as an inspiration and a living figure of veneration and is mirrored in the figure of Moorthy, the protagonist. However, this became another contentious issue as most of my students displayed hazy knowledge of Gandhi, his philosophy and contribution towards the nationalist movement. Their idea of Gandhi was mainly based on iconography or popular culture. It is not that the school books of the present times do not have elaborate chapters on the Indian nationalist movement or the role of Gandhi. But what is retained and reinforced in the memory depends on many cultural and ideological factors. One day, I asked the class what they associated most with Gandhi's philosophy and they answered 'ahimsa'. But when I probed further about what this ahimsa meant, one answered "if someone slaps you on one side of the face, offer the other also" and no other student was willing to add to this version of Gandhism most probably gained from the Bollywood blockbuster *Lage Raho Munnabhai* (Hirani 2003). To my amazement, I also discovered that though Gandhi's autobiography *My Experiments with Truth* was prescribed in the second semester of the same program, only five of them had read it fully. With such elementary knowledge, the class could hardly relate with the Gandhi who was the only thinker "to reach across a wide regional, cultural and linguistic span to turn the freedom movement into a genuinely 'all-India' phenomenon with mass participation" (Gopal 2009: 44). In fact, once, when I asked them about Gandhi and his Assam connection, I met with utter silence. Otherwise a politically aware group, which was willing to venture opinions on the world wars, the immigrant issue, the Assam movement, and even world politics, this kind of indifference indicated deeper fissures.

Though it is unfair to always rely upon the verbal responses of the student to fathom the depth of their understanding and breadth of their knowledge as many feel hesitant about sharing' their opinions in the class, my assumptions about their lack of awareness and casual approach proved to be more or less correct in the case of *Kanthapura* as I went through their seminar papers and answer scripts of the final examinations.

Boring *Sthalapurana* and post/modern engagements

As we read a text together, I occasionally stop and ask students if they are enjoying it. I asked this question about *Kanthapura*, and there was not a single positive answer. However, maybe feeling that I might be hurt by their lack of interest, one said that she was enjoying reading *Mrs Dalloway*, and many others also said the same. It must be noted that I was teaching them *Mrs Dalloway* as well in the same semester, which was a part of their compulsory paper on modern and postmodern fiction. Interestingly, when I was assigned to do these two very different types of texts with this group, I thought that *Mrs Dalloway* would be much more challenging because of its unconventional narrative style and unusual plot. I was very much confident about the success of *Kanthapura* in the class. However, the ground-level experiences revealed the opposite. Out of 60, more than 40 claimed to have finished reading *Mrs Dalloway* by the end of the session, and it was surely a sort of achievement in our kind of setup. This novel was also taught after exhaustive background sessions on the various aspects of modernist literature and was projected as a representative text of an age of fragmentation, anxiety and disillusionment. The teaching method was the same. After a detailed study of the first few pages and identification of the major concerns, the rest of the novel was discussed through themes of aging, sexuality, sanity, the impact of world wars, and feminism while paying particular attention to its stream of consciousness style. Some students even went out of their way to read on how menopause was dreaded as a disease during the early twentieth century, how frequent was the experience of shell-shock during the world wars, etc. The interpersonal relationships in the novel intrigued them and 'the many selves' each of the characters of the novel represented was what interested them most. If one feels that the yardstick of success in a literature classroom is empathy and an appreciation of the complexity the text represents, from my perspective this was a successful endeavour. However, both the students and I felt something was missing when we tried to deal with *Kanthapura*.

As mentioned earlier, *Kanthapura* is a *sthalapurana*, which relates the story of a rural community rather than of an individual protagonist. Its narrative mostly bypasses psychological exploration and mainly records external details of the awakening of a village to the call of the nationalist movement. Though Moorthy, the protagonist, is a young energetic man, he is too idealistic and unidimensional to appeal to the younger generation of our times. Without any love-interest or family drama, this story lacks the ingredients they associate with a well-told narrative. "The action of the novel takes place at some point in 1930s just prior to the iconic Salt

Satyagraha" initiated by Gandhi and correctly the novel has been called a historical novel (Gopal 2009: 47). And perhaps this is where the cause of the passive reception to the text might be located. Sanjukta Dasgupta relates two classroom teaching experiences where invariably the students "read a culture-specific narrative, by complacently rejecting the political and historical context" (2008: 233). Referring to her personal experience of teaching in an American university she says that despite the use of tools like maps, visuals and images, the response of average students was disappointing. Capturing the essence of the experience Dasgupta writes,

> It was indeed a revelation to perceive how students selectively ignore the context and prioritise the inter-personal relationships within the fictional narrative. As a result, the emotional relationships are privileged, the political and historical context appear of little or no significance as these fail to create the intended impact or impression.
>
> (233)

My experience was somewhat similar though here the privileged text and the ignored one were different. Dasgupta in this context raises a pertinent question: "*Can this detachment be due to cultural alienation and unfamiliarity?*" (233, emphasis added). While the discussions in the earlier sections validate this idea, perhaps one more point needs to be added: a sort of general trepidation towards historical narratives and ease with individual dramas, as was referred to by one of my students who said, "oh, it [*Kanthapura*] is all about history ... there is nothing *interesting* here."

The position of a text in the syllabus determines its reception to a great extent. As I was dealing with *Kanthapura*, the students were simultaneously reading *The Guide* and *Untouchable* in the same paper but with other teachers. In inevitable comparison, they found *Kanthapura* lacking in psychological appeal. In addition to the paper on post-independence Indian English Literature in the second part of the specialization, which was obviously more contemporary, another paper was on Modern and Postmodern fiction. This one had Joseph Conrad's *Heart of Darkness*, D. H. Lawrence's "The Fox", John Fowles's *The French Lieutenant's Woman* and Salman Rushdie's *Midnight's Children* in addition to *Mrs Dalloway*. These modernist and postmodernist texts were evidently much more intriguing and engaging with their uncertainties and their open or multiple conclusions.

Too long; read only the summary and important aspects

A common predicament faced by teachers of English Literature is that the students do not read the text. Especially if one is teaching a longish novel, it is an ordeal. In the present case, only two out of 40 students finished reading *Kanthapura* and around 25 could not/did not read beyond Chapter 5, where the first section of the novel ends. They simply lost interest and patience; and after a point even in the classroom it became more or less a one-sided exercise. I was compelled to narrate the significant episodes in the novel and relate them to the larger issues of the text, while the class mostly remained passive. As has been pointed out in the earlier sections, their disinterest was perhaps a result of too many factors put together. But what facilitated bypassing the text in the syllabus was the availability of alternative materials and the exigencies of our evaluation system.

As widely recognized, the present generation of students have a really short attention span. Habituated as they are to "vertical, extractive, rapid reading" (Lahiri 2017: 2) long sustained effort required to read a descriptive text like *Kanthapura* is a challenge in itself. What Madhumita Lahiri refers to as the TL; DR (Too Long; Didn't Read) syndrome seemed to afflict my class as well (2017:1). Ingeniously, they, in fact, appropriated my teaching methodology as their reading methodology. After reading the first few chapters from the text they conveniently shifted to either the summaries/ guides offered freely on/via Google or "cheaply published *kunjis* (mug-books or literally 'keys' to the texts)" easily available in the local market (Loomba 1992: 66).

The most commonly used *Kunjis* were by Raghukul Tilak, S. Sen and S. S. Mathur. Published by three different Indian publishing houses, these books are simply titled *Raja Rao: Kanthapura* and are available for a paltry 100–200 rupees. In general, covering the background information about the author and his other works, these guides provide detailed 'critical' summaries of the chapters, character analyses, elaborate discussions on the salient themes of the novel, and even ready-made answers to 'important' questions. As gathered from the students, some of the popular online web-pages – consulted by them for *Kanthapura* were litchart.com, enotes.com, and supersummary.com. In addition, they regularly surfed Google to find points about issues like, the role of Gandhi, the narrator and the narrative techniques, the language, role of women characters, significance of myths, caste system, etc. in *Kanthapura*. They could easily get material on the interpretation of the novel as a *sthalapurana* and historical narrative. In fact, a simple search on Google around these topics opens up a wide range of materials from blogs, open access online journals, and downloadable pdfs and words files from reservoirs like Shodhganga, and digital libraries like Scribd.

These alternatives in a way solve multiple issues for the students. Though heavily dependent on mostly uncredited sources and extremely simplistic in approach, these not only tackle the issue of disinterest and shortage of time, but with their summaries and interpretations prove to be very useful at examination time. Whereas the materials and articles that I had provided to the students from books (Naik and Narayan 2009; Riemenchneider 2005) and through portals like Jstor (Abraham 2003; Guzman 1980; Jain 1979; Knippling 1993; Komalesha 2009; Mukherjee 1993; Narain and Kaushik

1988; Srinath 2003; Trivedi 2006; Williams 1998) were well written and cogently argued, and took note of generic developments as well, according to them, these were "not to the point", or were too lengthy and were therefore not student friendly. In an ironic fallout, although only two students acknowledged that they had finished reading the novel, 12 of them presented 4 group seminar papers towards the closing of the semester as a part of the evaluation process. These papers were on the nature of the narrator, role of women, significance of myths and the charisma of Gandhi in the novel. None displayed any complexity in argument but were quite accurate about basic facts. *Kunjis* and online study guides were blatantly referred to in the Works Cited section along with one or two research articles. Interestingly, there was not a single seminar paper on *Mrs Dalloway*. It is not that *kunjis* or study guides on *Mrs Dalloway* are not available in the market or that the students did not consult any of them. But there was much more within the text and on the text which made the students read *Mrs Dalloway*. In fact, Ania Loomba has rightly pointed out that the deprecation of *kunjis* is finally an elitist position, if we take note of extremely poor library conditions, the inaccessible language of the texts and the critical books, and the inability of the students to buy books (1992: 79). In my specific context, the absence of reliable secondary material on *Kanthapura*, the heavy reading load of the syllabus and the limited number of classes allotted to complete the course in a semester of just about four months duration, were additional reasons that contributed to the students turning to these *kunjis* and short cuts. In the final examinations, the students were able to attempt questions on *Kanthapura*, and reproduce almost the same 'correct' answers only because of these 'egalitarian' guides.

Conclusion

Teaching *Kanthapura* was a revealing experience for me. It not only made me rethink my teaching strategies but also made me realise my own naïve assumptions about my students, as well as the limitations of the syllabus on offer. I feel that the location and constitution of the real classrooms must be kept in mind at the time of framing the syllabus, selecting the representative texts and adopting particular teaching methodologies so as to reach satisfactory and ideally planned for outcomes. In the case of literary works, historical, cultural and ideological distances and differences between the texts and the students are unavoidable. However, these fissures can be addressed effectively by underlining the finer nuances and located nature of the text. For example, a text like *Kanthapura*, though alienating, can also be used to teach difference across cultures. More challenging has been the pressure of covering the course within a short span of time that leaves little scope for a thoughtful, attentive reading and processing of critical materials and instead pushes students into the shortcuts of *kunjis* and freely available online resources. To counter these readymade options would require more good quality, reliable and accessible (read student-friendly) secondary material and changes in the evaluation system, which together might discourage spoon-feeding agencies. Finally, within the limited time allotted to this text in the class, how much justice could be done to the long, rich and multi-layered text of *Kanthapura* can never be assessed with any certainty. But it surely proved that teaching Indian Literature in an Indian classroom can be as demanding as teaching an English text of British or American origin might be, because the location of the classroom (even within the same nation) makes its unique demands on the reading process.

Works cited

Abraham, T. J. "Flawed Gandhism or Hindu Fundamentalism? No Cheers for "*Kanthapura*."" *Indian Literature* 47.4 (July–August 2003): 162–167. www.jstor.org/stable/23341162. Accessed 24 November 2018.

Anand, Mulk Raj. *Untouchable*. New Delhi: Penguin, 2001. Print.

Hirani, Rajkumar (Director). *Lage Raho Munna Bhai*. Vidhu Vinod Chopra Films, 2003.

Dasgupta, Sanjukta. "To Be or Not to Be or How to Be: English Department in Indian Universities." *Indian Literature* 52.6 (November/December 2008): 223–238. www.jstor.org/stable/23348445. Accessed 12 July 2018.

Dutta, Sanjukta. "Nationalism and Otherness: Reading Nation in the Literature Classroom." *The Global South* 2.1 (Spring 2008):71–90. www.jstor.org/stable/40339283. Accessed 12 July 2018.

Ghosh, Amitav. *The Shadow Lines*. New Delhi: Ravi Dayal Publications, 1992. Print.

Gopal, Priyamvada. *The Indian English Novel: Nation, History, and Narration*. Oxford: OUP, 2009. Print.

Guzman, R. R. "The Saint and the Sage: The Fiction of Raja Rao." *The Virginia Quarterly Review* 56.1 (Winter 1980): 32–50. www.jstor.org/stable/26436076. Accessed 12 July 2018.

Iyengar, K. R. S. *Indian Writing in English*. 1962. New Delhi: Sterling, 2014. Print.

Jain, Jasbir. "The Changing Image of Gandhi in Indo-English Fiction." *Indian Literature*. 22.4 (July–August 1979): 182–190. www.jstor.org/stable/23330052. Accessed 24 November 2018.

Joshi, Svati. Ed. *Rethinking English: Essays in Literature, Language and History*. New Delhi: OUP, 1994. Print.

Knippling, A. S. "R. K. Narayan, Raja Rao and Modern English Discourse in Colonial India." *Modern Fiction Studies* 39.1 (Spring 1993): 169–186. www.jstor.org/stable/26284402. Accessed 12 July 2018.

Komalesha, H. S. "Desi *Kanthapura*, Marga *The Serpent and the Rope*: Reassessing the Literary Lineage and Value of Raja Rao." *Indian Literature* 53.6 (November/December 2009): 202–217. www.jstor.org/stable/23348157. Accessed 24 November 2018.

Lahiri, Madhumita. "The View from Here – Too Long; Didn't Read." *English: Journal of the English Association*. 66. 252 (2017):1–5. https://doi.org/10.1093/english/efw065. Accessed 27 December 2018.

Loomba, Ania. "Criticism and Pedagogy in Indian Classroom." Sunder Rajan. *The Lie of the Land*, 1992. 63–89. Print.

Marathe, Sudhakar., et al. Eds. *Provocations: The Teaching of English Literature in India*. Madras: Orient Blackswan in association with British Council Division, 1993. Print.

Mathur, S. S. *Raja Rao: Kanthapura*. Agra: Laxmi Narain Agarwal, 2016. Print.

Mukherjee, Meenakshi. "The Anxiety of Indianness: Our Novels in English." *Economic and Political Weekly* 28. 48 (Nov. 27, 1993): 2607–2611. www.jstor.org/stable/4400456. Accessed 24 November 2018.

———. *The Twice Born Fiction: Themes and Techniques of the Indian Novel in English*. (1971)Delhi: Pencraft International, 2017. Print.

Naik, M. K. *A History of Indian English Literature*. (1982). New Delhi: Sahitya Academy, 2011. Print.

Naik, M. K. and S. A. Narayan Eds. *Indian English Fiction: A Critical Study*. New Delhi: Pencraft International, 2009. Print.

Narain, I. and A. Kaushik. "Charisma, Ideology and Politics: Gandhi in Indo-Anglian Novels." *The Indian Journal of Political Science*. 49.2 (April - June 1988): 204–220. www.jstor.org/stable/41855367. Accessed 12 July 2018.

Narayan, R. K. *The Guide*. New Delhi: Penguin, 2006. Print.

Rao, Raja. *Kanthapura*. Gurgaon: Penguin Random House, 2014. Print.

Riemenchneider, D. *The Indian Novel in English: Its Critical Discourse 1934–2004*. Jaipur: Rawat Publications, 2005. Print.

Rushdie, Salman. *Midnight's Children*. New York: Modern Library, 2003. Print.

Sen, S. *Raja Rao: Kanthapura*. New Delhi: Unique Publishers, 2014. Print.

Srinath, C. N. "Myth in Contemporary Indian Fiction in English." *Indian Literature*, 47.2 (March–April, 2003): 149–159. www.jstor.org/stable/23341397. Accessed 24 November 2018.

Sunder Rajan, Rajeswari., Ed. *The Lie of the Land: English Literary Studies in India*. Delhi: OUP, 1992. Print.

Tilak, R. *Raja Rao: Kanthapura*. New Delhi: Rama Brothers, 2011. Print.

Trivedi, Harish. "Raja Rao: The Twice-Born Novelist." *Indian Literature* 50.5 (September–October 2006): 8–12. www.jstor.org/stable/23340692. Accessed 24 November 2018.

Williams, P. "Imperial Vision: Anti-Colonial Revisions." *Critical Survey* 10.3 (1998): 114–123. www.jstor.org/stable/41556802. Accessed 24 November 2018.

Woolf, Virginia. *Mrs. Dalloway*. Delhi: Worldview Publications, 2002. Print.

8

PEDAGOGY, PERFORMANCE AND TRANSGRESSION
Samuel Beckett's *Waiting for Godot*

Namrata Pathak

Waiting for Godot in the class

The university where I teach is in the West Garo Hills,[1] a place known for its rugged beauty and evergreen hills. It is located in Western Meghalaya, one of India's northeastern states. Ensconced between Goalpara district on the north and northwest and Bangladesh on the south, the place exhibits an interesting cultural mosaic. Unlike Shillong, the capital of Meghalaya, which is cosmopolitan and accessible and is a popular tourist hub, the Garo Hills is little known and suffers from an anxiety about not been seen and heard. And if at all it figures in the public imagination it remains clearly marginal. Debates on the politics of identity and the now clichéd division between the centre (mainland India) and the periphery (the Northeast), and the complex uses of such a binary, an aspect that we overlook often, hence, occupy a pivotal place in my classroom discussions. The students are mostly Garos and Khasis. Apart from this major chunk we get a handful of students from Assam, Northern and Southern India and two or three from the neighbouring South Asian countries. In fact, it is a motley group with students of Meghalaya dominating the scene. This heterogeneity is a crucial point in my drama classes. To add to this, the composition of the classroom, the seating arrangements, and resulting spatial dispersal are closely aligned with crucial aspects of group behaviour and learner psychology that eventually become apparent in the way the class responds to texts that are prescribed.

What I have observed in my fairly long stint in the university as a teacher of English is a preference for Indian plays (in English and in translation). As I take up an English, European or American text, give the mandatory introductory lecture and establish the relevant context, I notice withdrawal, apathy or a purely mechanical attention in the classroom. In contrast, in the classes on Indian Writing in English, the students feel involved and are keen to interrogate and problematize the text, an outcome that every teacher desires and encourages. Such an engagement requires deep

 DOI: 10.4324/9781003146209-9

attention on the part of the students and this, I discovered, came naturally when texts from the two courses, Indian Writing in English and Literature from Northeast India, are taught. I observed that in such instances, the students breathe life into these Indian texts. They respond well, maybe because the Indian English texts embody their own experiential realities. They relate to the texts as they represent a slice of life that is familiar, not far flung, distant or alien. Not only are such texts steeped in a familiar topography and cultural setting, but they also refer back to a shared past. Each one of them has a sense of his/her past, even when this is inherently subjective, fragmentary, non-official, and only available in bits and pieces. And all of them know enough to understand and process their specific location/place in terms of popular historical events and mass sentiments. They have a fair idea of India and what it feels/means to be Indian (and a sense of the diversity of belonging especially when the perception of non-belonging is strong in the case of the northeastern states).The literacy of the students, we can say, is directly proportional to the evocation of empathy in the classroom, which is surprisingly missing in classes on British and Continental drama. Maybe that's why they are quite familiar with Aditi and Nibaran Bhattacharya[2] but estranged from the Parisian characters of Beckett in *Waiting for Godot*, a text that is central to the English syllabus in many Indian universities but that fails to stir any interest in them in the regular drama classes much to my surprise and dismay. Performing this text and prior to that, encouraging students to write their own script within its broad framework were necessary choices given this common lack of interest. This essay deals with the process of learning through such engagement and argues that the English text is brought closer to the student when they come back to it via perspectives developed from their own cultural and social locations. Once they have experienced the process of writing a script from the play, inserting elements from their milieu and bringing it close to their concerns and finally put up a performance the Beckett text becomes their own. And they go back to the original with an enhanced sense of understanding and interest.

Teaching and subsequently performing an absurd text like Beckett's *Waiting for Godot* in a classroom that is far removed from a conflict-ridden twentieth century Paris offers unique challenges. The first challenge was to reconfigure the text within a different socio-political framework – and this came about through repeated and multiple readings. The second challenge was to have 30 students actively participating in staging the play – handling stage props, writing a script within the newly emerging context, directing, and acting – and above all transforming the classroom into a theatrical space. Even as we (teacher and students) collaborated to stage the play I was conscious of the many intentions that were at work in the entire process – the text's, the author's the reader's. I discovered that we were increasingly being drawn into the text's complexities even as we worked to create an appropriate and relevant play-text for this specific location.

Waiting for Godot is part of the course on Modern Drama (ENG C: 405). This four credit course covers drama of the nineteenth and twentieth centuries. The objective is to introduce the Fourth Semester students to modern drama through a reading of six representative playwrights, to give them a sense of variety and also to acquaint them with the patterns of development of the form in this period. With this intention, various kinds of drama such as social drama, Irish drama, poetic drama, theatre of the absurd, theatre of protest, political theatre, and feminist theatre are incorporated into the course. These include besides Beckett, Henrik Ibsen (*Ghosts*), Bertolt Brecht (*Mother Courage and Her Children*), August Strindberg (*Miss Julie*), John Millington Synge (*The Playboy of the Western World*), Harold Pinter (*The Room/ Betrayal*), and Caryl Churchill (*Top Girls*).

My experience of teaching Beckett has been unique. Most students find *Waiting for Godot* "dull". The persistent "dullness" or stasis in the text according to some of them, makes them question its constituent elements and its composition. Why does the text appear so disarrayed and dispersed? What effect does it intend to produce? Students are discomfited by the text's refusal to live up to their expectations of internal cohesion and a linear developmental process. What they find is a presentation of a post-war setting but divested of any historically recognizable context with which they can connect. The anarchic sense woven into the text, as they see it, thwarts a meaningful and organised sedimentation in the classroom. This Beckett text appears always to be stuck in repetitions and for the students this is boring and monotonously patterned. It disrupts their productive/ constructive relation to the textual world. I have had to deal with this reception: Do they find the text difficult to relate to because it does not fulfil the designs of an ideal reading situation? Are they averse to the text because they feel threatened by and are unsure of the text's proclivities, the text being repetitive in terms of action, sequences of events, ideas, and portrayal of characters and their motives? Is it because they miss the action so familiar to them as the necessary causal development of a creative enterprise? Or is it that the taut social confines of their world, a sombre world of polarities and contrasts, force their rejection of a text that refers to a world that denies easy access? I am convinced that there must be something at work here that is worth exploring.

I try to understand and work out how a text that is structured so radically can be brought within the students' particular fields of perception instead of allowing it to remain incomprehensible, as it initially threatened to do. Every learner has a specific set of expectations, wanting to derive something meaningful out of a text. Driven by individual perspectives and notions, angles of vision, and varied intentions, it would not be wrong to say that they design a text of their own (in every reading of it in the class) which might be at odds with the text that the teacher places in the class. Each learner has a unique way of approaching a text. Whether the text matches their expectations, socially and otherwise, is inadvertently linked to a concept of integration – the students, by not letting a text like *Waiting for Godot* touch them in intimate ways are not only aiming to renegotiate the regimes of perception, but are looking for ways to distance themselves from it. In the case of *Waiting for Godot*, the reason for their inability and even their active rejection of 'understanding' might be the text's overwhelming sense of disintegration.

In a bid to meet the challenge of incomprehensibility, the only available solution seems to be to allow the students to enter the text in ways they want to or can, thereby granting them the freedom to recreate the text. This they do by grafting the text onto their own locale, chisel out its repetitions and make it conform to their sense of what such a play might mean, open up the elusive language to whatever degree they can and most importantly, reorient it so that it comes close to their understanding. In other words, all of them want a *Waiting for Godot* that can be easily understood and interpreted like Ratan Thiyam's *Nine Hills One Valley* and Arun Sarma's *Aditi's Autobiography*, two Indian/Northeast India texts that they approve of and prefer to Beckett's.

Also, engaging with the performative potential of the text gives them the scope to transform themselves into subjects of their own work, an act that is fun and invested with novel possibilities. Even better, it gives them a chance to let their imaginations soar, thereby opening up spaces in the text that they can explore. So together we decided on a performance of *Waiting for Godot*.

Waiting for Godot in the Garo Hills

The role of a director implies the choice of a vantage point, a cultural decision and a declaration of particular interest. Getting to direct a play like *Waiting for Godot*, gives the students a chance to work at repairing many of the wounds that these marginalized societies often bear. Such ideological repair work can be precarious but offers a fierce challenge. The 30 students, quite surprisingly, interpreted the performance space as a place of well-being, where they felt at ease and able to flex their imaginative muscles, a place that offered an occasion for unhinging the play and themselves from the constraints of a classroom. It was a space that carried the potential to fill the emptiness these students in a remote corner of the country experienced at every turn and it sharply addressed the disastrous effects of otherness, subjection, and exoticization. It was a space of empowerment for them. As they told me, the chief aim was to foreground the present socio-political context of Meghalaya and to render it contingent, by breaking the not-so-rigid boundaries between the "real" and the "unreal." More so, directorial manoeuvres tend to open the text up as a site of exploration in terms of generative signs, images, and symbols. The intention was to give in to a multi-layered schema of representation by filtering the "incongruities" and eventually doing away with them. This was done with the tacit understanding that the students would portray a slice of everyday life in the hills, seek solutions, and find answers – purposely avoiding the entanglements and complications of the politically charged space as witnessed in acts of violence (both abstract and concrete) and retaliations characteristic of a typical Beckett play.

Life in the hills has a special significance and needs a brief mention. Most of the students, when asked what makes their performance of *Waiting for Godot* different from a regular adaptation of the play in other Indian settings, pointed to the place to which they belong and how important it is for them to search for their roots. In order to understand their version of Beckett, they retorted, we have to know the nature of life in the hills. What does the place look like? It is a terrain of undulating views and evergreen trees. What do the hills hold for them – hope, joy, promise or a new beginning? Or for that matter, isn't it a fact that their existence is linked to a nostalgia for fullness and presence especially against the backdrop of marginalization and othering of the northeastern states? They talked about periodic discrimination and racist attacks faced by northeastern students in the cities of mainland India, elements that loomed darkly over their societies and families. Most of the factors that created havoc in their lives, the upsurge of insurgency movements, high handedness of the administration, violence, and poverty would not vanish overnight. A dark text like Beckett's does not do anything to effect a change. What would youngsters learn from focusing on meaninglessness, hopelessness and non-action? Moreover, they explained that a text that does not feature a single female character comes as a shock. Theirs is a woman-centric society. The Garo and Khasi societies are matrilineal. In Meghalaya, a comparatively small state in Northeast India, the largest tribe is Khasi, followed by Garo. In the societal structure of these societies, daughters have the sole right to the ancestral property and the youngest daughter of the family is chosen as the heiress and additionally there is no stigma attached to failed marriages. These aspects of the society give a different orientation to perceptions about women as is evident in the students' reworking of the play.

The students refuse to accept a minimal set-up in terms of the performance space. They say that, unlike Beckett, they want full details of the physical setting. A setting that could be anywhere but nowhere does not make sense. They do not understand what emptiness is. Why should there be a bare stage? The place in which they dwell can be one of the reasons behind the choice. The students choose Balpakram[3] as the place of action in the play. They want greenery all around. Lifeless barren sights and a leafless tree are unknown to them and so the idea of a tree as the only stage prop is rejected. The well-guarded sacred forests of the Garo Hills, doubly protected by laws of conservation by the government of Meghalaya along with the customs of the local people, makes this place totally different from the neighbouring state of Assam as well as from the Mymensingh district of Bangladesh that surrounds it. Luscious forests dot the banks of the rivers in the Garo Hills. There is a green canopy of thick foliage above the rivers and streams that flow through deep gorges.[4] Western Meghalaya also boasts of plateaus. The famous Balpakram plateau situated in the southeastern corner of West Garo Hills is a land of enchantments and mysterious powers. The deep gorges that cut into the plateau form a natural channel for strong wind blowing regularly from the South. Hence, the name Balpakram, which means 'blowing across'. According to the Garos the Balpakram plateau is an abode of dead spirits. It also houses different species of wild animals. Rare medicinal herbs grow abundantly in Balpakram. A wild life sanctuary has been set up by the Government of Meghalaya for the preservation of several species of wild animals. Balpakram is a place of rich lore and narratives that do not come to a close. This ever-expanding and self-proliferating discourse revolving round Balpakram finds a place in the performance of the students.

However, we had to work with the fact of Beckett's *Waiting for Godot* dispensing with all kinds of territorial reference points. There is no mention of the place to which the tramps belong. We don't know in which country the scene takes place, nor are we given the time of day. There is no hint about concrete spatial and temporal parameters. The reader is therefore unable to move logically from one object/place/sequence of action to the next. This dissolution of time and space, not to mention the detour, prolongation, and ultimate negation of the desired effect, frustrates the reader's expectation. The play opens with "Nothing to be done", (1) which has a disconcerting effect. It is spoken after Estragon's play with his boots in Act I. We realize at the onset of the play that this is a phenomenon that is likely to be repeated in the text. This uncertainty can be traced in lines like,

VLADIMIR: ...So there you are again.
ESTRAGON: Am I? (1)

The words convey an uncertainty about one's own identity, existence or a sense of belonging. This also obliquely unsettles the equilibrium that we seek in our everyday discourse. Also, Estragon is not willing to provide details or commit to a cause here. When asked by Vladimir about the place where he spent the night, Estragon, without any gesture, woodenly replies, "Over there." In contrast, choosing Balpakram as the place of action of the performance helps to anchor the performance in the students' own soil.

The classroom as performance space

We have a bright, well-lit performance space. The classroom is the stage. We do not want to use the auditorium, neither an elevation nor a proscenium arch. A tree in its full glory is placed at the centre. The tree boasts of shiny, green foliage. Branches jut out from the flowering tree. A few handmade paper birds are seen perched on the treetop. Colourful draperies and curtains adorn the room. Props like the murha or woven cane seat, hand woven-baskets, wooden boxes, utensils, sticks, newspapers, and flowers are reenergized into productive objects – the motive is to rearrange and re-present the spatio-temporal dynamics of the play in the classroom. We then attempt to rediscover the spaces of this particular society by creating a palpable space within a space. The urge is to use "objects" on the stage not only as things but in their relations with the people. Also, intentionally, most of the scenes of the play are enacted in spots that are close to the windows and doors of the classroom, integrating them into the play space in order to bridge the gap between a hostile exteriority and a known innerscape. The stage is decked with traditional attires of the Garos, Jaintias, and Khasis, which not only makes the stage vibrant and colourful, unlike the dull monochrome of the original, but also brings the text into a familiar zone that then facilitates the growing intimacy with the play in its new version.

Richard Schechner, in a foreword to *Teaching Performance* (2002) maintains that "the ways of studying performance emphasize activity rather than book or archival research. Participation observation – a technique adapted from anthropology but put to new uses in performance studies – is its own kind of practice" (xi). Not only this, the director is more Brechtian-Boalian as s/he does not believe in an "objective" viewpoint of life; rather the moorings are personal – s/he likes to work on the contours of her own culture/ other cultures (Western or non-Western) or even on an aspect of her own life. In the words of Schechner, while doing so:

> she or he is enabled to use criticism, irony, sympathetic engagement, and personal commentary. In a meaningful way, one performs one's fieldwork. It follows that those practising performance studies are actively involved in community life, often becoming advocates for, or coactivists with, those they are studying. Performance studies does not aspire to ideological neutrality. In fact, a basic theoretical claim of performance studies is that no approach or "position" is neutral. The challenge is to become as aware as possible of one's own position in relation to the positions of others – and then to take steps to maintain or change positions.
>
> (2002, xi)

What we wanted to foreground in the classroom was the interactive behaviour emerging in a performance – with the evocation of different meanings and reactions depending on how a performance is viewed, and how these can change from one context to the other –the prime thrust being the specific conditions and circumstances under which a performance is put up, the modalities of presentation, and even aspects of the site of performance, such as the shape and decor of the gallery or building. In performing Beckett, the 30 enthusiastic students went beyond mere adherence to the text. They followed up their departures in the setting with rebellion against the subjection of the text to the author. The text is restrictive. The students have their sights set on something that is protean and playful. They refuse to conform to the norms of the text or to what the text prescribes for them by refusing to internalize the text's norms and authority, seeking instead a collaborative swerve. This movement is initiated by their attempt at refashioning the text. The idea is to break free of a textual dependence, a nightmare that haunts most of the so-called law-abiding, docile learner – a stereotype that inhabits the master's programme in most Indian universities. In the opinion of the 30 students in this case, their performance is aimed at freeing the reader/performer from the pressures of legitimacy and normalization. For them, the rewriting of the play using their local context is an important act of transgression. They decide that they are going to make the first strong move by dismantling the political under-structure of the original. They agree on the need to write the text afresh. This new text would not be just a spin-off from Beckett. By pushing away the limits set by the text, they wish to give themselves room for exploration and even perhaps a raw form of resistance. In the process they seek to derecognize obligations, moral and otherwise. The performance text gives them the scope for fine experimentations. Their prime aim behind the performance in the classroom is to generate spectator mistrust by reinterpreting certain assumptions about "selfhood", "memory", and "empathy" with which they are expected to approach texts. First, the performers question the "place" where the tramps exist. Where do they come from? How can people who hail from Paris reflect our experiential realities? More so, what is Beckett's interpretive location? Can Beckett's text be sympathetic to a third world subject's position? If there is a linkage, solid and firm, between a subject and his or her economic and socio-political heterogeneity, how does a text like *Waiting for Godot* do justice to it? Since the Beckett text is one that appears in so many UG and PG syllabuses in India and has been a staple in the university where I work, these questions seemed legitimate to the students; and since they were compelled to engage with it, they were determined to make it their own.

Teaching or facilitating?

The rehearsals helped the students to develop their critical, descriptive, and analytical skills. These were done in myriad ways – through speech presentation, cabaret, story-telling, dance pieces, improvisatory role-playing, and ensemble. Each student was learning to work in a community, achieving familiarity with and communicating content and emotion, an important skill to acquire. Not only this, they were "learn[ing] to evaluate speech elements of volume, pitch, tone, rhythm, and pace and movement, elements of posture, pace, and spatial relations between people and between people and objects" (Stucky and Wimmer, 2002: 9). Such engagements geared them up for positive assertions and transformations. Engaging in elaborate discussions with the students, both inside and outside the classroom, was my role in this process. It served as a catalyst in reframing Beckett in certain egalitarian ways. In the course of our conversations, I discovered major divergences the students had made in the new performance text which I found quite interesting:

- The students did not want the messenger boy in the performance. The boy is obliterated without a second thought. From the start they have been emphasizing that they do not want a middle man to convey news about the arrival/non-arrival of Godot. The boy spreads insecurities and doubts. Hence he is not needed. This was a major departure because it was not only a character they were eliminating. They were attacking the play at a very basic level since this uncertainty was key to the play's original thematics.
- The involvement of the audience was another refreshing facet of the performance. The performers aimed to ask questions, simple and matter-of-fact ones, and seek answers from the members of the audience.
- Lucky and Pozzo do not turn deaf, dumb, and blind in the performance. Students declare that they do not like the idea of presenting a physically challenged duo in the serio-comic manner of the original. Vladimir is clever, active, contemplative, and is portrayed as a woman.
- The performance text is interspersed with casual dialogue. I observed that the students changed the language of the original text. The conversational language of the performance text is witty and it is a discourse of everyday life in the Garo Hills.

They gave an interesting dimension to the project, which was evident when they urged me to notice in their version traces left by momentary breaking down of hegemonic representation. I make it a point not to miss their rehearsals. Every day from 4 p.m., after the classes are over, pencils and sketch pens in hand, they huddle together, sit on the floor in circles, and address the Beckett text. The original text is the backbone and they read it many times – an incidental benefit in an era when we mourn that our students do not read their texts even once. They draw parallels with other texts they know and with their society. They compare and contrast. They dog-ear pages, strikeout some portions, and read aloud portions that intrigue them. They then start scripting the performance text. It goes on for a week. I hover around but try not to intrude while they mostly ignore my presence. I do my best not to upset the delicate balance between freedom and deference to authority they have managed to achieve in the classroom. But as the pedagogical figure my occasional promptings continue for a couple of days. From force of habit and the many years of teaching, I cannot help getting involved. I am an inquisitive onlooker, demanding justification for this change here and that change there. My string of "whys" and "whats" are not always well taken. They have taken charge of the interpretive process. My questions – "Why did you change this?" and "What is the need of this departure here?" are either met with knitted brows or casual dismissal and non-compliance. Eventually, their clear irritation and distress and their hard glances warn me to keep away from *their Waiting for Godot*. I realize they are beginning to resent my presence as obtrusive. My interventions, carried over from my usual classroom role as instructor, distracts them. Finally, I force myself to leave them alone, though the temptation to eavesdrop, to partake of the spectacle, to be there, and to know what the 30 of them are actually doing is very strong. I realize how strongly they feel that it is *their* performance.

But my interest is in the point of intersection between what I taught in the class and what they make out of Beckett. I noticed that at some level they had internalized the spirit of what had been discussed in the class. The theorists and theatre activists that they had learnt from through material in handouts given to them – Martin Esslin, Stanley Fish, Robert Young, Van Hall, Mark Fortier, and Richard Schechner – together made enough impact for them to be able to break out of the shackles of programmed interpretation. It was, in fact, the spirit of interpretive freedom that they seem to have imbibed from these theorists and that now gave them the courage to make their own text.

Turning Beckett's language upside down

Beckett's suspicion of the communicative potential of language is an important aspect of the play. In it language fails us and is empty. This failure of language not only has its foundation in pauses and punctuations, but it also opens up a maze of absences. The two tramps, Vladimir and Estragon, metaphorically embody this absence as what they are constantly looking for evades them. It is because of the uncanny presence of this absence that a deadening language is brought into play and lost at each moment. In the play what is at stake is the challenge offered to language that usually serves as a potent means of exchange of feelings, emotions, and ideas. Ironically, the language in the text, seems to be held in a linguistic trap, virtually a prison. The language seems to annul itself, racing ahead of its own cause and purpose. Sometimes it stands still and does not move an inch. It is quite difficult to glean any substantial meaning in moments like the following:

ESTRAGON: How long have we been together all the time now?
VLADIMIR: I don't know. Fifty years perhaps.
ESTRAGON: Do you remember the day I threw myself into the Rhone?
VLADIMIR: We were grape harvesting.
ESTRAGON: You fished me out.
VLADIMIR: That's all dead and buried.

ESTRAGON: My clothes dried in the sun.
VLADIMIR: There's no good harking back on that. Come on. (47)

The wish to erase memory here raises doubts regarding the authenticity of the past. We don't know if whatever is told to us is true or not. It might be a figment of Estragon's imagination, a piece of fiction. Losing the power to reminiscence is part of this existential situation, in a dead, barren earth that has lost the ability to nurture and nothing sprouts from it. Nostalgia, hence, is a prelude to nothingness.

When the play, newly minted, is performed in a classroom dominated by Khasi and Garo boys and girls, the use of local constructions like "mitela", "dongja", "namieba", and other such words is the first sign of awareness that this is an exercise in communication. This situation has interesting possibilities. At one level, by using words that are unfamiliar within the interpretive circle of the English text, they are playing with the idea of non-communication. But because of the local context and the shared language, these words have resonance in a way that takes the text beyond the norms of the absurd. So in a way they have understood the issue of communication as one that affects any culture in its relations with other cultures. The English text (and the fact of its French origins) and its basic alienation in their local linguistic situation is now re-presented with its mirror – language that is alien outside its local borders. Not only is there this unique substitution of English words with local equivalents, but there is a surplus of words, an excess that displays a vibrant, colourful spectrum – of languages, emotions, reception, horizons of expectation, actions – hinting at a densely packed, quite "optimistic" and "hopeful" text that has transformational possibilities for the existential situation of the present. What evolves is not nihilistic, dark, and sombre like the original. The performers believe that it is necessary to act on certain things in life and a protest is no protest at all if we cannot execute it actively and effectively. The students use a language that is simultaneously loamy and bouncy. This language is not only malleable, but it is also reshaped to fit into a form more adequate for the depicting of present realities. The performance for them would treat language as an important trope of celebration for spectacles of ordinariness. The performance is sympathetic to linguistic and ethnic differences. The classroom is turned into a site for the exploration of the psychical and interior. It propelled a "bare all", or "let's talk and change" movement pivoting on significant socio-political upheavals that the state had gone through in the two previous years. The performers read excerpts from books in Garo and Khasi (books by Wilberth D. Marak, Milton Sangma and the like), and news items from *The Shillong Times*, delivered impromptu speeches and even provoked the audience to respond and express themselves. What they produced was participatory, and full of significance. There were many diversions in the performance text that emerged from these forms of engagement, which eschewed a faithful adherence to Beckett. This was made clear at the start of the performance, which was set in a scene that was entirely different from the original:

Act One
Under the shade of a flowering tree in Balpakram. The soothing gurgle of a stream is heard. Four characters, the tramps, the master and the slave, meet and shake hands.

ALL: Good morning! Namieba! Namaste! It is 10 a.m. by our watches. Come, join us. We will do something together. We will do something together. We will do something together. We will make a change. We will make a change. We will make a change. This is a repetition, huh! But we are repeating because we have a reason to do so.

(*With concern*)

ALL: You can follow us, right? Are we not making our points clear? Yes, you find our language easy. It is very much the language that you use in your everyday life. We are very much like each other, aren't we? Yes, we are similar.

(*Beaming with happiness*)

ALL: Glad! We have much to tell you. Much! Lend us an ear.

(All excerpts from the students' play are from the version written for the project by Silba Marak and Yankitina Goldiva of the MA 2014–15 batch, of North Eastern Hill University, Tura Campus under the guidance of L.K. Gracy, a colleague from the English Department.)

Digressions and divergences

Here we have two outspoken but overtly positive tramps. We have a green tree, lush with foliage and this is how it appears in both acts. Here the repetitions, in terms of action, plot, and words, are done away with. The text is trimmed and manicured in a refreshingly new way from their constant erasures and additions. The narrative potential of the performance text is exploited through a robust "fullness". On the day of the performance, the rich culture of Meghalaya, varied and unique, catches our attention. This is the result of a multiplicity of folklore and oral tales that are incorporated into the performance text. Much to my surprise I observe that the performance does not bank on any social frameworks, defined gender or hierarchy. It is firmly grounded in the ecstasy of the moment. To give an example, the students' text uses the creation myth of the Achiks.

The two tramps, one male and one female, are given rhyming pairs of names. The male is called Achap/Abil (the young man) and the female is called Bile/Tom.e (the woman). Both are shown rolling layers of soil, digging, excavating, drilling and pouring water. They make three strips representing the earth, water, and sky each of which is involved in the creation of the earth. Soon the earth is covered with vegetation. The water reaches the brim. Fish swim in the water and animals roam the land. The sun shines bright in the sky. However, it is to be noted that the Achiks have their own versions of the creation myths. These narratives suffered several interpolations during the British regime and there was a decline of such myths as well as attempts to tamper with the distinct legends of migration of the Achiks that are orally transmitted from one generation to the next. This intervention created a counter movement among the natives, a fertile attempt to learn and document their own literature. Alan Playfair, in the context of the mythical explanation of the emergence of the Garos, explains:

> It is probably only a legend, but there does exist among the Garos a very distinct story of their migration from Tibet, of their arrival in the plains at the foot of the Himalayas, of their wanderings eastward up the Brahmaputra valley, and of their subsequent retracing of their steps until they came to the plains which lie between the river and the hills they now inhabit.
>
> (Marak 2016: 8)

The students instinctively understand the performance space as a potent site of resistance. In such a space, the act of going back to the creation myths of the Garos serves as a platform from which they can criticize current practices of manipulation and suppression. This stance, of course, is a reference to a colonial past even as it represents a desire to shed the baggage of long standing interventionist policies. The narratives of creation are of course subjected to socio-historical interpretations. But here in the performance we have new experiences carved out of traditional material from the past. Again, the tacit analysis of historical conditions also creates new links to "truths," to rules and to the self. An assertive attitude is evident as well as the desire to transgress. This desire is actualized in a series of practices that produce multiple and ever-new alignments and connections, thus enabling creative modes of transgression. The fertile and rich space of performance they have created provides ample scope for that.

Another remarkable deviation is observed in the delineation of Lucky and Pozzo (these two names are left unchanged by the students), shown as two men dependent on each other, standing in solidarity and eventually rising in rebellion against the Garo Customary Law, thus giving a twist to binaries like the insider-outsider, master–slave, and us–them. Lucky and Pozzo sermonise on the lopsided mechanism that the State upholds, the State's drive to expel "aberrant," "unnatural" subjects on the ground that this is acceptable and that is not, something that the Customary Law triggers and sustains, much to the bewilderment of the common public. At several points, the performance, thus, highlighted the contemporary political and social scene in Meghalaya. Modes of power define answers to questions like what makes a person, what it means to be gendered, or what rights a citizen has. The performance text was transgressive in the sense that the actors could rethink the paradigm of existence and experience themselves as agents of change. The performers overturned a text laden with its own historically situated ideologies by resorting to a democratic conglomeration of ideas and representation. This is an instance of refusing to fall into the trap of thinking and doing only what the text wants us to think and do. The students make it a point to show that their version of *Waiting for Godot* validates the right to live. It is life-affirming and emancipatory. Not only does the performance dispose of the original text's slippery language with its labyrinthine moves that perplex us, but also, its enchantment with mystification, forgetting, and failures of a temporal and spatial consciousness add to the frustration of the reader. The motive is to generate in the performance space the opportunity to articulate certain discourses that empower people and, in a way, also to breed modes of resistance and subversion of socio-political structures of power. The refusal to accept the Customary Law is one such instance. On 29 March 2017, the Garo Hills Autonomous District Council which administers the region under the Sixth Schedule of the Indian Constitution passed the Garo Customary Law Bill, 2009:

> The sixth schedule provides for decentralised self-governance and dispute resolution through local customary laws in parts of the North East. It allows village and district council courts to adjudicate most cases involving two tribal parties on the basis of local customary laws. Only the High Court and the Supreme Court have jurisdiction over suits and cases decided by these village and district council courts. The Bill codifies Garo customary laws into one Act that can be uniformly implemented across various clans and villages.
>
> (Saikia Web np)

One of the points of debate is how the Law defines a Garo. The Law, in fact, generated a debate on identity. According to the legislation, only a person born out of a legal marriage between a man and woman who belong to the Garo tribe will be considered a Garo. The unquestioning acceptance of the rules by a major chunk of the society, especially those at the lowest rung of the socio-economic ladder, throws light on the idea of disciplining in a state and this is crucial to the following section of the students' play text:

> (*Enter Lucky and Pozzo. Both embrace. They hold hands and speak in unison, fingers pointing up, glancing at the sky and giving us a feeling of crushed rebellion.*)

147

LUCKY: Isn't it undemocratic and xenophobic?

POZZO: What?

LUCKY: This mad game of preserving Garo identity. But is not the whole idea of pure-breed highly discriminatory? Isn't the world a melting pot of different cultures?

POZZO (LAUGHS): Note that there were only two women in the 29-member council. Can anything be as hilarious as this? Ha Ha! Ho Ho!

(Rolls on the ground and laughs)

Discipline makes individuals. It is a technique of power that regards individuals both as objects and as instruments of its exercise. Discipline helps in producing the docile yet productive bodies on the stage. Going by the "micro-physics" of power, the erring Garos who disobey the lawmakers fit into a typology of deviancy. The delinquent is the subject here who refuses to conform to the norms of the powerful, authoritarian lawmakers. In the realm of law making, given the modes of operation, the delinquent is not its failure but its success. The non-conformist subject is not simply the author of the crime, but also a member of a sub-species whose crimes cannot be explained as part of her being and character. Again, such a subject embodies a "useful" illegality. This illegality is deployed to further frighten the subjects away from political irregularities. In part, this narrative leans on a colonized assessment of the offender in the light of the scientific knowledge of the "normal." It seems people are frantically searching for a care or cure of the individual who is deviant, legitimized as much by knowledge as by right:

LUCKY: What is a living law, Pozzo?

POZZO: A law that eats, sleeps, cries, and dies.

LUCKY: No, a law that does not bite the dust. Like hope. Like the stars. Like the sun.

POZZO (POINTS AT THE TREE): Like that evergreen tree. It flowers all the season, yes?

LUCKY: Pozzo, in a matrilineal society, the Customary Law is detrimental to the multifaceted development of the women. What about the Garo women who marry non-Garo men? The Bill has many discriminatory legislative provisions. Can a woman be secure and exercise her fundamental rights without being bogged down by the politics of exclusion?

POZZO: But it can counter the rising migration from neighbouring states. The Bill is my weapon to terminate my foes.

LUCKY: I don't know. We are not a pure race. Borders are porous. Why to restrict the flow of new seeds, ideas, people and hope.

POZZO: Look! It prevents rape. The Bill prescribes a fine of Rs 3,330 for a man if found guilty of attempt to rape. Isn't the money hefty? We have only a few coins left with us. We cannot afford to rape. Ha HaHa! HoHoHo!

Lucky looks away.

Abil and Bile as agents of change

Of the two tramps, Estragon and Vladimir, renamed Abil and Bile, the latter is a woman. Unlike Vladimir in the original, Bile is not obsessed with her hat, nor does she have stinking breath. She is the more intellectual of the two. She reads books and is worldly wise. But what is kept intact in the new rendition is the fact that she looks after Abil in almost a "maternal/ wifely manner, feeding him", covering him with a coat and "singing a lullaby to put him to sleep (Prasad 2012: xxii). The same orientation is discerned in the original text,

> They constantly bicker with each other like a couple of long standing – husband-wife, mother-child or just old friends. These are precisely the pairs of roles that circus clowns play as part of their routine. Vladimir and Estragon are different from each other but you can't think of one without thinking of the other; they need each other to play out their various roles, for they are *their* roles as is everyone.
>
> (Prasad 2012: xxii)

The students' text is about the woman being in control. She is knowledgeable and has authority. However, what is striking is the woman's response to Abil's (Estragon's) rhetorical question, "We always find something, eh Didi, to give us the impression that we exist?" (61),

BILE: Yes, but this waiting won't do, Abil, this passing of time and the non-events that populate our world. What is there in existing, in waiting, in killing time? Aren't we fooling ourselves? I joined the Women's Commission yesterday. I have been writing books on women's empowerment. It's time to work.

ABIL: But we are waiting for Godot.

BILE: Godot is not coming. You know. I know. We know.

ABIL: Then what to do?

BILE: Let's talk sense. Let's distribute textbooks in the school adjacent to the Rishipara locality. Poor people dwell in that area. The village headman cannot do much to work for such a cause. The underground water in Dobasipara is polluted by the paint industry. Let's meet the Municipality Board people and devise plans to counter the effect. First, we are going to repair your roof. Dark clouds are gathering up. It's going to pour down heavily. Come, let's work.

ABIL: But we are waiting for Godot.

BILE: Let's face it, you and I. Godot is not coming.

There is a visual and aural appeal in this scene. Remarkable for its use of light, the performance restricts stage space so that the audience's vision of the play is controllable, constantly switching from wide angle to close focus. The scene releases emotions that have varied consequences. We can contend that translating an obstinate proscenium into a small-scale performance space creates special resources for stirring the audience. We encounter two tramps quite conscious of their plan of action. Bile, a woman, is far sighted and decisive. But Abil is shown as intensely myopic, on the verge of blindness. The idea of seeing and not-seeing acquires subtle significance in the wake of episodes of conflict in Meghalaya, emerging from the negative reception of the Customary Law and attempts at neutralizing its enormous effect on the public. However, Bile not only throws light on how power tilts in a lop-sided, irregular world, and the inevitable fragility of regulations, but also hints at the porosity of borders in a state like Meghalaya, as well as the multiple affiliations of power.

In the original Beckett text, a post-war setting serves to showcase the hopelessness of modern life and Vladimir's questions in Act II of the play are full of disturbing implications:

VLADIMIR: Was I sleeping, while the others suffered? Am I sleeping now? Tomorrow, when I wake, or think I do, what shall I say of today? That with Estragon, my friend, at this place, until the fall of night, I waited for Godot? That Pozzo passed, with his carrier, and that he spoke to us? Probably. But in all that what truth will there be? (83)

There are significant differences in the portrayal of Vladimir and Bile. A confident and self-assured Bile's waiting for a Godot who never comes has a very different impact from the original. Bile makes it clear that people must act and work and not make the waiting a central aspect of their existence. In that sense the very idea of a central and determining point in the play is displaced. In the original Beckett play, on the other hand, the tramps are not sure whether Godot will come. They don't remember whether Godot promised to meet them in this place or a different one. Also, they are oblivious of what day it is. But they wait:

if one day is like another, and one place like another, then how do you identify time or place? Who are they (and how does one decide that about anybody?) and what are their real names? But, then, what are names, what do names mean, and how do they decide anything? What does it matter if a leafless tree is a willow or not? Everything is just something to talk about, even if desultorily. The only role for language is to keep silence at bay and, along with other action, to pass the time.

(Beckett 2012: 157)

Godot will come and this seems to determine their behaviour – it is not an incidental fact as it is for the students' version.

Not waiting for Godot

Scenes of waiting in the Beckett play establish an everyday routine in which uncertainty serves as an ordering principle. Within this economy, each member is required to do the job assigned or play the role allotted. This is something that never appears hopeful and is never accompanied by gratitude, compensation, acknowledgement, and reward. We know that the person called Godot is not going to come. Waiting is dependent on the expected presence of the person waited for and this creates a network of faith, trust, and dependency. The moment we obliterate the person, there is nothing left to be waited for. The entire act of waiting is rendered pointless and futile. The students feel that we cannot go about living like Estragon and Vladimir, waiting interminably for someone to turn up without knowing whether the person would come or not. Given the fact that the two tramps wait for Godot regularly, every day, waiting seems to an ethical duty for the tramps. The question that haunts us in *Waiting for Godot* is: why do the tramps think, desire, and say the impossible? This is precisely what the 30students in their performance interrogated. They did not wait for Godot!

It should be borne in mind that their performance was not a complete rewriting of Beckett; rather, there was an effort to unsettle the original text by tugging at the loose ends (for the students these seemed to be quite clear) and animating the play through an array of local events. They made the text Meghalaya-specific. Whether it was a lack that hollowed it out or a pleasure that filled it, the chief agenda of their performance was not to show what composes it, but what it does, how it functions, and what it produces. Instead of hinting at an all-pervading emptiness or a barren existence of humankind from which there is no respite, the performance did quite the opposite – filling up this emptiness with the urgent concerns of *their* time.

Notes

1 The Garo Hills were formed as a separate administrative unit in 1866 with Captain W.J. Williamson as the first Deputy Commissioner. It is a major constituent of the present state of Meghalaya. The Garo Hills are situated between 25°9' and 26°IT of North latitude and between 89°49' and 91022' of East longitude. It has an area of 8164 sq.km. The Garo Hills form the western extremity of the range separating the valleys of Brahmaputra and Surma. On the western side these hills rise sharply and attain the highest elevation of the Nokrek Peak of the Tura range. Nokrek Peak is 1457 metre (4652 feet) high from the sea level. It is the highest peak of the Garo Hills and the second highest in the state of Meghalaya. The northern side of the hills has a low elevation towards Brahmaputra.

2 Aditi and Nibaran Bhattacharya are characters of the well-known trilogy, *SriNibaran Bhattacharya*, *Aditir Atmokotha* and *Agnigarh*, by the eminent Assamese playwright Arun Sarma. *Aditir Atmokotha* was recently incorporated into the paper on 'Writings from the North-East' in NEHU.

3 Balpakram is at an elevation of 1206 metres. The Balpakram plateau has several salt lakes. Areng Patal, in Balpakram, is a huge rock that is said to attract any living being that goes near it, and once a man enters into its hollow there is no return. The Goncho Dare rock cliff canyon is also believed to be the home of evil spirits.
4 Simsang is the largest river in the Garo Hills. The other name for the river Simsang is Someswari. Some other rivers of the region are Moheskheli, Diram, Didrang, Rongai, Ildek, Galwang and Rongkai. The region has beautiful waterfalls and lakes. Rongbangdare, Rongdong, Damre are some of the waterfalls of the Garo Hills. Ta 'sek, Jolding, and Dekachang are a few lakes of the region.

Works cited

Beckett, Samuel. *Waiting for Godot*. Longman Study Edition. With an Introduction and Notes by G.J.V Prasad. London: Faber & Faber, 2004. Print. (All the quotes from Beckett are taken from this book).

Chhakchhuak, Linda. "Is the Garo Customary Law Bill Saving the Tribe or Breaking It?" in *The Wire*. (n.d.). https://thewire.in/politics/garo-customary-law-tribe Accessed on 25 November 2018.

Dawson, Kathyrn and Lee, Bridget Kriger. *Drama-Based Pedagogy*. Bristol, UK: Intellect, 2018. Print.

Dolan, Jill. *Geographies of Learning. Theory and Practice, Activism and Performance*. Middleton, Connecticut: Wesleyan University Press, 2001. Print.

Esslin, Martin. *Theatre of the Absurd*. Harmondsworth: Penguin, 1968. Print.

Hull, Van Dirk (ed). *The New Cambridge Companion to Beckett*. New York: Cambridge University Press, 2015. Print.

Marak, Caroline R. (ed). *Creation Myths of the Seven Tribes of the North-East India. Indian Literature in Oral Languages*. New Delhi: Sahitya Akademi, 2016. Print.

McKean, Barbara. *A Teaching Artist at Work. Theatre with Young People at Educational Settings*. Canada: Pearson Education Trust, 2006. Print.

Nicholson, Helen. *Applied Drama, The Gift of Theatre*. London and New York: Palgrave Macmillan, 2014. Print.

Perks, Robert and Thomson, Alistair (eds). *The Oral History Reader*. Second Edition. London and New York: Routledge, 2006. Print.

Saikia, Arunabh. "In Meghalaya's Garo Hills, a Bill to Codify the Tribe's Customary Laws Could Hurt Women the Most" in *Scroll*, https://scroll.in/article/834180/in-meghalayas-garo-hills-a-bill-to-codify-the-tribes-customary-laws-could-hurt-women-the-most Accessed on 25 November 2018.

Stucky, Nathan and Wimmer, Cynthia (eds). *Teaching Performance Studies*. With a Foreword by Richard Schechner. Illinois: Southern Illinois University Press, 2002. Print.

van de Water, Manon, McAvoy, Mary and Hunt, Kristin. *Drama and Education. Performance Methodologies for Teaching and Learning*. London and New York: Routledge, 2015. Print.

Woodson, Etheridge Stephani and Underiner, Tamara (eds). *Theatre, Performance and Change*. London and New York: Palgrave Macmillan, 2018. Print.

9

TEACHING POSTCOLONIALITY THROUGH *THE GRASS IS SINGING*

Lakhipriya Gogoi

The teaching of English Literature in India varies according to the place and time in which it is carried out. The reading of an English text in a classroom where text and language carry the baggage of the colonial past even as it has global appeal affects the nature and performance of the class. At times the classroom is pervaded by the serenity of a Wordsworth poem while at others it becomes volatile discussing *Midnight's Children* (1981). It reads, re-reads and reinvents texts written hundreds of years ago and also the ones that are contemporary. The teacher has to be an integral part of these pro-cesses. In the mostly traditional classroom situation the lecture format is common with the teacher doing most of the talking while the students scribble notes and nod their heads in agreement. I try to break out of this apparently normal dynamic of the class whenever possible by inviting thoughts, comments and queries on the topics of discussion. Sometimes the students participate and respond to the various strands of discussion that a text entails and yet I have mostly failed to create a truly interactive environ-ment inside the classroom. Nevertheless, the classes that become vibrant with such discussions provide many occasions to ponder over my role as a teacher. The teaching of the literary texts of another culture has been accom-panied in my mind by a concern over what such texts actually give to students – especially, what are the benefits for them of achieving familiarity with the milieu and the conduct of everyday life and personal relationships in a literary text. It has begun to appear to me that the socio-historical con-text in which characters function make students reflect on contemporary issues of our time as they are engaged with in diverse cultures. Reading English literature with such objectives in mind, it often becomes necessary to devise strategies to deal with students' changing perceptions to the text over time. I have noticed that students also change their responses to texts depending upon the broad thrust of a course of which the text is a part. An instance from the class would make this clear. In a course tracing the growth

DOI: 10.4324/9781003146209-10

of English fiction in the modern and the postmodern periods, I taught women-centric novels like *To The Lighthouse* (1927) and *The French Lieutenant's Woman* (1969) to MA third semester students and I remember them, mostly girls, empathizing with the protagonists of the novels, Mrs Ramsay and Sarah Woodruff respectively. It was especially the character of Sarah Woodruff that fascinated them. Two girls were so impressed by the character that they declared in the class that they wanted to be like her. When I asked them what it was that they liked most about her, they unanimously answered that it was her 'freedom' or rather, 'confidence' to do whatever she wished to do with her life irrespective of the time when she lived. While reading the character of Sarah as an oppressed woman in Victorian England, who either did not care or was able to transcend the societal norms of her time, my students simply viewed her as a woman like them. They identified themselves with Sarah as they read their own lives as equally dictated by their society, and especially by embedded patriarchal norms. They read these novels as accounts of women oppressed by patriarchy and the eventual rejection of these patriarchal norms by a strong woman as mirrors for their own societies and their own desires to overthrow such oppression. Yet this same group of students revealed a surprisingly different attitude towards Mary Turner, the central woman character in Doris Lessing's *The Grass Is Singing* (1950) that they read in the next semester.

Reading the novel under the course titled "Colonial Transactions" in which postcolonial fiction is taught they primarily saw Mary as representative of the White oppressors of the native people of Southern Rhodesia. They initially approached the course designed to familiarize them with postcolonial theory and its concerns with questions of race, gender, nation, migration, ethnicity and language without addressing the nuances of these notions. They thought justice was done when she finally lost her life at the hands of Moses, her black servant. The students for whom the white identity of Sarah was not a matter of concern while empathizing with her struggle to live freely in a patriarchal society saw another white woman Mary Turner in a plantation farm in Southern Rhodesia as a colonizer instead of an equally marginalized woman. I wondered what made these students take different positions in reading almost similar stories of women and develop certain frames to look at the characters. Was it because the strong-willed Sarah appealed more than the weak and submissive Mary? Or was it because the former has not been presented by Fowles as a participant in the racial binary whereas the latter stands out as a member of the White settler community in Southern Rhodesia during the time of Apartheid? I noticed that the question of female identity that the first novel espouses does not invite much attention to the issue of race; and instead problematizes the relationship between men and women around the question of class; whereas, in Lessing's novel female identity is entangled with related question of race. Had *The Grass Is Singing* been prescribed in the same course as *The French Lieutenant's Woman* as part of English fiction instead of being offered as a postcolonial novel, would their responses towards these women characters have been different? Understanding and working with this apparent anomaly in the response of the class was the big challenge that I saw before me.

Postcolonialism – theory and literature – is an important part of most English Literature courses in the country and Dibrugarh University is no exception. It requires students to develop familiarity with the colonial experience by reading critical works that address the project of colonialism and its aftermath. The diversity of such experiences acquaints them with the heterogeneity of purposes behind colonization and provide the knowledge of certain discourses that analyse the agencies of anti-colonial ventures under one rubric. Understanding that the productions of postcolonial theory and literature are embedded in diverse geographical, cultural, political and economic histories helps them situate their own reading positions. Besides recognizing themselves as members of a once colonized country and hence sharing a strong sense of empathy with people with similar experiences, the students also learn to perceive deviations. Nevertheless, such aberrations in reading experiences and expectations lead to different interpretations of theoretical concepts like identity, hegemony and power in the postcolonial context. In the course of discussing Lessing's novel all these concepts that are overtly applied in binaries such as coloniser/colonised, master/slave and white/non-white are readdressed by the students.

Teaching *The Grass Is Singing* at a time when the locale in which it is received – early twenty-first century Assam – is fraught with similar issues of identity and power that the text addresses, revealed several intersections between the South African text and this reading context. It occurred to me that the problematic of identifying Mary as the outsider and Moses as the insider can be read as a manifestation of similar identity politics of determining the indigenous and non-indigenous groups of Assam. At a time when the process of putting together the National Register of Citizens in the state on the basis of rights over land is underway (at the time of writing) the reading of Lessing's text made us aware of how across time and culture the questions of insider/outsider and the ideology of language remain the same. While trying to address these in the light of postcolonial discourse, the classroom discussions led to various other realizations that made me rethink mainstream theories of postcolonialism and their implications in contemporary times. I explored the dominant issues of race, language and gender through Lessing's text as part of the mandate to teach postcolonial theory. In the process, on several occasions I found that sociopolitical issues in Assam offered the class new insights into postcoloniality. With this as our reading context, the students and I negotiated the complexities of the South African English text in our attempts to understand postcolonialism.

I

Teaching English Literature in a region where English is a second language and moreover to a group of students who have had a cursory education in English Literature (at the undergraduate level in college), is difficult. A majority of students at Dibrugarh University come from rural areas with limited exposure to the English language and its literary culture. Their practice of English remains confined mostly to the reading and understanding of textbooks prescribed in schools and colleges. At the same time they very often associate a sense of elitism with the language due to its global appeal. This appeal on the one hand fascinates them and draws them to pursue English as a major subject at the BA and post-graduate levels; on the other hand, they often fail to overcome the difficulties and strangeness of the language. In the last seven years I have seen many of our students struggling to overcome their fear of the language. Compounding this fact is their lack of interest in literature, notwithstanding their choice of discipline. The popular trend in Assam has been that a student who scores good marks in English in the final examination at the secondary level (10+2) opts for English as a major subject without realizing that the textbooks of English meant for Classes Eleven and Twelve are no preparation for an Honours/Major Course. Owing to this inability to differentiate between real interest and marks scored in the subject as criteria to pursue English, many students fail to achieve even a minimum competence in the discipline. Moreover, the linguistic-cultural impact that English has in the everyday lives of these students outside the classroom is insignificant compared to the influence and overall domination of the Assamese language. As a result of these factors, students come to the MA English programme with very poor knowledge of the history and nature of English Literature. In the interviews held for admission we come across students who call Shakespeare a novelist or a writer of the seventeenth century and continue to persist with these mistakes even after they have made it into the programme. Almost every year only 20 to 30 per cent of the students enrolling for the course reveal genuine interest in the subject and come with the habit of reading literary texts outside the prescribed syllabus. In such a situation, it becomes a daunting task to not only overcome their fears and their disinterest but equip them with a critical apparatus that will enable their participation in classroom discussions. And yet, the satisfaction of seeing them working to master the language and develop critical thinking is encouragement enough to evolve strategies that will facilitate the learning process. Trying to teach my students to be responsive to the emotional appeal of the subject I often find it useful to adopt strategies to bridge the gap between the alien culture that a text introduces and their own by drawing analogies between events and experiences from the text and the ones that the students go through in their own surroundings. Such attempts to study English texts in conjunction with local issues and concerns convert the otherwise rigid classroom into a relatively comfortable space. It becomes especially helpful when the text being studied comes laden with issues that are pertinent to the region.

Assam, a state in the northeastern region of India, has a complex socio-political and cultural history. The predominantly tribal nature of the state is evident in its diverse cultures and languages. The various tribes such as the Ahoms, Kacharis, Bodos, Misings, Rabhas and many others, all with their own dialects and cultures, have mostly lived in harmony with only occasional conflicts. In terms of caste hierarchy – the four dominant categories of Brahmin, Kshatriya, Vaishya and Shudra – however, all these tribes are considered as lower castes in relation to the mainstream Assamese caste Hindus and Brahmins, and hence a sense of social alienation had been a part of their socio-cultural experience. The rigid caste norms that prevailed in the Assamese society in pre-colonial times did not change much during the colonial period and continue to be much the same even today. The sense of alienation and exploitation on various fronts felt by these ethnic groups gave rise to separate identity movements in the post-independence period leading to the formation of different forums and organizations. Alongside the now well-known Assam Movement of the 1980s for the assertion of linguistic identity and to raise awareness against the influx of illegal immigrants from Bangladesh, Assam in the last few decades has seen many identity movements led by various tribal groups. The intriguing questions of identity and rights that these movements raised surfaced in our classroom discussions as points of reference while reading the issues of race, language and gender in Lessing's text.

The assertion of Black identity in the novel *The Grass Is Singing* in the context of Southern Rhodesia was read in conjunction with the identity movements led by the tribal groups in Assam. The differences of place and time were negotiated in these discussions in order to address the impor-tance of the issue in postcolonial times. Another important issue that Lessing presented in the novel was the question of language as an agency in colonial oppression. The contemporary politics of Assam centring on the status of Assamese language and identity provided us with an occasion to understand it as a significant domain of postcolonial studies. The ques-tion of gender also appeared as a crucial aspect of the novel as Lessing was the only female novelist in the course and also because she chose a white woman as the central character. Thus, teaching the text at a time when identity politics and language were urgent issues in Assam, I could not avoid these intersections of the text and our present context as valid points to address what postcolonialism is all about. This enmeshing of contexts pointed to three important phases of the text's production and proliferation, namely the colonial period that it depicts, the first half of the twentieth century when it was written and the second decade of the twenty-first century when it is read and discussed in a classroom of Dibrugarh University.

II

Given the conditions in which English is learnt and the many reasons for opting to study it at a higher level the experience of the classroom is worth some attention. Every year in the beginning of a new academic session I insist that the students read the texts prescribed in the syllabus so as to develop comprehensive knowledge in the course that can be used to take the engagement to the next level instead of simply preparing notes for end-semester examinations. Such familiarity with the texts prescribed is likely to be uneven and vary from student to student, but it is necessary to their participation in the classroom discussions. Whereas 20 per cent of them follow these suggestions, others struggle to cope with the entirely new dynamics of the classroom. In my attempts to make them comment or ask questions in the class, I encounter several hitches – such as their hesitation to speak because of inability to express themselves in English, their lack of knowledge about the text concerned or sometimes the practice of discussing English texts in the Assamese language in the BA programme they have completed to come here. The lack of a sustained reading habit poses a further challenge. In an effort to overcome some of these challenges, I have sometimes brought into class discussions other texts such as a film or a song that students may be familiar with in order to help them understand the issues we wish to discuss from a different perspective. In fact, screening of movies that are adapted from texts prescribed in the syllabus has been a regular practice in the department – a popular way of familiarising students with the alien cultures of England, Ireland, the USA or other such countries. Sometimes these films serve the purpose they are expected to; occasionally, however, they can prove to be problematic as students tend to consider the film an adequate substitute to the text. Nevertheless, the films help to develop a casual and conversational situation in the class, even when we run the risk of encountering direct references to the film or song used in the class in written assignments, students having misconstrued the purpose of the film screening as introduction or comparison. In these attempts to familiarize the students with the multiple ways of interpreting a literary text the practice of referring to events happening in their own milieu offers an opportunity to talk about otherwise alien issues. Notwithstanding the dilemma that drawing references from local contexts in order to read culturally alien texts at times trivialize the critical attention the texts demand, I try to make the students look at the texts as opportunities to understand their own culture as well. This gives me an entry point into the text where I try to make use of the prior knowledge that the students come with, which sometimes may have nothing to do with English Literature and its history.

The other texts in the course where *The Grass Is Singing* features are Alan Paton's *Cry, the Beloved Country* (1948), Chinua Achebe's *No Longer at Ease* (1960), Ngugi wa Thiongo's *A Grain of Wheat* (1967), J. M. Coetzee's *Foe* (1986), Rohinton Mistry's *Such a Long Journey* (1991),

Amitav Ghosh's *The Glass Palace* (2000) and V. S. Naipaul's *Half a Life* (2001). The various issues that the texts address, especially questions of post-colonial identity and the onslaught of modernity, give the students occasion to read all these texts in conjunction as well as in isolation. Based on their familiarity with the traditional British Literature written in various ages and having developed an acquaintance with English literary criticism and theory in the first three semesters the students are expected to achieve critical understanding of postcolonial literature and theory through these novels. Given the students' general fascination with novels the course offers them opportunities to discover the diversity of colonial experiences and their consequences in different parts of the world even as they increase their understanding of India's colonial past. The stories of human lives and institutions affected by colonisation in various societies such as the Nigerian, the Rhodesian, the Burmese and the Indian offer a diverse yet comprehensive understanding of the various issues that postcolonial literature addresses.

I have mentioned that we primarily focused on three important issues that are addressed by Lessing and out of these 'race' was the first issue that I took up. As an entry point to the novel I decided to talk about the apartheid era that the novel projects. I found that their vague familiarity with issues like apartheid owing to the knowledge of anti-apartheid movement in South Africa led by Nelson Mandela and its visual presentation in movies and documentaries helped the students to enter fairly easily into the milieu of the novel. Their reading of the novel *Disgrace* (1999) by J. M. Coetzee at BA level also came in useful now as they quickly moved from a basic awareness about racism to the nuances of the complex black-white relationship in *The Grass Is Singing*. The disturbing relationship between Mary Turner and Moses and the general treatment of the natives by the white community that the novel depicts was a much discussed topic in the initial classes. It occurred to me that Lessing's sensitive handling of the questions of gender and race might remain confined to just textual discussion with little additional benefit unless we learned to see their similar implications in postcolonial India. Given our experience with such issues in contemporary India and the likelihood of students encountering incidents that would demand a response from them, it seems to me that this added dimension – an extra-literary dimension – was essential to a meaningful classroom engagement.

I told the students to carefully go through the first occasion that the text offers to think about the black–white relationship in the context of Rhodesia when Lessing highlights the awkward silence within the white settler community about the reported murder of Mary Turner in the first paragraph of the novel. She makes the readers notice that the news has been treated as ominous by the people of 'the district'. Their unease and unwillingness to let it pass make the readers curious about the lingering fear and apprehension within the community. The doubt that rather than Moses, the murderer, they might be judging Mary as being responsible for such an end to her life is carried by the students from the very beginning of the narrative. This hint given by the text had been discussed in the class as a starting point as well as an overall framework to understand the complex relationships between whites and blacks in the apartheid era. Although the students did not have any personal experience of colour-coded racism in their own society, they could relate to it through their exposure to the dynamics of 'caste' in Indian society. They could understand why the neglect of a well demarcated boundary between themselves and the natives by the Turner family lead to their social exclusion. The nuances of the phrase "Poor Whites" (10–11) as a blemish on white society and its currency during the apartheid years were understood by the students as manifestations of similar situations in the caste-ridden Indian society – as cases involving poor Brahmins and other high caste people. The tragedy of the Turner family for them became the story of a poor caste Hindu family in their own society whose members, because of poverty, are unable to maintain their caste superiority and keep themselves segregated from the castes below them in the social hierarchy, in the process bringing shame to their community. At the same time the division between the Afrikaners and the British is also made quite clear in the novel and this provides a different understanding of white identity and of the problem of racial distinction being a matter of white against black. Lessing states: "There was no great money-cleavage in those days (that was before the era of the tobacco barons), but there was certainly a race division. The small community of Afrikaners had their own lives, and the Britishers ignored them. 'Poor whites' were Afrikaners, never British" (10–11). This division between the whites was a matter of great interest to the students who had not, up to this point, imagined the possibility of division amongst the whites. This realisation of superiority–inferiority outside of the overall black–white dynamic fascinated them as they could see the layers of meaning embedded in the question of race and its role in determining identity in the colonial times. The fact that it was still in practice at the time when Lessing wrote the novel and even in their own societies made them see the link across these diverse times and places.

Their own observation of caste hierarchy in Assamese society helped them contextualise the author's questioning of the racist attitude of the whites in the novel. Doris Lessing presents the dilemma that Mary is faced with as she goes through the difficulties of farm life, and especially as she is compelled to allow a native to be her saviour. Her feelings of guilt and subsequent redemption add to the complex question of race in postcolonial literature. We tried to address this interweaving of race and gender as Lessing reveals the 'white ruling-class hypocrisy' (186) through Tony Marston's observation in the novel to which students paid particular attention:

For in a country where coloured children appear plentifully among the natives wherever a lonely white man is stationed, hypocrisy, as Tony defined it, was the first thing that had struck him on his

arrival. But then, he had read enough about psychology to understand the sexual aspect of the colour bar, one of whose foundations
is the jealousy of the white man for the superior sexual potency
of the native; and he was surprised at one of the guarded, a white
woman, so easily evading this barrier.

(186)

This perspective helped them observe that the question of 'gender'
emerges as equally important as that of 'race' in understanding
postcoloniality. They could see that Mary Turner becomes a victim of the
politics of both race *and* gender. The easy acceptability of a relationship
between a white man and a black woman was inverted in her case to that
of a black man and a white woman as she surrendered herself both physically
and mentally to a black man. Such depictions of the gender roles in
postcolonial literature were also understood by the students in the context
of their own societies. They brought into discussion common events of
'honour killing' in the northern parts of India and dire consequences in
cases of inter-caste relationships in Assamese society as equivalent instances
of caste and gender binaries. As members of a society where caste remains
a dominant marker of identity and where the consequences of violation of
caste norms lead to social criticism and ostracism, the students responded
with sympathy and understanding to the text.

Apart from *race* and *gender*, the other dominant question that the text
presented as crucial was the issue of *language*. The superiority attached to
the English language and its use to dominate the non-English speakers of
Southern Rhodesia is addressed by Lessing in the incident where Mary
becomes enraged on hearing Moses answering her command in broken
English. Once again, we addressed the complexities and difficulties
involved in homogenizing such issues across all experiences of colonisation by giving examples from colonial Assam. I spoke to them of the con-
flict between vernacular language and English and of how language
becomes one of the crucial areas of debate in postcolonial theory. Gauri
Viswanathan's *Masks of Conquest: Literary Study and British Rule in
India* (1989) that they read in the third semester and essays such as Homi
K. Bhabha's "Signs Taken for Wonders: Questions of Ambivalence and
Authority Under a Tree Outside Delhi, May 1817" (1984) and Abdul R.
Jan Mohamed's "The Economy of Manichean Allegory: The Function of
Racial Difference in Colonialist Literature" (1985) offered them new
insights on the reception of the English language in the colonised countries. Our discussions invariably led to the issue of language politics in
contemporary Assam. The perceived threat to the Assamese language
especially in the wake of the Citizenship Amendment Bill, 2016 and the
large scale protests against it in the entire northeastern region were
brought into our discussion to address the interweaving of language and
identity in the postcolonial context.

III

In the initial classes, thus, I invited their attention towards these three important aspects of the novel that more or less covered the major issues that the other novels of the course also address and hence offer a glimpse of the concerns of postcolonial literature. I told them that *The Grass Is Singing* offers a strong sense of "white postcolonial guilt" (Wang 2009). The students seemed particularly interested in this phrase. They saw Mary as a representative of the white settlers who once exploited the native plantation labourers of Southern Rhodesia. On the other hand, they empathised with Moses and felt able to identify with the colonised native people of Rhodesia, reading their exploitation at the hands of whites like Charlie Slatter as manifestations of the whites' authoritarian attitude towards non-whites that historically in their conception also included Indians. They were quick to position themselves on one side of the coloniser/colonised binary. A general sense of solidarity that once-colonised societies share regardless of the ramifications of colonisation and the differences of place, culture and language was evident in their interpretation. They found it interesting that Mary Turner, the authoritarian white woman who once lashed a whip across the face of Moses, believing that he had disobeyed her command as a member of the master class, finally accepted death at his hands. What they ignored in asserting such a simplistic justice was that Mary had assumed the role of a white master only temporarily in her otherwise miserable life and unhappy marriage. Mary Turner, until the episode when she exerts her white supremacy over the plantation labourers in the absence of her husband, Dick Turner, does not live the stereotypical life of a privileged white woman. While taking a stand against her they focused on her single act as white master to the black natives, ignoring the fact that during her life before marriage she had no acquaintance with people from the other race. As Lessing puts it, 'race' for her always meant:

> the office boy in the firm where she worked, other women's servants, and the amorphous mass of natives in the street, whom she hardly noticed. She knew (the phrase was in the air) that the natives were getting 'cheeky'. But she had nothing to do with them really. They were outside her orbit.
>
> (35)

Moreover, all the failed attempts of Dick to earn a decent living and the memories of her happy independent life before marriage made Mary feel she was a victim of circumstances. The position taken by the students primarily represented the reading strategies of a cultural group that identifies with similarly positioned people and share in the same history of colonial oppression and resistance.

To make them assess Mary outside the frame of the master/servant dynamic, I drew the attention of the students to Lessing's intensive study of female psychology. The choice of a white South African woman, for whom "the word 'Home' spoken nostalgically, meant England" (32), as the protagonist of the novel was discussed in the class. Lessing's familiarity with the location of Southern Rhodesia and the dynamics of black–white relationships there had been understood as the reasons behind her choice of Mary Turner to talk about the complex questions of race and gender. To draw a connection with other novels in the course, I referred to the treatment of these issues by other writers such as Achebe and Coetzee. The discussions on the question of gender vis-à-vis the issue of race in the text posed various challenges for me. I noticed that my efforts to engage the students with the historical and critical insights of a discourse like Feminism sometimes lead to the production of facile notions about women being always marginalised and oppressed. An invariably practised method in initiating such discussions has been to ask the students about gender as an issue and to link it with their everyday experiences. Whereas, on the one hand, it leads to the possibility of interpreting the issue outside its textual and theoretical frame, on the other hand, it can also dilute the rigour that is required in reading such critical theories. Leena Pujari in her essay "Doing Sociology of Gender in the Classroom: Re-imagining Pedagogies" (2017) addresses the issue and talks about the challenges she faces while teaching a course called "Sociology of Gender". She says that it becomes very difficult to replace the positivist approach with a critical Feminist pedagogical approach where constant engagement of the students even outside the classroom becomes necessary. Similar problems of disengagement and disconnection that the students go through while understanding the contents of a literature syllabus in relation to their lives outside the classroom affect the reading and teaching of a text. It poses difficulties in keeping the discussions effective and relevant even while teaching the theory underlying such themes.

To discuss gender in a literature classroom is to consider a text as a pretext to make the students think about their social milieu and everyday reality where unknowingly they too participate in producing gender binaries or play roles in gender politics. I asked them to think about this crucial aspect of the novel by referring to the detailed account of Mary's childhood where the father remains an absent figure and the subject of her mother's complaints. Lessing emphasises the hatred of men that Mary seems to have internalized since her childhood as a result of the irresponsible behaviour of her father who is identified as the sole reason behind their impoverished lives. The drunken father figure and his neglect of the family evokes in her a sense of intolerance and indifference towards men in general that later affects her own married life and her relationships with all the other male characters of the novel. This vital aspect of Mary's character was ignored by the students while assessing her as representative of white supremacy. What they also ignored while taking note of the Mary–Moses relationship as a conventional master/servant or coloniser/colonised relationship was that besides being a servant, Moses also enters her life at a point of time when she finds it extremely difficult to deal with a life of penury with another unsuccessful man, Dick Turner. Overlooking this traumatic past of Mary, the woman, they read her as a white master figure who was cruel towards the blacks of Southern Rhodesia and consider her murder by Moses as justified as it gives a sense of power to the latter. The powerful notion of the colonised striking back at the colonisers is celebrated in such assumptions and blurs the nuances of the coloniser/colonised dichotomy.

I insisted that the students think of the character of Mary as a woman regardless of her race. I made them go through the details of her early life spent with her parents and later on her own as an independent woman. Mary's mother, according to Lessing, "made a confidante of Mary early. She used to cry over her sewing while Mary comforted her miserably, longing to get away, but feeling important too, and hating her father" (33). She also "inherited from her mother an arid feminism, which had no meaning in her own life at all, for she was leading the comfortable carefree existence of a single woman in South Africa, and she did not know how fortunate she was" (35). Her sudden decision to end this happy comfortable life of a single woman was triggered by another group of women who commented on her spinsterhood. A sudden and desperate urge to prove her womanhood hastened her decision to marry Dick whereas she was still not free from the traumatic experience of her parents' marriage and its consequent bitterness in the family. The students could see in this episode other forms of patriarchy where women also act as collaborators in the production of patriarchal notions in which marriage is associated with a woman's worth. Incidents like this which they could observe in their own lives made it possible for them to rethink the conventional notion of patriarchy beyond the general perception of men's oppression of women and see how it emerges as an important question in the gender politics within postcolonialism. Lessing does not portray the lives of other white women on the plantation except for making brief remarks on the wife of Charlie Slatter, a successful and authoritarian British settler. The absence in the novel of other white women's lives, both Afrikaner and British, prevents the reader from imagining the collective lives of white women in Southern Rhodesia and yet it is made clear that Mary was never welcomed by the white society. In fact, the lives of native women too were not depicted except for one casual remark on their physical appearance. The growth of Mary Turner as a woman in *The Grass Is Singing*, thus has been contrasted with the lives of other *men* in her life. Given this assumption, the students started analysing her character from a feminist point of view in which they understood her as a doubly oppressed woman. The comment made by Charlie Slatter, "Needs a man to deal with niggers. Niggers don't understand women giving them orders. They keep their own women in their right place" (23), in a very intimate and informal voice set the tone for such readings of the question of women in the colonial set up. Her attempts to run away from the miserable life on the farm and the subsequent compulsion to embrace the same life were read carefully by the students. They saw Mary's revulsion at the disobedient Moses as a woman's anger against the oppressive forces of patriarchy. They assessed her as a woman trapped by the forces of patriarchy where the feeling of attraction towards another man cannot be separated from the question of racial supremacy. They read Mary's twin sense of satisfaction and guilt expressed frequently as an instance of how her life is trapped between the dictates of race and gender. Lessing states:

> There was now a relation between them. For she felt helplessly in his power. Yet there was no reason why she should. Never ceasing for one moment to be conscious of his presence about the house, or standing silently at the back against the wall in the sun, her feeling was one of a strong and irrational fear, a deep uneasiness, and even – though this she did not know, would have died rather than acknowledge – of some dark attraction.
>
> (154)

Such complex pictures of women appear relevant in the students' contemporary societies as well, making it easier for them to address such issues outside the textual-theoretical framework.

IV

Lessing's inclusion of a 'progressive' young white man named Tony Marston as an important character opened up the avenues for debates on another dominant issue, that of identity. It emerged in the discussions not just as a theoretical framework offered by postcolonial theory but also as one of the relevant issues of the time. Tony Marston's so-called 'progressive' mind has been critiqued in the novel as, despite his rejection of the race division in South Africa in principle, he shudders at the sight of Mary being undressed by Moses or at their close proximity inside the Turner household. He finds it difficult to believe that a white woman, even when she is emotionally upset, can build an intimate relationship with a black servant whereas at the same time he accepts that similar exploitations of black women by white men is a common sight in the farms. The colour bar that is ingrained in the mind of this educated, progressive youth becomes a subject of inquiry in the postcolonial agenda of race and identity. The students seemed very displeased that white men like Charlie Slatter, Sergeant Denham and Marston show such disgust for Moses only because he is a black. They empathised with the latter as a victim of racial discrimination. The ideal or textual position that the students took at this point compelled me to remark that when we assume such positions we must not forget that we too very often participate in this process of discrimination. I mentioned the racist jokes that many of them share in social media platforms without ever thinking about it. I reminded them about the gamut of pictures and memes where black people are harassed and objectified every day on Facebook and WhatsApp that we share and laugh at. It helped the students realise the nuances involved in such acts of taking a position in the textual world which remains unaffected if we do not take into cognition the surrounding world in which the text is being read. The homogenised identity of an oppressed people that they earlier shared with Moses while identifying the white colonisers as the common oppressor was refuted after such readings that introduced them to the diversities of the colonial experience and its legacy in different parts of the world. In fact, they found themselves in a position similar to that of Tony Marston, caught between ideology and practice.

The discussions progressed from the rights of the natives in Southern Rhodesia to issues of identity and ethnicity in contemporary Assam. The sensitive issue of Assamese identity in the period after the Assam Movement (student-led protest across Assam on the issue of illegal immigrants) and the subsequent unfolding of events like ethnic conflict and violence among various linguistic minorities was not only a historical reality but is very much a current issue that students would be able to associate themselves with. At the same time, other ethnic movements in the wake of the Assam Movement had begun to occupy the everyday consciousness of people and these were also available for ready reference. Mention of the ethnic violence in Bodoland in 2015 in which conflict between the Bodo community and other non-Bodo communities living in Bodoland led to mass killing had also made the students aware of the violent possibilities of a politics of identity. The question of the native people's right over land that Lessing hints at gave them an opportunity to relate it to the numerous identity movements led by various ethnic communities in Assam, all of which were in some way connected to land. The defiant behaviour of Moses in the early part of the story and his gradual change of plan to take revenge on Mary and the final act of homicide were read by some of the students as a native's rebellion against the outsiders in his land. Parallels were drawn between Moses' position in the text and that of the indigenous people of Assam who time and again have felt threatened by immigrants and have regularly protested against their inclusion within the constitutional framework. The Assam Movement and others that followed it, along with the recent protests against the Citizenship Amendment Bill, 2016, were discussed as such assertions of rights over land. Several mass protests by farmers under the banner of an organisation named Krishak Mukti Sangram Samiti (in the state capital and several other places of Assam since 2010) against the building of big dams and indigenous rights over land were mentioned in our discussions. The mass gatherings at places like Dhemaji, Doyang-Tengani, Guwahati and other places in the recent years have served as instances of indigenous people's appeal for rights over land and these episodes made the students realise the politics involved in the insider/outsider dynamic. The sympathy that the students expressed equally for Moses and for various minority groups in Assam who feel they are threatened in their own land offered an occasion for looking at the undercurrents in the postcolonial notion of identity at one's own location.

Nevertheless, given the shyness of students – especially with their often uncertain English speaking skills – such concerns did not result in the kind of heated debate that often takes place in a classroom in History or Political Science (colleagues from these two departments have given such accounts). The constant pull of the texts that demand to be read in terms of their contextual reality that yet enable the reader to take note of and understand anew her own location decide the nature of what happens in the English Literature classroom. Teaching postcolonialism through its theory and literature in a classroom in this particular location made me rethink the entire dynamics of syllabus making. A text chosen with the specific purpose of introducing the students to new and important schools of thought like postcolonialism made it necessary to constantly negotiate the boundaries between text and the context both of the text and of the reader.

V

These various strands of reading occurred in the course of classroom discussions and in each of them, alongside the textual reality it was the position of the students in their contemporary society that guided them towards these varied interpretations. The picture of the colonial past in Southern Rhodesia, the legacies of such experience especially in the domains of race, language and gender in the first half of the twentieth century as witnessed by Lessing herself did not remain as distant events but were brought home to these students from twenty-first-century Assam quite intensively because of the receptive ground that had been created by their own local experience of similar situations. In fact, a connection was established between these three phases – the colonial times in South Africa, the early twentieth century experiences of Lessing and the early twenty-first-century happenings in Assam – where politics of power and identity were identified as larger operative forces. The text in this sense no longer functioned only as an occasion to study postcolonial theory with reference to the various frames of understanding offered by theorists; rather, cutting across the boundaries of cultural and temporal differences, it became a space where the living realities of the students could be acknowledged as valuable reading positions. In this process of reading the natives in South Africa as counterparts of the tribal groups of people living in Assam, the practice of English language as reflective of the current formation of linguistic identities such as Assamese and Bengali and the precarious positions of women across these societies, we realised that beyond postcolonial theories of race, language and gender, postcolonial literature itself offers multiple ways of addressing these issues.

The MA fourth semester syllabus in which the course on postcolonial fiction features consists of three other courses out of which two courses are on critical theory and contemporary critical thought and the fourth is an optional course that students select out of three different courses on American Literature, Indian Writing in English and Linguistics. The simultaneous reading of these other courses also framed the students' approaches to the text. If their reading of *Foe* in the same course gave them the opportunity to study the relationship between Susan Barton and Friday as another exposition of the interracial relationship like that of Mary Turner and Moses, their exposure to theories such as Psychoanalysis and Ecocriticism in the Critical Theory courses provided them with further tools to analyse the novel along the lines that our discussions of it had opened up. I came across seminar papers that adopted a psychoanalytical approach to the Mary–Moses relationship or undertook an ecocritical reading of the novel with reference to the plantation farms – additional insights that enhanced and consolidated their subversive readings of the novel and of their location instead of shifting their focus as might have been expected.

Given the rigid framework within which higher education at the universities and other institutions is conducted in India, a text prescribed in a syllabus is not something that can be approached at leisure and expanded upon over many sessions of interaction in the classroom. The text and the course is caught up in other dimensions of the teaching–learning process such as stipulated time for completion of the curriculum and set processes of examination and declaration of results – goals that have to be met and that interfere with the actual process of teaching that a teacher might like to undertake over the period of time she thinks necessary for her students to fully comprehend a text. The traditional mechanism of evaluating a student's knowledge of a subject on the basis of answers written in response to questions asked from a text plays a significant role in both the teacher's and the student's approach to a text. Further, the process of comprehensive and continuous evaluation in the Choice Based Credit System mandated nationwide by the UGC ensures that students are perpetually under the pressure of performing well in examinations. There is little scope within these structures to take time over a text, to reflect and understand and see the larger issues the literary text often points to. The complaint from students that they do not have enough time to study is really a result of these pressures. As a result they tend to collect readily available notes and summaries of the prescribed texts from unreliable sources on the internet. Such practices sometimes discourage a teacher from making a detailed study of the text in the class and serious concerns about the lack of students' interest in reading the actual text very often emerge in conversations among faculty members. It is therefore against all these factors, or rather by keeping these factors in mind, that the English teacher has to take the literary text to the classroom, hoping that she will be able to capture their interest by bringing the text as close as possible to the concerns closest to them.

Works cited

Lessing, Doris. *The Grass Is Singing*. London: Harper Perennial, 1950. Print.

Pujari, Leena. "Doing Sociology of Gender in the Classroom: Re-imagining Pedagogies", *Sociological Bulletin* 66.2 (2017): 145–157. https://doi.org/10.1177%2F0038022917708389. Accessed 22 October 2018.

Wang, Joy. "White Postcolonial Guilt in Doris Lessing's *The Grass Is Singing*." *Research in African Literature* 40.3 (2009): 37–47. https://muse.jhu.edu/article/268793. Accessed 12 January 2013.

10

UNCOMFORTABLE QUESTIONS AND ANSWERS

Teaching *Death in Venice*

Jeetumoni Basumatary

Teaching Thomas Mann's *Death in Venice* to a batch of postgraduate students turned out to be an unexpected, but delightful experience of venturing out of our comfort zones to look at our issues with middle-class society and its values. While I deviated from my usual practice of teaching, the students were able to read a European modern text by using knowledge from their local surroundings and relate to it in a better way. The present essay is about how I would have taught Thomas Mann's *Death in Venice*, and how I actually taught it to a batch of postgraduate students two years ago. I talk about how during the lectures, I tried to draw from various things that the students may have been familiar with, sometimes even using images from popular Hindi cinema. I begin by presenting the composition of my classroom, their diverse social backgrounds and their possible literacies. I then go on to talk about how I prepared to meet this class for Mann's *Death in Venice* and the teaching method I had decided to adopt. This is followed by a discussion of the method actually used in teaching the text and the result achieved, as well as the reason that led me to put aside my own standard method and adopt a new one.

I

While it is common to see students coming from various ethnic backgrounds in any Indian classroom, in Assam such diversity has its own unique composition. The students of my classroom at Cotton University belonged to various ethnic and linguistic groups such as Assamese, Bengali, Bodo, Karbi, Dimasa-Kachari and Rabha. The difference or diversity lay not only in their cultures and languages, but also in their social background. As a result of this diversity, the students had different beliefs and value systems, social behaviour and different levels of literacy. While some students were the third or fourth generation in their family to acquire higher education, some were first-generation learners and had different levels of confidence irrespective of the kind of knowledge they had or did not have. The diversity

DOI: 10.4324/9781003146209-11

of the classroom was such that while some had smoothly made their way through an English medium school and had got admission into a relatively premium institution like Cotton University, there were others who had to battle unfavourable conditions in order to emerge from remote places to study in a university located in the city. If a few grew up reading classics like *Alice in Wonderland* and *Treasure Island*, there were others who had not even seen these classics in television adaptations or heard the names of the books. There were yet others who might have done exceedingly well in an Assamese Literature or any other course, but had opted for the English course because of its market-value. Such diversity becomes critical for a teacher facing a group of students who not only belong to different ethnicities, but also come from varied social classes. To look at all of them as equally equipped for English Literature studies at the postgraduate level was virtually impossible and to lead them towards an understanding of a text such as Thomas Mann's *Death in Venice*, was a challenging task.

I was also facing students most of whom, having done their undergraduate level at the same university, may not have read anything of Modernism since it was only an optional paper at the undergraduate level. As the students came from diverse socio-cultural backgrounds with certain prior knowledge, ideas and notions, some of their perceptions on various subjects may have undergone often radical adjustments during the course of their three-year BA Major course in English Literature. A large section of the students appeared to lack the ability to read a text critically or recognise references and allusions despite the three years spent studying the discipline, qualities most essential for reading a highly symbolic text like *Death in Venice*. However, it was also evident from their responses that this lack of critical thinking in relation to their prescribed text did not extend to their day-to-day interaction with their surroundings. The composition of the class thus posed a challenge, wherein I had to try and identify a commonality among the students from diverse backgrounds and then attempt to build a bridge between their existing literacy and their reading of *Death in Venice*.

II

Death in Venice was a part of the Modern European Literature paper prescribed for the postgraduate students at Cotton University (then Cotton College State University). In this particular paper, the students were introduced to the major aesthetic developments of the late nineteenth and the early twentieth century Europe, such as Naturalism, Realism, Symbolism, Aestheticism, Imagism, Expressionism, Dadaism and Surrealism, apart from studying some major works such as Charles Baudelaire's "The Albatross", Rainer Maria Rilke's "Archaic Torso of Apollo" and Federico Garcia Lorca's "Sleepwalking Ballad". Apart from Mann's *Death in Venice*, the students also read texts such as Kafka's *Metamorphoses*, Dostoevsky's *Notes from the Underground*, and *The Outsider* by Albert Camus. In other words, the paper provided the students with a fair understanding of the concerns and trends in European Literature of the late nineteenth and the early twentieth century. *Death in Venice* is about an aging writer who suffers from writer's block and impulsively goes on a holiday to Venice, falls in love with a young boy and is unable to leave despite rumours of an epidemic. The novella has a lot to offer for discussion in the classroom such as homoeroticism, repression and frustration, obsession with propriety, art, the relationship of an artist with his work and his society, outward form and inner decay of the protagonist as well as the society. Written in a style that Mann himself calls 'Mythos plus Psychologie', it is highly symbolic and full of references to classical mythology and philosophy. While the mythological framework draws on Nietzsche's *The Birth of Tragedy*, Plato's *Phaedrus* and *Symposium* are the sources for the novella's philosophical references. Mann also derives from Freud's various works in order to delve into the psycho-physical world of his protagonist.

With *Death in Venice*, I imagined very lively and interactive sessions in the classroom about art, death, decadence, the inter-textual nature of the novella and everything else that the text had to offer for discussion. I enjoy teaching texts that are dense with inter-textual references and those that throw up an extensive range of matter for discussion. I wanted to take the students through a comprehensive reading of the texts by encouraging them to recognise the symbolic significance of various references brought in by the author. By looking at the various inter-textual references and understanding their significance within the text as well as outside it, I believed that I would be able to make the students see the relevance of reading such a text as a part of the syllabus.

The three main readings of *Death in Venice* are psychoanalytical, autobiographical, and aesthetic (specifically as a neoclassical discussion of art), all of which make use of the various allusions and references to other texts. The three main interpretations notwithstanding, *Death in Venice* shows us the predicament of the modern man torn between irreconcilable extremes, living in a disenchanted world threatened by war and destruction. In Georg Lukács' words, Thomas Mann presents to us a bourgeois Germany and in *Death in Venice*, he presents a representative bourgeois artist and his predicament. Apart from reading Lukács' *Essays on Thomas Mann* (1964), especially the chapter "In Search of Bourgeois Man", I also read "'Myth Plus Psychology': A Style Analysis of *Death in Venice*" (1956), where the writer André von Gronicka speaks about Mann's peculiar style of combining the real and the transcendent, leading readers beyond the real and the psychological to a magical world of apocalyptic vision. In a somewhat similar tone, Lukács calls Mann a realist while labelling the form of his writing as 'unnaturalistic' (Lukacs). The other two essays that I looked at as a preparation for my lecture were, Tom Hayes and Lee Quinby's "The Aporia of Bourgeois Art: Desire in Thomas Mann's *Death in Venice*" (1998) and Gary Johnson's "*Death in Venice* and the Aesthetic Correlative" (2004). The above readings, I hoped, would help me in interpreting the text for the students as a modernist one that portrayed the conflict between affirmation and resistance to bourgeois ideals. I had hoped to dwell on this conflict by bringing in the Nietzschean binaries of the Apollonian and Dionysian characteristics of an artist, as well as the Freudian analysis of repression. With Gary Johnson's "*Death in Venice* and the Aesthetic Correlative", I would have introduced the students to the new ethnographic and cultural turn that criticism on *Death in Venice* was taking lately, as interpreters were not only recognising the European north and south dichotomy between German bourgeois restraint and Venetian abundance, but also identifying Aschenbach, the protagonist, as a precursor of the early twentieth-century homosexual.

III

While the prospect of teaching such a text appears to be very attractive due to the various aesthetic developments and literary concerns and trends, the same qualities may stand as an obstacle to a successful interaction in the classroom for various reasons. An acquaintance with modernism and its major trends from undergraduate courses would draw better informed if not more nuanced responses than in the classroom situation where no such familiarity could be assumed. My own experience of teaching texts like Mary Shelley's *Frankenstein*, Alice Walker's *The Color Purple*, or Toni Morrison's *Beloved* to undergraduate students of a Delhi University college had taught me that a mere analysis or interpretation of the texts is not enough. I needed to help students towards a critical reading of the texts so that they would also understand their significance in the overall discipline of the humanities. At Cotton University, with a different undergraduate course as preparation I realised that interpreting the text required much more groundwork and the gulf between the world they read about in their texts and the world they were in needed more effort to be bridged. This disjunction between the world of the texts and the world of the readers appeared to be much higher in my current classroom than in the Delhi college, irrespective of the places students came from. This gulf was between the metropolis and the smaller city, between different degrees of exposure to cultures and lifestyles – to cultures other than Indian, to urban lifestyles, expectations and opportunities and the availability of everything – books, films, ideas – on a larger scale. In the Cotton University classroom, there were students who despite having spent three years studying English Literature at the undergraduate level had read little else besides the prescribed texts. A host of other factors contributed to the general malaise that students seemed to have, especially in the humanities, where the immediately discernible opportunities and 'scope' for employment were limited. There is a reduced capacity for imaginative thinking and for empathy, qualities required to benefit from any course of study. The difficulties in the classroom often stem from factors like these. The challenge is, of course, much more evident when students are faced with issues and ideas that are still not commonly talked about in the 'sheltered' worlds they come from. For instance, how does one interpret a text like *Death in Venice* for a class that goes into an uncomfortable silence or breaks into giggles as soon as the word 'homosexual' is mentioned? How does one interpret for the students, the layers of meaning hidden in the language of Webster's *The Duchess of Malfi*, seeing them look furtively at each other and smile at the mention of phrases like 'lusty widow', 'phallic symbol' or 'rape imagery'?

These problems appear to be more challenging in institutions situated in remote places far away from the metropolis, and where the divide between the world of the texts they read and their immediate existences is considerable. In addition to that, most students may have enrolled in the discipline because they believed it would be the easiest of all subjects, or because they wanted to learn how to speak the English language. On the other hand, many of us English teachers, walk into a classroom, especially at the post-graduate level, with the preconceived notion that our students would know and comprehend the language and have certain foundational knowledge about what English Literature is. Some indeed do, but in a place like Assam, there is always a large section of the class with whom we have to begin from scratch. Getting students to read the entire text on their own, help them to understand it well enough so that more complex issues can be brought in and to teach the texts taking into consideration the other kinds of literacies they come equipped with, are the initial challenges. Therefore, initial lectures are on the text – a close reading of the text accompanied by examples and references from their surroundings and from things with which they are familiar to aid comprehension. So, a class on the nature of the court in *The Duchess of Malfi* may involve a reference to Indian politics or even the institution's student politics, and a lecture about Tadzio rising from the sea after his swim in *Death in Venice* may involve a mention of a female film-star rising seductively from the sea. Together we try to get close to the text and its world before going on to supplementary material. Interpretations and critical reception of the text are only referred to after the students have read the text on their own.

I began by introducing students to the three main readings (psychoanalytical, autobiographical, and aesthetic) of *Death in Venice*, hoping to lead them through the text and push them towards a critical consciousness that would help them to establish a connection between the study of literature or a text like *Death of Venice* with their own lives and milieu. Having decided to begin with the autobiographical interpretation of *Death in Venice*, I gave an introduction to Thomas Mann, and read excerpts from his *A Sketch of My Life* (1961). This involved telling the story behind the writing of the novella, from Mann's initial intention to write about Goethe's love for a much younger girl called Ulrike von Levetzow, to the development of the story into that of his own love for Wladyslaw Moes, whom he had met in the Grand Hotel des Bains at Venice when he had visited the place with his wife in the summer of 1911. The transformation of the story from a heterosexual love story of Goethe and Ulrike to the homosexual love of Gustav von Aschenbach, an aged writer, for Tadzio, a much younger boy, has its source in Thomas Mann's own suppressed homosexuality. The mention of the word 'homosexual' in connection with Thomas Mann drew a few reactions from the students, which are worth mentioning here. While there were a few in the class who looked down and pretended not to have heard the word, there were two boys sitting in the front row who nudged one another and could not hide their giggles. My first reaction was to scold the boys before I realised that while they found the very mention of the word 'homosexual' funny, the rest of the class had gone into an uncomfortable silence. This made me think that while during the course of their past three years in the discipline of English Literature, the students might have been accustomed to many such words that are considered taboo in our society, the word 'homosexual' might still be a very new one in their vocabulary and the idea of 'homosexuality' associated with a figure of authority such as the author of the text they are reading, still unthinkable. This might be the result of the kind of the sanitized education system we have in India, as well as the society we live in where discussions of sexuality are virtually taboo. Unlike students in the more urban-metropolitan milieu of Delhi University who would have read Chugtai's "Lihaf" or Alice Walker's *The Color Purple* by the time they reached the MA class, the three-year undergraduate programme in English at Cotton University offered no occasion for them to become easy with such notions.

Though homosexuality has a long history in India, it was criminalized by the British through a section introduced into the Indian Penal Code in 1864. The Indian subcontinent in the nineteenth century came under the influence of England's Victorian morality and values. While there is a wide range of literature available in India about homosexuality and the transgender or eunuch community is a visible presence, there is a great degree of illiteracy about it among people. Societies throughout India, irrespective of their exposure to liberal ideas, are still hesitant to speak aloud when it comes to matters such as sexuality. It is not considered acceptable in decent society to talk about such matters in the open or acknowledge having any knowledge about them. So to be confronted with a discussion on homosexuality in the sacred environment of the classroom must have disconcerted the students. They responded by looking intently at their desks and pretending not to have noticed what I said. The ones who went off into uncontrollable giggles must have conjured up in their minds the stereotypical image of a eunuch or the mostly farcical or serio-comic representation of same sex relationships in popular Bollywood cinema. A large section of people in India, especially in places away from the metropolises, still conflate male homosexuals and transgenders in the same category. While lesbianism is still largely non-existent in their perception, male homosexuality is associated with notions of lost masculinity. A homosexual man, then is associated with the image of a eunuch or 'hijra', an unnatural presence in society, and hence considered marginal and laughable.

IV

The initial response of the class compelled a change in method. Instead of introducing the students to the psychoanalytic, or the aesthetic aspects of Mann criticism, I decided to use *Death in Venice* as a channel for the students to confront the set notions of their societies and raise questions about seemingly unbreakable customs, by focussing on Lukács' reading of Mann's work as representative of bourgeois concerns. Nietzsche's dichotomy of Dionysian and Apollonian attributes of an artist and Freud's theory of repression of passions and their possible outburst were incorporated into our discussion of the modern man's affirmation and rejection of bourgeois ideals and values. However, I led the class through the text, chapter by chapter, and picked up for discussion parts that would force them to reflect on their surroundings.

Death in Venice announces its climax, the death of the protagonist in the very title. After the title, the rest of the novella appears to be like a long obituary, prefiguring the approaching death of Aschenbach through various images. There is a sense of doom and foreboding from the very first line which goes, 'On a spring afternoon in 19—, the year in which for months on end so grave a threat seemed to hang over the peace of Europe …' (197). The reference could be to World War I and the threat that looms over Europe is its disintegration. The threat of war over Europe was also a threat arising in the early twentieth century to the ordered middle-class society that had continued from the nineteenth century. The suggestion I gave to the class was to look at Aschenbach, the 50-year old, uptight, aristocratic European, a national writer with his firm belief in a life of discipline as symbolic of an ordered nineteenth century Europe that breaks into chaos in the early twentieth century. While the threat that looms over Europe is war, the one that hovers above Aschenbach is the potential disintegration of his restrained and disciplined life into wantonness and sensuality.

The mention of Aschenbach as a 'national writer' led us to the discussion about what makes a writer, a national writer. A student began by pointing out that a 'national writer' must be recognised by the state, win a nationally recognised award apart from being popular. On being asked whether a national writer would be pro-establishment, they all agreed and when prodded further as to the implications of being pro-establishment, the students at first looked surprised that such a question should be put to them. We talked about the various writers who have returned their awards received from the Sahitya Akademi, the apex literary body of India, in protest against the growing intolerance in the country, and the possibility of being a nationally proclaimed writer as well as a spokesperson for truth,

176

but not necessarily always pro-establishment. During the discussions, examples of works like Salman Rushdie's *The Satanic Verses* (1988), Rohinton Mistry's *Such a Long Journey* (1991), and Wendy Doniger's *The Hindus* (2009), which were banned or faced official disapproval for opinions expressed in them, were brought in, in order to try and understand what makes a book acceptable or unacceptable. Aschenbach, it is said, is always restrained, doing what is expected of a man of his class, writing what would appeal to his audience and propel him towards his much-desired fame. His readers recognised themselves in his heroes "who work on the brink of exhaustion, who labour and are heavy-laden, who are worn out already but still stand upright" (205). More than being pro-establishment, he is acutely desirous of being accepted as a good writer by his readers, which is why, as required by the middle-class readers, Aschenbach chooses to "repudiate knowledge as such, to reject it, to step over it with head held high" (206). At this point in the discussion, the students, now equipped with the understanding that Aschenbach caters to the middle-class, are led back to the reading of the protagonist as a symbol of the ordered nineteenth century Europe. This return is necessary to look at the protagonist of *Death in Venice* as representative of the bourgeoisie, and his psychological repression as symbolic of bourgeois Europe's repression or moral uprightness. Aschenbach's constant illness despite a disciplined life symbolizes the rot beneath the facade of middle-class morality and respectability. The storm that seems to be brewing can then be interpreted as the threat of war that looms over the smug European bourgeoisie, or as the sudden outburst of Aschenbach's repressed passions.

Through Gustav von Aschenbach's character, Mann shows us the modern man who lives under constant pressure to maintain a facade of rational and ordered middle class values, while his subconscious mind refuses to adhere to those values. There are several moments in the novella when Aschenbach's extreme restraint and self-control threaten to break down and leave his inner passions exposed, until we reach the fourth chapter when he finally surrenders to those passions. His attraction towards the young and beautiful Polish boy at Lido, his inability to escape from Venice despite the threat of cholera, his failure to warn the Polish family about the impending danger and ultimately his happy return to Lido after an attempt to leave the island, are all moments when his repressed nature threaten to break free and reveal itself. From the fourth chapter onwards, we see Aschenbach feeling relaxed and happy even in inactivity; something that had agitated him in his youth, burdened as he was by his ambition for fame. His open acknowledgment of his emotions also arouses in him a desire to write again. The narrator tells us that Aschenbach had been wanting to write about "a certain important cultural problem" for some time; but now he had a strong desire to write it in his own words in the presence of Tadzio using "the boy's physique for a model as he wrote" (239). In discussing Aschenbach's mental conflict, Freud's "Civilization and Its Discontents" was brought in, in order to highlight the predicament of the modern man who is frustrated by the restriction imposed upon him by society, and who is under a serious threat of disorder due to the repression of his powerful instincts. Aschenbach's extreme form of self-discipline and his obsession with gaining fame through his literary works were seen as attempts of his unconscious mind to hide his most basic impulses. His momentary lapse into a hallucinatory day-dream of the tropical landscape after seeing the red-haired man outside the mortuary chapel provides us a glimpse into his *id*, his unconscious, where his two basic instincts, Eros (moist and warm tropical landscape symbolizing sensuality and fecundity) and Thanatos (the death–desire represented by the cemetery as well as the red haired man outside the church attached to the cemetery, like Satan, luring him towards the forbidden are located). In Aschenbach's frustration or failure to write, we see an artist whose desire for serving his society through his work has led to suppression of the dark impulses inherited from his Bohemian musician mother. His cold, calculated and artificial art is a result of stifled spontaneity. His formalist art affirms bourgeois values and reflects the repressive structure of bourgeois society.

Considered from the point of the Nietzschean opposition between the Apollonian and Dionysian elements of the artistic worlds, Aschenbach is an essentially Apollonian artist relying heavily on form, clarity and restraint. The Dionysian impulses of emotion, spontaneity and sensuality are disregarded by the protagonist, and his darker erotic and libidinal energies are inhibited. In the protagonist of *Death in Venice*, we see no hint of what Nietzsche calls 'Kunsttriebe', the ideal 'artistic impulse' born out of a fusion of the Apollonian and Dionysian impulses and achieved by Aeschylus and Sophocles in their great tragedies. Instead of attempting to build a fine balance between the two impulses and create great artistic work, Aschenbach attempts to suppress the Dionysian for the sake of the Apollonian. As a result, his art is not a result of spontaneous creation, but of studied effort consisting of two or three hours of his early morning hours, spent daily, at the altar of art.

V

Aschenbach's story allowed my students to think about individual liberty vis-a-vis the society. While I had begun by struggling to find a common ground of reference for the students coming from diverse backgrounds, I realised that the issue of an individual's conflict with his society can be the starting point. We explored the necessity of individual liberty or freedom from societal pressures for the expression of spontaneity not only in art, but also in our day-to-day existence. The notion of 'being true to the self' was posed against middle class notions of morality and propriety. While the classical references and the symbolic nature of the text could not be avoided, Aschenbach's predicament as a modern man overwhelmed by his class and society's pressures became the central focus of our discussions.

Questions such as whether a writer should be concerned about being read and accepted by his or her audience, whether he should be careful not to express any opinion that might hurt the public's sentiment, and write only that which is acceptable and pro-establishment, or whether he or she should write truthfully were explored. The responsibility of a writer as well as that of a person towards his or her society was brought up during one of the discussions. The students were asked to think about their own society's notions about propriety and acceptable behaviour, as well as about the middle-class preoccupation with respectability and reputation. Moral and upright behaviour, respect for elders, obedience towards them and not talking back or asking questions are some codes of conduct deeply embedded in Indian society. While urban societies in the metropolitan cities have been able to shake off or negotiate with some of these middle-class values, they are still largely prevalent in the rest of the country. During the discussion in the class, many students spoke about their own experiences, and shared what they would have wanted to do in certain circumstances and what they actually did, bound as they were by their knowledge of what was expected of them. Some of the students spoke about occasions when they were asked by elders not to behave in a particular manner or say certain things in front of certain people. They also spoke about how often they have had to censor themselves with the fear that what they say may be wrong or would be disliked by somebody. Many of them had never asked a question in the class, never argued or debated with elders and even if they thought about politics, human rights or the general conditions of their time and place had never articulated such thoughts.

Aschenbach's homosexuality, its suppression and the author's frustration were discussed as a reflection of Thomas Mann's own frustration. While Mann's position as a representative German writer made it almost impossible for his early commentators to look at his sexuality, the author himself was open about it, if not publicly, at least in his diaries. The tendency of scholars and commentators to provide symbolic value to the presence of homosexuality in Mann's works changed significantly with the publication of his diaries which revealed his truth. The blind eye turned by commentators towards Mann's sexuality was referred to in the class as an example of middle-class tendency to refrain from speaking about subjects considered to be taboo. This was done to further our discussion about the way middle class morality and values tend to govern nature and behaviour in society. It was also an attempt to make the students confront their discomfort with the notion of homosexuality and look at it without the lens of society's heteronormative values.

The class had already expressed their opinion about homosexuality in one of the earlier classes through their awkward silences and giggles. After the discussions of the novel, we now confronted anew the acceptability of homosexuality and especially the ability to talk about it without subjecting it to normative judgements. Aschenbach attempts to disguise his sensual attraction towards Tadzio in platonic terms by placing himself in the position of Socrates. The students were hesitant to voice aloud their opinions on being asked why Socrates's admiration for young boys should be antithetical to his wisdom, and why Socrates cannot be considered both wise and a lover of male companion. As the students reflected on this problem, they also came round to reconsider what is acceptable or normal behaviour, and who decides these things. They recalled the several occasions when we have judged a person on the basis of his or her attire, or other superficial aspects without realising that 'good' or 'bad', 'acceptable' or 'unacceptable' behaviour may often be arbitrary social constructs. To bring the idea closer home, the girls in the classroom were asked to think about the various occasions they have been judged on the basis of their hairstyle, make-up and attire, or the number of times they have been ordered by an elder to behave like a 'decent girl'. The boys were asked to think about how they may have refrained from shedding tears, or expressing their emotions as they tried to conform to an interpretation of society's expectations.

Our discussions led to the conclusion that homosexuality is part of a person's being 'true to the self'. It is in a person's nature. Just as a person's choice of attire, hairstyle, makeup, food habits, etc. are instances of normal behaviour, so is his/her sexuality. Emphasising the man-made nature of society's customs and values, it was pointed out that like so many other aspects, even the normative nature of the man–woman binary is a mere assumption established by patriarchal society. As a result of this assumption, heterosexual relationships are considered to be normal while other kinds of sexualities are rejected. Homophobia exists due to society's discriminatory tendency to frown upon all that is considered non-normative. The fact that homosexuality has been present in India throughout history in society, art and literature was brought up during one of the discussions to tell the students that it is not a modern phenomenon derived from western civilization. That Section 377 of the Indian Penal Code that criminalised homosexuality is a British colonial legacy and had its basis in Britain's nineteenth century Victorian morality, also came up during the discussion. The above-mentioned moral laws were allowed to continue until 2009 and then reinstated in 2013 due to the cultural intolerance of homosexuality. As a counter to a still prevailing mindset that had initially interfered with our reading of *Death in Venice*, we noted developments like gay rights activism, the annual pride parades and the gradually more nuanced representations of same sex relationships in mainstream cinema. As we read through the novel I discovered that my tacit intention beyond teaching the literary text, was also to 'normalise' homosexuality in the perception of the students, and the text acquired a rich undercurrent from our brief foray into findings in modern medicine and psychiatry that looks at same-sex orientation.

In addressing a group of youngsters who had been cultured in obedience and discipline, being apolitical and providing unquestioning respect, such a discussion proved to be enriching. Many of the students realized that what appears to be normal may be wrong and deserve some rethinking and that being political and being a rational human being are the same and cannot be boxed into different categories. The discussion about the responsibility of a writer or a person towards society, and the practice of Aschenbach to write about what pleases his readers were done to bring home the perception that while it is important to be polite and respectful to one and all, and while it is a natural human tendency to desire appreciation and acceptance, it is also equally important to have a voice and raise it for truth without any fear. As we concluded reading the novel, the students appeared to realise that questioning and doubting accepted beliefs and long-established notions and values, and returning to them or moving away after a better understanding, is an acceptable part of their education. The discussion on homosexuality I believe, managed to remove, if not all, at least some of the students' prejudices.

While the first lecture on the text may have given the impression of a difficult road ahead, it ended on a satisfying note. The response of the students to the introductory lecture had made me wonder at the purpose of engaging with such a text for a group of students who are merely going to read it as a story of an old man in love with a young boy in a foreign land. However, the discussions that came up in the course of the lectures and the rethinking and reassessment of our cultural, social and gender orientations were deeply fulfilling. It was a semester where we burst the comfortable bubbles of conventional thought, shaking long-established notions about respectability and 'good' or restrained behaviour, looking at them objectively and returning to them with a changed perspective. Even if the students do not retain any of the discussions on art, the artist's relationship to his art or the quest for the sublime, they perhaps learnt to question set ideas especially those that are against people or groups perceived to be different, to answer uncomfortable questions and to be comfortable speaking about the unspeakable. With this, *Death in Venice* would have done its job and validated its presence in the syllabus for students of Assam.

Works cited

Freud, Sigmund. *A General Introduction to Psychoanalysis*. Translated by G. Stanley Hall. New York: Horace Liveright Publisher, 1920. Project Gutenberg Ebook. Accessed 10 January 2017.

———. *Civilization and its Discontents*. Translated by Joan Riviere. New York: Dover Publications Inc, 1994. Print.

Gronicka, André von. ""Myth plus Psychology": A Style Analysis of Death in Venice." *The Germanic Review: Literature, Culture, Theory*. 31.3(1956):191–205. https://doi.org/10.1080/19306962.1956.11786846. Accessed 10 January 2017.

Hayes, Tom and Lee Quinby. "The Aporia of Bourgeois Art: Desire in Thomas Mann's Death in Venice." *Criticism*. 31.2(1989): 159–177. www.jstor.org/stable/23113351. Accessed 21 February 2017.

Johnson, Gary. "Death in Venice and the Aesthetic Correlative." *Journal of Modern Literature*. 27.3 (2004): 83–96. https://doi.org/10.1353/jml.2004.0076. Accessed 21 February 2017.

Lukács, Georg. "In Search of Bourgeois Man." *Essays on Thomas Mann*. Trans. Stanley Mitchell. London: Merlin Press, 1964. Print.

———. *A Sketch of My Life*. Translated by H.T. Lowe-Porter. New York: Random House, 1960. Print.

Mann, Thomas. "Death in Venice." *Death in Venice and Other Stories*. Translated by David Luke. London: Vintage Books, 1998. Print.

Nietzsche, Friedrich. *The Birth of Tragedy or Hellenism and Pessimism*. Translated by William August Haussmann. London: George Allen & Unwin Ltd, 1910. Project Gutenberg Ebook. Accessed 10 January 2017.

Plato. *Symposium and Phaedrus*. New York: Dover Publications Inc., 1993. Google Book Search. Accessed 2 March 2017.

11

A PORTRAIT OF THE RESEARCHER AS A YOUNG TEACHER

James Joyce's *A Portrait of the Artist as a Young Man* in the classroom[1]

Jinan Ashraf

A curious passage marks the opening paragraphs of Book IV of James Joyce's *Finnegans Wake* (1939), where a hand emerges from the cloud—in the midst of what seems to be an apocalyptic showdown of indiscernible forces, a veritable Armageddon where the resurrected "Eireweeker" seems to face the "wohld bludyn world" (*FW* 593.3)—drawing out a chart "expanded" (593.19), the contents of which are not immediately accessible to the reader. Like most passages in this daunting work, I found it difficult to proceed through this section without spending some amount of time pensively eyeing the text and diligently turning pages back and forth to look for a clue that I might have missed. What this particular description did recall to my mind, however, were diverse images from across the scriptures: of Biblical Moses and the Commandments, of the Abrahamic "Book of Fate", and the Koranic *lawh-al-mahfouz*, all of which variously imply a chart or preserved tablet of one or other kind with a set of inscriptions. The nature and scope of these inscriptions (on the one hand .... written) inviolable, and on the other, always poised on the brink of being "expanded", drawn out, or written, amused me because it drew my attention to a conception of destiny that was, in my understanding of the Abrahamic notions at least, paradoxically inevitable and contingent at one and the same time. And yet, one of the glosses on this passage (Campbell and Robinson 1944: 339) alerted me to the instance of the chart being blank, "unwritten", signalling a *ricorso*, or the beginning of a new cycle of history about to take its course.

There I was, arched over the text contemplating the notion of a *palimpsest* of history, one that was always-already written, variously overwritten, yet to be written, and hence unwritten, when my co-supervisor first suggested to me the idea of teaching a representative Joyce text to his II year MA students in his four-credit survey course on "Twentieth-Century British Literature and Thought". This text was to be *A Portrait of the Artist as a*

DOI: 10.4324/9781003146209-12

Young Man (1916), Joyce's first successful experiment in the form of the novel that I thought took the concerns of *Dubliners* to its logical end (or beginning, as we may venture with Joyce). As a new researcher and aspiring teacher, the sense of excitement and gratitude that followed was immense. This was soon to quickly transition, however, into an overwhelming sense of awareness of the various challenges and difficulties of introducing a writer of such complexity as James Joyce, and teaching—if such a thing could be attempted at all— a work of intricate texture such as *A Portrait of the Artist as a Young Man* (hereafter *Portrait*). I recalled how circumspectly even such twentieth-century-thinkers as Derrida, that fine writer of the high *Joycean* line, treaded while addressing an audience on the subject of Joyce, speaking, not a little warily, of a "hypermnesia" that bound those who, like him, were overwhelmed and obliged, at once, by the Joycean oeuvre: the feeling of "not [yet] having begun" to read Joyce, of "being as it were at stake ... from the outset" (Derrida 2001: 352). How was I then to begin to prepare myself for a work of this kind?

As a cursory glance at the syllabi offered by English departments across the country would reveal, selections from across Joyce's works figure broadly in modernist course outlines and are taught predominantly at the undergraduate and postgraduate levels: usually a short story from *Dubliners* (1914), most commonly "The Dead", or *Portrait* (1916), and in some parts of the country, even *Ulysses* (1922). Whether these texts are taught with the aid of online annotations, glossed over due to time constraints of the semester-bound course, or examined in parts to illustrate motifs, symbols, or characters, today students of English Literature are often called upon to demonstrate their acquaintance with Joyce's works, or in most cases, *at least* the earlier works. These early works are often considered more accessible than the ones to follow later, set as they are in the method of "scrupulous meanness". To questions such as "Can Joyce be read at all?", answers prove futile; it certainly does not help the more pressing fact that in spite of this overwhelming question, his works *still* figure in our syllabi, and for the most part, teachers and students in this part of the world are still at odds with each other in deciding whence to proceed when confronted by Joyce's *spectral* presence in their classrooms as well as their literatures.

Therefore the broader question that I was grappling with, while examining the relatively lesser addressed question of teaching and learning collaborations on Joyce texts across the country, was how best I could work with a diverse classroom profile and how I could conceptualize an effective learning design for the students. I was well aware that the classroom comprises a mixed group of students coming together as a class from diverse regional and educational backgrounds, with differing levels of proficiency in the English language. In most cases, the students chiefly *receive* the reading assumptions and habits that have traditionally guided reading and pedagogical practices as well as choice of texts in the English classroom. Although the students have, on previous occasions, come across a variety of texts that have all been demanding in their own ways, in different degrees for different students, the question at hand was what these students have by way of preparation to interact with a *Joyce* text, one that demands a different, and often exacting, set of reading and language skills from students of language and literature. How best could a teacher proceed in attempting to bring a purportedly *difficult*, culturally different text "home" to a diverse group of students, for whom the "us/other" dichotomy was only too familiar in their daily lives?

"Preparatory to anything else": decisions and revisions prior to teaching

I recall an episode in the last chapter of *Portrait* where Stephen Dedalus imagines, "restless and helpless", an English classroom hard at work at the bidding of a dull pedagogue. He envisions the sight of his classmates "meekly" bent over their note books, recording, painstakingly, "nominal definitions", "essential definitions", "examples" or "dates of birth or death", "chief works", and "a favourable and an unfavourable criticism side by side" (195). This scene strikes me as an enduring description of pre-dominant scenes of instruction in English classrooms *anywhere* in the world, and strikes close to home because the *teacher-as-preacher* pedagogical model most sustained in *Portrait* is also one that perhaps generations of Indian students of English Literature across the country might be able recall in their experience of education in colleges and universities of various national accreditations, one that perhaps still persists in several institutions even today.

How can the English classroom then be made participatory, responsive, and alive to the text that they are studying? What preparatory lessons can the teacher herself draw from harsh portraits of pedagogy pervading the very text that she intends to "teach"? These were some of the questions that I was beginning to consider at length, in addition to questions related to designing the most effective ways to enable the students to contextualize the writer and his works for themselves. Identifying the gaps that seemed to have emerged in their conceptions of reading was also a pressing question that needed to be addressed immediately in order to facilitate an understanding of modernist fiction firstly and Joyce next. What the class required, then, was a series of connecting links from the novels that they were *familiar* with. Drawing on their prior knowledge and experience of having read texts from a little before and after the 1910s, the class could gradually work themselves through to a discussion of the key concerns of modern fiction before arriving at Joyce's own timeline, where students could begin to briefly examine the Anglo-Irish tradition that was to frame some of his most powerful literary concerns. A trajectory such as this would perhaps equip the students with a kind of working background to the changes in the novel prior to the beginning of the twentieth century in order to be able to contextualize and place Joyce and his reputation for "obscurity" against the larger question of the tendency in modernist fiction to "contrive means of being free" (qtd. in Bradshaw 2008: 11) to set down what the author chooses to, in a mode of self-expression that the author finds best suited to the task at hand. Here, the students could also begin to ask themselves why it was necessary for modern writers to do this, and how these terms were met.

I was also beginning to realize that it would be necessary to involve the class in an engaging discussion around the development of the "thought" implied in the title of the survey course "Twentieth-Century British Literature and Thought". The clue to this, I began to reason to myself, would be the political discussion at the heart of *Portrait*, seen in the Christmas dinner episode in the Dedalus household against the backdrop of Parnell's fall in the late nineteenth century. This episode takes its cue from the long drawn liberal debate of mid-nineteenth century British politics that culminated in the pressure for/against Home Rule in Ireland in the early twentieth-century. Some background or sense of this debate was necessary, I felt, for students to appreciate the varying political strands taken by Simon Dedalus and Mr Casey, on the one hand, and Dante, on the other, in the early episodes of *Portrait*.

Class on *Portrait* at the University of Hyderabad, October 2018

On first stepping into the classroom, I was curious to find out what the students had made of reading *Portrait*, particularly those who were encountering the work for the first time. In the discussion of the reading experience that followed, I found that a majority of the students had succeeded in wading through all five chapters of the novel, but not without a little difficulty, as most of them eventually confided, often turning to obliging passages of explanation in their variously annotated editions of the text. The students confessed that whilst some of the dense passages in Latin and certain obscure references to Irish history flew past them, they *did* find themselves taken irresistibly on board on account of the impressions of the young Stephen and the language that seemed to change as he grew up into a young man. The students also pointed out how certain phrases and usages in the text—such as when Uncle Charles "repaired to his outhouse" (67)—seemed to them odd or unfamiliar, and were unsure as to what to make of sentences that carried such peculiar turns of expressions. As students began to warm up to the discussion, opening up and talking about their particular problems with the reading of the text, one of them made bold to quip:

Why does Joyce write the way he does?
How does one begin to answer this question? And yet, this was a question that was as real as it was urgent. I could only hope that the class,

including myself, would be able to address the question by proceeding to examine a few crucial factors that led to Joyce's formulation of his theory of fiction. For this, I told them that often the clue to understanding one modernist writer was to look at them through another. Writing a little before Joyce and offering astute commentary on matters literary and social was the writer Virginia Woolf, who, in such essays as "Modern Fiction" and such series as *The Common Reader* attempted to lay out some of the common concerns of modern fiction and reading in general in an era that was beginning to take stock of, and even question, its predecessors. And yet one had to ask what it was about the novel form that had irked the likes of modernist writers such as Virginia Woolf, James Joyce, Dorothy Richardson, and Wyndham Lewis.

The tyranny of coherence and linearity that has had the conventional writer "in thrall" often has us in its grip as well when we read a novel. The pursuit of a "go-ahead" plot is one that readers have grown accustomed to, and have often found difficult to do without. The conventional novel has traditionally appealed to us readers for various reasons: for its neat arrangement of events in a time-sequence, for its linear pattern of a well-defined and discernible beginning, middle, and end, and for the distinct entourage of characters that come to the aid of plot. But, more importantly, the novel has been read ravenously for its straightforward plot, offering readers a neat tie-up and rationalization of causes and effects of events in a story, followed by a rough and ready estimation of its possible meaning(s). Drawing from Woolf, I tell them that writers have for a long time been asked to "provide a plot", "provide a love interest", and an "embalming" air of "probability" (qtd. in Bradshaw 2008: 8) to make the novel appealing to readers. But the question that Woolf raises is whether life was "like this": one where people, places, and circumstances are, at one or other time, known or knowable. For the modernists writing in the 1900s, the conventions of the novel, so steeped in the rigid representation of character and reality, seemed ill-equipped and even "hostile" (Parsons 2007: 2) to the depiction of living in a new age, replete with technological, social, and political changes.

What would happen, I ask my students, if a writer was free to set down what he/she chose to? What would happen if, instead of ascribing to a set of conventions established long before their time, the author was to take up the exploration of the "unknown" and the "uncircumscribed" (qtd. in Bradshaw 2008: 9)? What Woolf seemed to be suggesting here was that it was time that modern writers began discussing the "proper stuff" of fiction, which was "a little other than custom would have us believe" (qtd. in Bradshaw 2008: 9). The problem that was emerging before modernist writers, then, was how they could begin to "contrive means of being free" to write about what the author chose to, whether it was something "hitherto ignored" or set in a "different outline of form" (qtd. in Bradshaw 2008: 11) not always comprehensible to their readers.

187

Yet another modernist writer who spoke keenly of the changes in modern fiction and hailed the need for new forms, new tools, and new parallels was T. S. Eliot. For wasn't it Eliot after all who said that *Ulysses* (1922) had given him the "surprise, delight, and terror" that he required? What made Joyce's works so significant for Eliot was its pointed recognition of and dissatisfaction with the shortcomings of the traditional form of the novel. Joyce's works marked a radical departure from these conventions as he inaugurated his freedom as a writer to set down, as Woolf had already pointed out for us, a subject matter of his choice with the "courage to say what interests him [most]" (qtd. in Bradshaw 2008: 11) with "uncompromising inventiveness" (Parsons 2007: 1).

The modernist writer's freedom to choose and execute (echoed in Woolf and Eliot) is also a predominant theme in *Portrait*, as when Cranly recalls Stephen's theory of art: "To discover the mode of life or of art whereby your spirit could express itself in unfettered freedom" (Joyce 2010: 272). In Joyce, there are other conventions too besides the novel form that he rigorously engaged with, conventions not always confined to the literary, but expanded to encompass and address the immediate, the social, the cultural, and the linguistic. Take, for instance, this passage from *Portrait*:

> When the soul of a man is born in this country there are nets flung at it to hold it back from flight. You talk to me of nationality, language, religion. I shall try to fly by those nets …
>
> (Joyce 2010: 224)

This statement by Stephen Dedalus is often taken to be "Joyce's modernist manifesto" (Ellmann 2010: 18) and I tell my students that along with questioning, and finding inadequate, the form of the novel that writers had inherited, Joyce was also preparing to signal his departure from inherited modes of thinking about nationality, language, and religion. Why was this? In order to learn a little about Joyce's break from and re-imagination of the questions of nationality, language, and religion, it was necessary to contextualize *Portrait* within the larger modernist concerns of the twentieth century and the "Irish question" in particular.

On the shores of Ireland: Contextualizing *Portrait*

There is often a tendency to gloss over the historical background of a work, whether as part of an exercise in practical criticism, or due to the time constraints of the classroom, or simply because the text invites the readers to explore some larger and more pressing issues. However, what constitutes one of the most *effective* approaches to a critical appreciation of Joyce's works, for Joyce scholars such as Matthew Hodgart for instance, is the historical (contextual) approach. This is because Joyce's texts usually encompass a range of historical and philosophical references that often elude direct access, particularly to first-time readers. The way I began to see it, a preliminary background to the polemics of the Irish question would form a crucial context for *Portrait*. I took the class through a brief early history of Ireland, engaging them in a discussion of terms such as "invaders/colonizers", "natives", "ascendancy culture", "peasantry", "famine", "land", "nation", "agrarian uprising", and "folktales" (while also pausing to examine the many 'English' portraits of the Irish and the Indians that were catered to suit a growing English readership and imagination), traversing the Irish landscape from the arrival of Christianity through to the Viking invasions and Norman Conquest in the twelfth century and the religious schisms and national movements that gained momentum over the course of its history from the sixteenth century through to the nineteenth and twentieth centuries, when the island's political identity consolidated in movements that placed ardent pressure for/against Home Rule.[2] Of particular interest to us as a class tracing the political terrain of liberal thought and its connections with the British empire, particularly with reference to Ireland and India, was the culmination in Ireland of liberal thought in the *Protestant Ascendancy* that established the *Anglo-Irish* tradition of that keen satirist Dean Swift, who began to vehemently articulate the concerns of his country through several pointedly critical pieces.

Seen in the light of this context, and not in a vacuum where definitions, nominal or otherwise, float in an empty abyss, Swift's passionate and biting satirical portraits seemed to make sense. The students were able to see, and even venture to anticipate reasons for, the various tangential strands of political and religious consequences that led up to the fall of Charles Stewart Parnell—whom Mahatma Gandhi had once exalted as the able leader of a people for whom liberty, above all else, was most significant—in the nineteenth century. Here the students began to draw comparisons between India and Ireland as two lands colonized by a single imperial British master, as countries that were partitioned over differences in the right to assert freedom from British rule, as traditions rooted in a strong oral and folktale culture—there seemed to be more than what students thought they could learn about a country not their own, split at the core for centuries by the Western liberal rhetoric of "us" versus "them", the "white, privileged able-bodied reformer" versus the "savage", "to-be-reformed" other, stripped of land, siphoned of their own resources.

We gradually worked our ways through Oscar Wilde, whose satirical texts the students had previously studied (and took great delight in) in their undergraduate classes, then paused to reflect on W. B. Yeats and the Irish literary revival. This was to help the class examine Joyce's attitude towards the literary and nationalistic endeavours directed by his contemporaries. In order to approach differently the question that kept ringing in our ears as a class, "Why does Joyce write the way he does?", we went through some of Joyce's earlier critical works to sample a few of his formative concerns and preoccupations with art, one that students would see manifest, in different ways, later in *Portrait*. In such early papers as "Drama and Life" presented before the Literary and Historical Society of the University College Dublin, Joyce demonstrated, deriving strength and inspiration from the works of Henrik Ibsen, the inklings of what would be later his primary concern with the novel: an uncompromising presentation of his concerns in a mode of expression of his choice, unhindered by what was usually considered taboo. We next began to talk about how these early writings, including *Dubliners*, gradually paved the way for the urtext *Stephen Hero*[3], how the two differed from each other, and talked a little about Ezra Pound's significant role in the publication of *Portrait*.

It seemed a little odd to the students that Joyce did not seem to share some of the concerns of his Irish successors and contemporaries. Why, for instance, did he not join the Irish Academy of Letters? He certainly did not seem to be sympathizing with the British imperial forces either. What was one to make of this? Why does the biblical *non-servium* echo throughout the text? What connotations, religious and political, present themselves before us when Stephen's battle-cry "non-servium" is brought to light? What does he not serve? The next class, then, would not be a continuation of a series of lectures on context and background studies; nor was it to be a religious listing of themes, motifs, and symbols. Instead, the students would attempt an on-going dialogue with the novel, one where they would speak and be spoken to by the text that they were reading. The teacher would become the facilitator of discussion, raising questions, orchestrating the flow of arguments, and directing lines of thought, before both parties coalesce before the text as complicit allies in reading.

Playing with words: classrooms as portals of discovery

Walking into class the next session, I was anxious to see how many students had come prepared with their second/next round of reading *Portrait*. The first few minutes of the class was devoted to the reading experience, in keeping with the routine of the last session, and my delight knew no bounds when students told me that they found it easier to approach the text from the preliminary *historical* approach of the last session. They found the reading process better orchestrated, now that they were aided by a sense of the Irish context, and could locate modernist writers (though these writers could not for the most part be brought under an umbrella term) in a larger network of interrelated concerns. The students felt better equipped to relate modern writers from Ireland more or less by political position as well. *Portrait*, the students realized, was (in the sense that Eliot sees it) Joyce's first novel, a manifesto where he addresses and re-defines the terms of his art. How was the class to proceed so as to truly appreciate the novel?

For the first text-based class, I decided, drawing back from the lectern, that it was time for the students to engage in a 'play' with the text, beginning with the title of the novel. The class was encouraged to take down each word of the title and assess it in terms of its etymology and trace its denotative and connotative values. The class was also asked to see, after having drawn their own inferences from the title, whether the present title, and not, say "A Portrait of the Young Man as an Artist" was more befitting for the text. Does the title serve its purpose? Does it introduce/raise questions fundamental to the novel/give readers a sense of the subject of the novel? With these questions, the students drew into a heated discussion amongst themselves, with some making a case for Stephen, while others against. Making my rounds around class, I was witness to a discussion of words that were beginning to escape the rigid black and white binaries of mere denotations; here, in the classroom, as in Stephen's world, words began to multiply in the search for *subtleties*, they began to be 'political', in the way that Stephen's use of the word 'tundish' before the Dean of Studies could be said to possess an inimitable political gravity. Each word, students began to realize, seemed to offer something else; synonyms, of such words as portrait ("picture", "depiction") or "artist" ("craftsman", "artisan") are not *quite* the same. Within the four walls of the classroom, I began to feel a sense of something bigger than myself and the students at play: words being dealt with conscientiously, unlike Stephen's memory of the dull ring of the students meekly scrawling definitions in the English classroom.

At the end of the discussion, such questions as "What is a portrait?", "Who or what is the subject of this portrait?", and, conversely, "Who is the artist of the portrait?" began to emerge, which the students began to cross-examine with their peers. Some moments caught them by surprise as when, during the discussion, I had my own, instantaneous moments of sudden realization: in asking the question, "Is this a *commissioned* portrait?", we began to talk about money, and consequently, that word *price* seemed to echo frighteningly in the classroom.

—What *price* does the artist pay for this portrait? I asked.

The students were silent for a while as the question rang through the classroom before offering such answers (some of which make an appearance or echo resoundingly in *Portrait*) as 'blood', 'sweat', 'tears', 'human relationships', 'family', 'comfort', 'true friend', and finally, 'life'. To the question, "What does he pay this price for?" the students recalled Stephen's maxim of "silence, exile, and cunning" and answered: for a mode of self-expression that was "free" and "whol[e]" (Joyce 2010: 273). The artist, then, to recall Maurice Beebe's argument, "dies to a certain kind of life" so that he may be "reborn into another" (qtd. in *TCLC* 163). This exercise in spinning the roulette of words, so to speak, to see which word best fits the context and why consequently led us to make the revelation, echoing our lessons from Woolf, that the artist exercises a conscious *political agency* in the choice of words/materials to respond uniquely to a given artistic cause.

Portraits of *Portrait*: classroom activities and exercises

One of the most engaging discussions of the previous session on the play with the title was upon the question of the many kinds of 'portraits' in *Portrait*. At the symbolic level, the students ventured to guess, the novel was a portrait (a picture-in-words) of the coming of age of Stephen Dedalus as a young man responding to the calling of art as vocation. But was that the *only* portrait to emerge? Operating at various other symbolic levels, the students tell me, are portraits of "saints and great men" (Joyce 2010: 62) decked on the walls of Clongowes Woods and "old" portraits on the wall of his house (22), particularly that of Stephen's grandfather (41), each of which functions in different ways in making a claim upon the impressions of the young Stephen. I am eager to elicit different responses, however, as I ask: "Do the portraits of the saints in the hall mean the same to Stephen as they do to, say, the rector?" The rector and Simon Dedalus seem to carry different portraits with them, each his own. How objective is a portrait, then, and just how many portraits of a portrait are there?

I was slowly making my way to a discussion of some ways in which one could begin to read *Portrait*. The aim was to raise certain basic questions (and elicit responses from the students themselves) about *Portrait* through classroom activities, as opposed to my giving the students "points" from critical essays that they could religiously note down without discussing or contesting them. The point was that in the bid to access the text quicker (through textual glosses and some such), the teacher and the students mustn't circumvent *the* text in question in the classroom. Therefore, for this session, I asked the 40-odd students to seat themselves in groups of five in circles, passing around a handout that I had prepared, containing a sample set of questions for the students to ask themselves as they read through the text. First, the students had to critically examine, offering illustrations from select passages, whether the "first two pages [of the novel] enact the entire action in the microcosm of the novel" (qtd. in Beja 1973: 126); second, they were to record how "a catalogue of senses, faculties, and mental activities is played against the unfolding of an infant conscience" (qtd. Beja 1973: 126); and third, the students had to point out the "difficulties of distance" (Booth 1961: 325) that present themselves to readers with regard to the narrator/ reflector in *Portrait*. With regard to the first exercise, the students were asked to come up with a sentence/ combination of sentences that could be said to contain the "seed" of *Portrait* in these pages: in other words, to point out those sentences that seemed to best anticipate what they took to be the key concern(s) of the novel.

Portrait, as the students begin to venture to guess, seemed to begin innocuously enough, in the strain of any and every story, with the lines "Once upon a time" (7). But very soon, the students realized, the commonplace story has become unfamiliar, distant, foreign: it is the story of a little boy and a curious "moocow", which the reader simultaneously translates as the combination of the sound "moo" (signifier) with the associated mental concept of an animal ("cow") that produces such a sound (signified). In the next few lines, curiously, the tone seemed to shift, and there seemed to be an almost imperceptible shift in narrative voice, giving the students the sense that this was no ordinary narrative, but a personal record, or some such kind, of impressions of words, sounds, people, places, objects in a particular private universe, either recorded or recollected. Their interests sufficiently piqued by the curious features of the text—particularly the stylistic convention of the long dash in place of direct quotations signalling dialogue—the students began to bend inquisitively over their copies of *Portrait*, flicking pages back and forth with brows furrowed, asking questions, taking a leap and landing on a different page in the same chapter, or a different section in a later chapter, all the while attempting to elucidate a point or two to a fellow group member. It began to dawn on the students that the first two pages, like many of the pages to follow later, seemed to be pervaded by sense imagery. Each of the senses seemed to help the young Stephen Dedalus discern "empirical realities" (qtd. in Beja 1973: 126): at a very young age, Stephen encounters the adult world of politics, religion, and language, all of which seemed to elude his understanding. The students also observed how words and names in particular seemed to hold a terrible power over Stephen's imagination, recalling the jingle on the eagles, and the names of Davitt and Parnell whom the young Stephen Dedalus knew nothing of as yet:

> Words which he did not understand he said over and over to himself till he had learnt them by heart: and through them he had glimpses of the real world about them.
>
> (Joyce 2010: 69)

Stephen's vocabulary had not yet discovered the "poetry" of Doctor Cornwell's Spelling Book, and was as yet far from the poetic hold of Shelley or Byron, operating instead in a system of binaries: "rose/green", "warm/cold", "father/mother", "small/big", and "strong/weak". The students observed that this binary played out in a finale in a sentence at the end of the second page: "He kept on the fringe of his line, out of sight of his prefect, out of the reach of rude feet, feigning to run now and then" (Joyce 8), locking this sentence as the "seed" of contention in Stephen that would only play out on a more dramatic scale later, one that could be said to *contain* the controlling images/emotions/symbols/motifs/themes in later chapters. For Stephen, as the students pointed out, there were two options: to keep to the line (succumb to authoritative figures: his peers, the Church) or transgress the line (break off from tradition), and the words "out of sight" and "out of reach" seemed to echo his later decision to become an exile. These words also seemed to point to the "flight" motif in keeping with the Dedalus myth, and which Stephen's surname invariably invoked.

If the opening pages set the spatial and temporal co-ordinates for the reader (in addition to anticipating some of the key thematic concerns of the novel later on), then each of the chapter endings seemed to evoke a pattern of *epiphanies*. The students observed that there was some insight/vision that Stephen held true at the end of each chapter, which would inevitably be flouted in the next. Thus one observes Stephen challenging his passive submission to authority through active vigilance and questioning of (religious) authority at the end of chapter one; readers next find Stephen mustering authority and standing up for himself before his batchmates and submitting, by the end of chapter two, to the *siren* voices of the prostitute; Stephen then seems to revel in sin, only to seek priesthood as vocation by the end of chapter three; he falls "to err[ing]" by the end of chapter four once again, this time resolutely; and by the end of chapter five, he seems to have embraced art as vocation.

While observing such shifts in the structural pattern of *Portrait*, the students were also keen to note the specific problem of the narrator/reflector of the text, asking of the text such profoundly simple questions such as "Who speaks, and to whom?", which seemed only to fetch results that showed us how much more complex the text was than what met the eye. Some students ventured to claim that Stephen was the reflector throughout the novel, whilst another quipped that perhaps it was an older Stephen, one you could almost see beginning to write the novel, recollecting memories, carefully choosing materials for a self-portrait, parodying his perceptions of reality through language that could be said to best suit each phase of his growth. Yet another student drew the class' attention to the quality of meta-commentary present in the title. Perhaps, one student ventured, the narrator is the implied author? Here I drew their attention to the question of words in the gravitational field of the *nearest speaker*, an argument posited by Hugh Kenner and later taken up by Denis Donoghue (Donoghue 1981: 64). To illustrate, I took a passage from the Christmas scene in the first chapter of *Portrait* where the phrase "in a jiffy" appears bereft of the long dash that Joyce employs to demonstrate dialogue (29). The narrator of *Portrait* seemed to incorporate the words of the nearest speaker into the narration as *the speaker* would have the sentences articulated. In this case, the voice belonged to Stephen's mother, who uses the phrase "in a jiffy" to alert them that dinner would soon be served.

Thinking about race, gender, class, and language

One of the most enduring passages from *Portrait* that students were most alive to was the episode with the Dean of Studies, that oft-cited encounter between the colonizer (the 'English') and the colonized (the 'Irish') in a debate on the usage of the words "funnel" and "tundish" in the English language, where the latter outdoes the former in argument and intellectual rhetoric in the language of the imperial master. Having read the text in light of its historical background in the introductory lecture, the class was encouraged to think about questions of "foreign versus domestic/native", "centre versus periphery", "liberal versus conservative", "English versus Irish Gaelic" pervading *Portrait*. Does Stephen Dedalus, reminiscent, in many ways, of Gabriel Conroy from "The Dead", seem to offer a(n) (in)different response to the national question, or is it one of strategic counterfeit? Does *Portrait* offer us an examination of the colonial experience, and if it does, how different is it from our own? What questions of race and ethnicity emerge, and could Stephen's enduring adage "non-servium", along with the final battle-cry to forge the "uncreated unconscience" of his race in the "smithy" of his soul (Joyce 280), be said to be a political assertion of his full and final break with the imperial forces of Rome (Church/religion), England (language), and to an extent, his own country (homeland/nationality)?

The students next proceeded to a careful examination of the 'portraits' of women pervading *Portrait*. Here they attempted to read closely for instances where the text could be said to point to an all-pervading, unquestionable "female essence" (McCaw 2008: 117). The students were quick to observe how the binary of the 'profane' and the 'spiritual' that ran through all the chapters seemed to extend to the depiction of women in the novel as well. There seemed to be a pervading tension between the figure of the "whore" on the one hand and that of the "virginal mother" figure on the other. The students pointed out how the mysterious E-C, Dante, Mrs Dedalus, and the Roman Catholic Church merge as figures associated with the "virginal mother" from whom absolution ought to be sought when Stephen erred. A woman in Stephen's conception, students ventured to observe, was either a figure profane (in the image of a "prostitute", causing to err) or a subsuming "mother figure" that could either absolve his sins (his mother, E-C) or admonish him (Dante, the Church). The students were quick to notice also the recurrence of the words "queer" and "strange", and pointed my attention to possibilities of a suppressed sexuality and homoeroticism in Stephen, recalling the episode between Stephen and Cranly in chapter five, and several instances of a crippling heteronormative sexuality that Stephen's 'non-servium' could also be said to be addressing, in a way that was reminiscent of Joyce's predecessor Wilde. The final session on textual approaches was drawn to a close after discussing the text in terms of the depiction of economic circumstances, social status, and class, pausing to examine terms from the novel such as "magistrate" and "gentleman" (9) "peasants" and "turf and corduroy" (19), the Jesuits and their fashionable mode of clothing (94), and the deteriorating social and economic circumstances of the Dedalus family against the backdrop of a country that was struggling, in the face of its economic base being decided by a minority class politics, to break away from its imperial chains. The students were encouraged to examine reasons, for instance, for why Simon Dedalus was too quick to remind Stephen how it was important to be hailed a "gentleman", or why

Stephen was warned frequently against the Protestant children. Were they reasons attributable to religious tension alone, or could one sense also at the heart of *Portrait* a question of differences in social class associated closely with different religious denominations?

As the session began to draw to a close, I wondered to myself what it was about *Portrait* that seemed to arrest, to seize entirely, and draw students to a close examination of the text, and conversely, a close attention to themselves. What forces seemed to encompass its appeal? Looking at the students and listening to their questions and observations at the end of the session, I was left inspired. Here was a group of students who were beginning to make connections both within the text and without. For in spite of its complexity, the students seemed to have thoroughly enjoyed the novel, seeing perhaps their own portraits in *Portrait*, learning to look at themselves half-apologetically perhaps, or with a little pride and more than one's share of irony, inspired by the luminous glow of Stephen's youthful ambition given the constrains of a confining sense of poverty and the demands of a convention, once held dear, that one was beginning to question. In other words, the text that we were reading had ended up reading ourselves. *Portrait* perhaps appealed to the students because it was poised precariously on the brink of that question that Cixous so aptly pointed out: one of "What shall I be?" (219). As Beebe recalls, *Portrait* contains seeds of revolutionary potential to offer to the young: the novel has the potential to hone one too many "a young writer or would-be artist" that has found a "mirror" in the novel (qtd. in *TCLC 163)*. It certainly did inspire a "would-be teacher".

The "smithy" of the Joyce text: final reflections on teaching and research

As I was filing my papers by the lectern at the end of the session, wondering to myself how so many things could have been done differently perhaps, and far better, I realized that there was a thin line of students trickling next to me. I looked up enquiringly and discovered one or two students requesting for clarification on Stephen's notion of epiphanies, yet another student on extra reading material, and a few others who told me that they would like to read more of Joyce, and perhaps one day even tackle *Ulysses*. How do I begin to explain to myself what had happened, both to the students and to myself?

The words "forge" and "smithy" that occur at the end of *Portrait* seemed to offer an interesting way to explain what had perhaps transpired in the classroom. These words seemed to imply a certain rigidity of the "workpiece" (iron for the blacksmith, for instance) that was at one's disposal and had to be brought under necessary conditions after which the material was ready to be "forged". Thus when Stephen refers to "forging" the "uncreated conscience" of his race (Joyce 2010: 280), he seemed to imply his ardent desire to bring the tempered and fixed concerns of his homeland (nationality,

196

religion, and language) to the "smithy" that was his craftsman's "soul" so that he could begin to make something "beautiful" of what were mere rigidities, incapable as yet of being forged, requiring the temperament of the artist and the hearth. Perhaps here Joyce had something of the Blakean motif of the blacksmith in mind, for all of Stephen's resolve "not [to] cease from Mental Fight" till he had "built" Ireland's conscience.

It is no surprise then to begin to reflect on *Portrait* as the smithy in which readers, teachers, and learners are crafted and made under the conditions of the classroom. The "rigidities" of the workpiece under question here are our time-held notions of the conventions of the novel, our reading practices, and most certainly the way we begin to think about the teacher and student dynamics in the classroom. The Joyce text puts us under immense pressure in asking of us to shed our scales as readers and demanding of us a response to reading and language that was never demanded of us prior to this encounter. *Portrait* heightens our sensitivity to the difficulties and challenges of reading and appreciating modernist texts, and in doing so asks us to respond and collaborate with the author in equal measure.

There was most definitely a sense of having been forged or crafted as readers by the end of the session on *Portrait*, owing in most ways to the fact that Joyce writes the way he does. I was reminded of how some of the Joyce scholars I now frequently turn to (whenever passages in *Wake* give me some trouble, as they are wont to do) such as William York Tindall and Matthew Hodgart, themselves life-long researchers of Joyce, inaugurated their long Joycean calling with the teaching profession, sharing their love for Joyce for the first time in the classroom, and picking up a few things on reading Joyce with the students along the way. This rewarding experience of teaching and learning a Joyce text has certainly awakened me to the potentials of the classroom. In some future time, at the end of the sessions on *Portrait*, my teacher would tell me: "When one teaches, one is both a learner and a teacher at once—a unique experience gained from the knowledge only a classroom generates". The knowledge transaction that takes place in the classroom is valuable to what we bring and take away to/from the Joyce text that we read together as a class, one that can only be generated by the teacher and students working in tandem as readers of and active collaborators with the text.

After the classes on *Portrait*, I have realized how many of the methods with which I have always worked as a researcher have been particularly useful to the teaching and reading of Joyce in the classroom. As in research, a teacher is confronted with the problems of having to *observe* trends in the classroom and *identify* gaps, whether in learning or the syllabi or resources available; the teacher also has to *survey* the literature and locate the specific concerns of the text for the benefit and understanding of the students, and together pay close attention to the text or materials collected/problems or gaps identified. Raising basic questions such as "What does the class need?" or "What does this text demand of us, and how do we go about it?" are crucial to addressing the more immediate concerns of both the classroom and the text. The teacher and students also need to *sample* both the text that they are confronted with in the classroom as well as those that are incidental to the text.

All of these eventually lead to a realization in teaching and reading, as in research, that one is part of a larger network of (reading) relations that facilitates our learning; that reading is more *socious* than it is individual; that it is a system of *relations* rather than an activity. The motif of the "smithy" then seems to me pertinent to the Joyce text both as a researcher and teacher. Returning to the *Wake* passage that had held me captive prior to the teaching experience, suddenly the lines that I'd been grappling with did not seem to me so odd or strange. I began to think that perhaps the metaphysical question of the "hand from the cloud" expanding a mysterious tablet, the contents of which may or may not appear clear, only invites our attention to something that I had learnt very recently through the teaching experience: that we are all of us involved in a collaborative effort as teachers and learners, readers, and writers of the *world* that we are trying to make sense of as *text*.

Notes

1 I am grateful to my teacher, Professor K. Narayana Chandran, for offering me several occasions to teach and interact with his MA students, the most recent being the opportunity to teach his II MA students such a challenging text as James Joyce's *A Portrait of the Artist as a Young Man*. I thank him for his advice, feedback, and timely intervention in helping me design the course outline for these sessions, for the many lessons on research, reading, and teaching methods, and for constantly urging me to write about the process through it all.

2 For keywords I looked to Welch 1996, where I found the following entries useful: Protestantism (482–484), Catholicism and Catholics (90–91), James Joyce (277–281), *Portrait* (479–480), and the Irish language (265–267); for a literary and source history of Ireland, I consulted Hyde 1899; Johnson 1980; and Jeffares 1982; for a sense of Irish folklore and mythology, I found it helpful to course through Glassie 1985 and Gregory 1996.

3 Stanislaus Joyce 2003 provides a biographical account of Joyce, offering insight on *Portrait* as a work of art/creative fiction.

Works cited

Beebe, Maurice. "James Joyce: The Return from Exile". *Twentieth Century Literary Criticism* 8 (1982): 163. Print.

Beja, Morris, ed. *Dubliners and a Portrait of the Artist as a Young Man: A Casebook*. London: Macmillan, 1973. Print.

Blake, William. "Jerusalem". *Poetry Foundation*, n.d. Web. 26 October 2018. www.poetryfoundation.org/poems/54684/jerusalem-and-did-those-feet-in-ancient-time.

Booth, Wayne C. "The Problem of Distance in *A Portrait of the Artist*". *The Rhetoric of Fiction*. Chicago: University of Chicago Press, 1961. Print.

Bradshaw, David, ed. *Virginia Woolf: Selected Essays*. New York: Oxford University Press, 2008. Print.

Campbell, Joseph, and Henry Morton Robinson. *A Skeleton Key To Finnegans Wake: Unlocking James Joyce's Masterwork*. Novato: New World Library, 1944. Print.

Cixous, Hélène. *The Exile of James Joyce*. New York: David Lewis, 1972. Print.

Derrida, Jacques. *Writing and Difference*. London: Routledge, 2001. Print.

Donoghue, Denis. *Ferocious Alphabets*. Boston: Little, Brown & Company, 1981. Print.

Eliot, T.S. "Ulysses, Order, and Myth". *Open Modernisms*, 1922 Web. 26 October 2018. http://openmods.uvic.ca/islandora/object/uvic%3A64/datastream/PDF/view.

Ellmann, Maud. *The Nets of Modernism*. New York: Cambridge University Press, 2010. Print.

Glassie, Henry. *Irish Folktales*. New York: Pantheon Books, 1985. Print.

Gregory, Lady. *Complete Irish Mythology*. New York: Smithmark, 1996. Print.

Hyde, Douglas. *A Literary History of Ireland: From Earliest Times to the Present Day*. London: T. Fisher Unwin, 1899. Print.

Jeffares, Norman. *Anglo-Irish Literature*. Dublin: Macmillan, 1982. Print.

———. *Finnegans Wake*. London: Faber & Faber, 1975. Print.

Johnson, Paul. *Ireland: Land of Troubles*. London: Eyre Methuen, 1980. Print.

Joyce, James. *A Portrait of the Artist As A Young Man*. Dehradun: Maple Press, 2010. Print.

Joyce, Stanislaus. *My Brother's Keeper: James Joyce's Early Years*. Boston: DaCapo Press, 2003. Print.

McCaw, Neil. *How to Read Texts: A Student's Guide to Critical Approaches and Skills*. New York: Continuum, 2008. Print.

Mitchell, Andrew, and Sam Slote, eds. *Derrida and Joyce: Texts and Contexts*. Albany: State University of New York Press, 2013. Print.

Parsons, Deborah. *Theorists of the Modern Novel: James Joyce, Dorothy Richardson, Virginia Woolf*. New York: Routledge, 2007. Print.

Welch, Robert, ed. *The Oxford Companion to Irish Literature*. New York: Oxford University Press, 1996. Print.

INDEX

For Product Safety Concerns and Information please contact our EU
representative GPSR@taylorandfrancis.com
Taylor & Francis Verlag GmbH, Kaufingerstraße 24, 80331 München, Germany

www.ingramcontent.com/pod-product-compliance
Lightning Source LLC
Chambersburg PA
CBHW071106100726
47908CB00008B/2287